Freedom – Treason – Revolution

AF795672

BRITANNIA

TEXTS IN ENGLISH

edited by Jürgen Klein

Vol. 10

PETER LANG

Frankfurt am Main · Berlin · Bern · Bruxelles · New York · Oxford · Wien

Christoph Houswitschka (ed.)

Freedom – Treason – Revolution

Uncollected Sources of the Political and Legal Culture of the London Treason Trials (1794)

PETER LANG
Europäischer Verlag der Wissenschaften

Bibliographic Information published by Die Deutsche Bibliothek
Die Deutsche Bibliothek lists this publication in the Deutsche Nationalbibliografie; detailed bibliographic data is available in the internet at <http://dnb.ddb.de>.

Cover Illustration:
Isaak Cruikshank (1764-1810/11)
No Reform, No Reform.
Etching with hand-coloring
21.2x29.7 cm image
Published April 9, 1795 by S.W. Fores
Courtesy of The Lewis Walpole Library,
Yale University, 793.1.8.1

Cover design:
Horst Dralle, Hamburg
hdralle@t-online.de

ISSN 0179-1648
ISBN 3-631-38979-5
US-ISBN 0-8204-4394-8

© Peter Lang GmbH
Europäischer Verlag der Wissenschaften
Frankfurt am Main 2004
All rights reserved.

All parts of this publication are protected by copyright. Any utilisation outside the strict limits of the copyright law, without the permission of the publisher, is forbidden and liable to prosecution. This applies in particular to reproductions, translations, microfilming, and storage and processing in electronic retrieval systems.

www.peterlang.de

REFORM ADVISED.
good Constitution
I am your Friend John Bull you want a Reform
John Bull you are too Fat
REFORM BEGUN.
Eat it you Dog & hold your Tongue you are very happy
REFORM COMPLEAT.
now he is quite happy
Oh Delightfull you may thank me you Dog for sparing your Life—thank me I say.
H—O—H French Fraternity

Illustration

Preceding page:

Thomas Rowlandson (1756-1827)
Reform Advised. Reform Begun. Reform Compleat.
Etching
41 x 25 cm, image
Published January 8, 1793 by John Brown
Courtesy of The Lewis Walpole Library, Yale University, 793.1.8.1

Text:

Reform Advised
John Bull: The blessed effects of a good constitution
First Jacobin: I am your Friend John Bull you want a Reform
Second Jacobin: My Hon.ble Friend speaks my Sentiments
Third Jacobin: John Bull you are too fat
Reform Begun
John Bull: A pretty Reform indeed you have deprived me of my Leg and given me nothing but Frogs to eat I shall be starved I am no Frenchman.
First Jacobin: Eat it you Dog & hold your Tongue you are very happy.
Second Jacobin: That's right my Friend we will make him Happier still.
Third Jacobin: He is a little leaner Now
Reform Compleat
First Jacobin: now he is quite happy I will have a Jump
Second Jacobin: Oh Delightfull [sic] you may shank me you Dog for sparing your Life – thank me I say.
John Bull: O – H – O –H French Fraternity

An awakened mind is one of the most important purposes of education
William Godwin, *Enquiry,* 1797, p. 5

The people must grow wise, in order that the people may rule
Henry Yorke, *The Trial of Thomas Hardy for High Treason,* 1794, I, 201

Mankind now read too many books to be permanently injured by any
John Thelwall, *Sober Reflections,* 1796, p. 336

It is, in my opinion, impossible to judge of a man's principles, either by the books he reads or circulates. The only fair conclusion that can be drawn from the circulation of books, is, that those who circulate them, wish to promote a spirit of inquiry
John Wilks, *Athalia*, 1795, p. 16

Preface and Acknowledgements

Texts for this anthology were collected during a research sabbatical that was supported by the Thyssen Foundation. Without this generous grant, I could not have spent four months in the British Library typing in texts which I later used for my habilitation project, *Die Rechtskultur der Trials for High Treason von 1794 und die Literatur der Demokratisierung*. I am pleased, and I am grateful to acknowledge permission from the British Library to publish these texts from their collection.

The title *Freedom – Treason – Revolution* uses three of the most widely used and most differently interpreted terms of the 1790s. Thomas Rowlandson's (1756-1827) etching "Reform Advised. Reform Begun. Reform Compleat", which was published by John Brown on January 8, 1793, is a satirical variation of the topic of this anthology presenting both interpretations as the contradiction between words and deeds. The order of the title may suggest what both the loyalists and the radicals believed and feared would be the course of events in England in the decade following the French Revolution. Whereas the radicals thought that the government had conspired against the constitution and, therefore, that revolution may be inevitable, the loyalists supported the King and his prime minister, who believed that the radical movement had committed an act of high treason against the crown and the British constitution in attempting to provoke a revolution through propagating parliamentary reform.

This anthology not only illustrates the dramatic circumstances under which several leading members of the radical reform movement were accused of high treason in 1794, but also presents a selection of the various reactions and commentaries that eventually disrupted the government's attempt to destroy the reform movement. The events that unravelled in the legal culture of the year 1794 were accompanied by a broader political debate. Edmund Burke's *Reflections on the French Revolution* (1790) and Tom Paine's *Rights of Man* (1791-1792) had polarized British society. Burke's *Reflections* provided much of the intellectual groundwork for a primarily conservative belief in strong and stable state institutions. Paine's bestseller was inspired by the American experience and may be regarded as the beginning of the working-class political movement.

The anthology concludes with two sections of radical and loyalist texts which contributed to the broader political debate of the 1790s and which have thus far not been anthologised. They show that both sides used propagandistic rhetoric and arguments in a very similar manner. The whole society was permeated by conspiracy theories. The pathos of the political language is as familiar to our contemporary ears as it is obvious in its intentions. Nevertheless, certain social concerns and political agendas of that time remain essential for peace and freedom to this day – concerns about the dissolution of societal values and institutions through radical reforms on the one hand, and striving for democratisation, participation and social progress on the other hand.

The original spelling and punctuation of the sources has been maintained. "*Sic*" had been used to confirm original misprints and variants the reader might find questionable or suspicious. Books which appear more than twice and in different parts of the book are included in a short bibliography at the end of the book.

My thanks go to the staff of the British Library for helping me to gain access to its unique collection; to my academic mentor, Prof. Uwe Böker and to Prof. Jürgen Klein for his support. I would also like to thank Julie A. Hibbard and Julia Söhlemann for proof reading. For any remaining mistakes, the blame is mine.

Bamberg, December 2003

Contents

Illustration **6**

Text: **6**

Preface and Acknowledgements **9**

Contents **11**

I. Introduction **19**

Freedom – Treason – Revolution **20**

The Legal Culture of the Period before the Treason Trials **23**

The Reform Movement of the 1790s and the Treason Trials of 1794 .... **24**

II. Freedom of the Press **29**

1. "Long, long live the Blessings that spring from the Press," from: *The Blessings of a Free Press, A New Song*. [London], [Dec. 31, 1792] **30**

2. "If we possess that unimpaired, we can never be enslaved. If we lose it we cannot be free," from: *The Trial of Daniel Isaac Eaton for publishing a supposed Libel intituled Politics for the People, or, Hogs Wash: at Justice Hall in the Old Bailey, February Twenty-Fourth, 1794*. London: published by the defendant, Daniel Isaac Eaton, 1794......... **35**

3. "In Thee the gen'rous Monitor we find," from: William Pinn, *Poems on Various Subjects: in which is a Most Beautiful and Novel Description of his Majesty's Review of the Kentish Volunteers. August the First, 1799*. Chatham: Printed by C. Townson, 1800. .... **36**

III. Revolution in France and War with Great Britain **41**

1. "The War with the French People is both Impolitic and Immoral" (1796), from: William Hodgson M.D., *The Case of W. Hodgson, now*

Confined in Newgate for the Payment of Two Hundred Pounds, after Having Suffered Two Years' Imprisonment on a Charge of Sedition, Considered and Compared with the Existing Laws of the Country: by himself. **London: printed for the author, and sold by D.I. Eaton and others, 1796. .... 43**

2. "Christian Warfare Defended and Recommended," from: ***A Sermon Intended to Have Been Preached Before the Vice-Chancellor, and the University at St. Mary's Church, Cambridge, on the 28th of February, 1794, the Day Appointed for a Solemn Fast.*** **London: printed for C. and G. Kearsley and sold by W. Page, 1794. .... 45**

3. "Many of his political opinions would astonish our countrymen, who [...] cherish their prejudices," from: ***A Tour through the Theatre of War, in the Months of November and December, 1792, and January, 1793. Interspersed with Military and Other Anecdotes. To Which is Subjoined an Exact and Authentic Account of the Death of Louis XVI. The Second Edition.*** **With the Addition of an Appendix. London: J. Bew, 1793. .... 48**

4. 'Twenty thousand meet on a plain and shed each other's blood - without the least animosity', from: ***The Curses and Causes of War, Pointed out; and the Approaching Cessation of Both Determined.*** **Spitalfields: R. Hawes, for the Moral and Political Society, 1795. .... 52**

5. "... when he entered in such a horid guise, His Mother shriek'd," from: Robert Merry, ***The Wounded Soldier, a Poem.*** **By Mr. M-y. London: printed for T. G. Ballard, [1795?]. 56**

6. "Freedom advances near," from: ***A New Song, to an old Tune,*** **-- viz. "God save the king." [London], [November 1792] 60**

IV. English Politics and the French Revolution 63

1. "TOM PAINE and PRIESTLEY wou'd/ Deluge the throne with blood," from: ***Sedition, Levelling, and Plundering; or the Pretended Friends of the People in Council.*** **London: Printed and sold by S.W. Fores, who again opened his Exhibition Room, to which he has added several Hundred old and new Subjects, [1792?]. 64**

2. "Tell me then, ye sons of discontent, what are your wants?" from: *Principle and Practice Combined: or, The Wrongs of Man. An Oratorio. As it was often performed by the Jacobines of Paris, with great Applause. The Music selected from modern French Airs.* By one who feels himself a Patriot. London: J. Parsons and J. Barker, 1792..........66

3. "Bring the Gold, the Fees then bring, And you shall Loyal find us," from: *The associators, at the Crown-and-Anchor, in the Strand. A song.* [London, 1793]...73

4. "I right made wrong, and wrong I said was right," from: *The Last Dying Words of Tom Paine, Executed at the Gullotine in France on the 1st of Sept. 1794, with A Description of the genuine Water for Converting the Jacobines. Verses on the Death of Paine, and A Dialogue between a Jacobine and the Devil.* London [1794]...........................74

5. "... every idea of absolute perfection in Government is chimerical," from: William Augustus Miles, *A Letter to Earl Stanhope.* London: printed for G. Nicol and J. Sewell, 1794.........................78

6. "Jesus Christ was a Revolutionist," from: Mark Wilks, *The Origin and Stability of the French Revolution. A sermon. Preached at St. Paul's Chapel, Norwich, July, 14, 1791.* Second edition. [Norwich?]: Printed for the Author, 1791...80

V. The Trials for High Treason of 1794 83

1. "... the object of these societies was to proceed in contempt of Parliament," from: *Debates on the Report of the Committee of Secrecy in the House of Commons. On the 16th and 17th of May, and in the House of Lords, on the 17th and 19th and 22d of the same month, 1794.* Edinburgh: J. Robertson, [1794]...84

2. "There can be no government where all men live upon terms of equality," from: *An Account of the Treason and Sedition, Committed by the London Corresponding Society, the Society for Constitutional Information, the other Societies of London, Sheffield, Norwich, Manchester, Bristol, Coventry, Nottingham, Derby, Birmingham, Dublin, &c. &c. their correspondence with the Convent on and*

Jacobin Societies at Paris; sending Deputies to France; admitting Barrere, Roland, and St. André, into the Society for Constitutional Information; also a dangerous letter to Mr. Sheridan, Chairman of the Society, calling themselves the Friends of the People; and The Whole of the Two Reports, Presented to the Hon. House of Commons, by The Secret Committee. **[London]: Printed for J. Downes, No. 240, Temple-Bar, Strand, [1794]. 92**

3. "Each day's Publication will be sold for One Shilling," from: ***A Copy of The Bill of Indictment Found Against Thomas Hardy, Thomas Holcroft, John Horne Tooke, John Richter, John Augustus Bonney, Matthew Moore, Stewart Kyd, John Thelwall, Jeremiah Joyce, Richard Hodgson, Thomas Wardle, John Baxter For High Treason with A List of the Grand and Petty Jurors, and the Names of the Witnesses, Who Have been Subpœned on the Part of the Crown.*** **London: J. Bell, 1794. ....94**

VI. The Accounts of the Accused Reformers 99

1. "It is our business to pursue what is right," from: Jeremiah Joyce, ***A Sermon Preached on Sunday, February the 23d, 1794. By Jeremiah Joyce, twenty-three Weeks a close Prisoner in the Tower of London, to which is added an appendix, containing an account of the author's arrest for "treasonable practices" his examination before his Majesty's most honourable Privy Council; his commitment to the Tower, and subsequent treatment.*** **London: printed for the author, and sold by J. Ridgway; H. D. Symonds; and D. Holt, Newark, 1794. ....100**

2. "It may be the language of the law, but surely common sense revolts at it," from: Thomas Holcroft, ***A Narrative of Facts, relating to a Prosecution for High Treason; including the Address to the Jury, which the Court Refused to Hear; with letters to the Attorney General, Lord Chief Justice Eyre, Mr. Serjeant Adair, the Honourable Thomas Erskine, and Vicary Gibbs, Esq. and the defence the author had prepared, if he had been brought to trial.*** **London: printed for H. D. Symonds, 1795. ....107**

3. "When the Ministers had made an effort to support their false accusations of High Treason," from: Thomas Hardy, ***Memoir of***

Thomas Hardy, Founder of, and Secretary to, the London Corresponding Society for Diffusing Useful Political Knowledge among the People of Great Britain and Ireland and for Promoting Parliamentary Reform, From its Establishment in Jan. 1792 until his arrest on a False Charge of High Treason On the 12th of May 1794. **Written by Himself. London: James Ridgway, 1832. ....117**

VII. The Legal Culture of the Trials for High Treason 119

1. "What is the proper definition of a juryman, by the laws of England, in the case of high-treason?" from: *A Calm Inquiry into the Office and Duties of Jurymen in Cases of High-Treason: with Seasonable Remarks. Earnestly Recommended to their Attention in the Present Crisis.* London: Printed for J.S. Jordan, 1794. 120

2. "Let Freedom's fair name/ Each bosom enflame," from: *Trial by Jury, A New Song.* London. 127

3. "All tyrants dead, and heav'n born LIBERTY," from: *A friend to the distressed Patriots. On the Death of Mrs. Hardy, Wife of Mr. Thomas Hardy, of Piccadilly; Imprisoned in the Tower for High Treason. She expired in Child-bed on Wednesday, August 27, 1794, and declared in her last moments, that she died a martyr to the sufferings of her husband.* London: J. Smith and J. Burks, 1794. 129

4. "Boast, BRITAIN, thy JURIES! thy glory!" from: Morganwyg Iolo, *Trial by jury. The Grand Palladium of BRITISH LIBERTY. A song, sung at the Crown and Anchor, Feb. 4 1795, in celebration of the late trials for High Treason, and Triumphant Acquittals of Thomas Hardy, John Horne Tooke, and John Thelwall; and in honour of their Counsel Thomas Erskine, and Vicary Gibbs.* By Edward Williams, "author of Poems, Lyric and Pastoral, lately published" [London, 1795]. 132

5. "ERSKINE and GIBBS! whose names, to Nature dear,/ Ages unborn may gratefully revere", from: William Hayley, *The National Advocates, a poem. Affectionately inscribed to the Honourable Thomas Erskine and Vicary Gibbs, Esquire.* London: J. Debrett, 1795.....................133

6. "Has not the cry of treason! treason! been vociferated through every part of our distracted island?" from: Mark Wilks, *Athaliah; or the Tocsin sounded by modern alarmists: two collection sermons, towards defraying the expense of the defendants in the late trials for high treason: preached on the nineteenth of April, 1795, in St. Paul's Chapel.* Norwich, [1795]. 146

7. "May the People ever keep a watchful eye," from: Charles Stanhope, Earl Stanhope. *Substance of Earl Stanhope's speech, delivered from the Chair, at a meeting of Citizens, at the Crown and Anchor, on the 4th of February 1795 to celebrate the happy event of the late trials for supposed High Treason; and published at the request of the Meeting; and the Toasts together with an appendix by Earl Stanhope respecting the trial by jury.* London: J. Burks, J. Smith, and T. Spence, [1795]. 160

8. "In an age so agitated by political convulsions as this," from: Anthony Pasquin [= John Williams], *Legislative Biography; or, an Attempt to Ascertain the Merits and Principles of the Most Admired Orators of the British Senate. Being Intended as a Companion to the Parliamentary Reports.* London: H.D. Symonds, 1795. 166

9. "Imprisonment is attended, in many cases, with circumstances singularly distressing, and notoriously unjust," from: George Dyer, *A Dissertation of the Theory and Practice of Benevolence.* London: printed for Kearsley, 1795. 171

10."I shall not be satisfied with general declarations of their love to the constitution," from: *Two Letters: The First Containing Some Remarks on the Meeting Held 5th November, 1809, to celebrate the Acquittal of Messrs. Hardy, J.H. Tooke, Thelwall, and others, in November 1794: with an Abstract of the Facts Proved on Those Trials, and also of the Confession of James Watt, Executed at Edinburgh for High Treason in October 1794. The Second containing A Short Comparative Sketch of Our Practical Constitution in Ancient Times and The Present; with some Observations on certain Assertions made by the Modern Reformers.* By A Freeholder of Cornwall. London: J. Hatchard, 1810. 187

VIII. Radicals and Reformers 193

1. "But Reason and Philosophy,/ Began to plant Democracy," from: *The Tree of Liberty, A New Song. Respectfully Addressed to the Swinish Multitude, by their Fellow Citizen, William England.* London, [1794?] 194

2. "Hang them, and bang them, and hang them up all!" from: *Brother Burke to Brother Wyndham, A New Song, for the New Year.* London, [1794?] 198

3. "The Law is the only expression of the public will," from: *The Rights of Men and Citizens [and other songs and prayer].* London: printed for Citizen Lee, [ca. 1794?] 202

4. "Thus shall thou speak unto the children of Albo," from: *The Book of Bobs. Being a Serious Caution to the Pensioned Tribe of Albo.* London: Printed for R. Bedford, and Sold by all the Patriotic Booksellers [1795?]. 209

5. "We live in times when any sentiments in favor of Liberty are dangerous to their author," from: James Sansom, *Oppression; or, the Abuse of Power, with the Recovery and Establishment of Freedom in America and France. A Poem. Interspersed with Occasional Strictures on many of the most Celebrated Characters of the Present Age. Addressed to the Reforming Societies in Great Britain.* London: Printed and sold by J. Davenport, 1795. 213

6. Thomas Spence, *The End of Oppression; or, a Quartern Loaf for Two-pence; being a Dialogue between an Old Mechanic and a Young one. Concerning the Establishment of the Rights of Man.* London: printed for the Author, and Sold by T. Spence, [1795]. 224

IX. Loyalists and Reactionaries..229

1. "So well balanced is our Constitution," from: *Opinions Delivered at a Numerous and Respectable Meeting in the Country, Lately Held for the Purpose of Signing a Declaration for the Support of*

***Government in the Present Lamentable Crisis.* London: R. Edwards, 1793. ....231**

2. "Tis time the World should grow more sage," from: Sir John Ramsea, *The Head and Limbs. A Fable.* London: Harrison, 1794. 233

3. "To defend poor Old England -- Huzza! boys, huzza!" *King, Liberty, Laws. (Tune, -- "Hearts of Oak.")*. London [1794?]....238

4. "A race of Democrats [...] Atheists, Assassins, Traitors, Regicides," from: Dickinson, Charles. *The Travels of Cyllenius. A poem. In Sixty-six cantos.* London: Printed for the Author, 1796. 242

Bibliography 251

I. Introduction

This anthology includes literary, legal and political texts mainly from the 1790s. They illustrate the dramatic circumstances under which several leading members of the radical reform movement in London were accused of high treason in 1794. The various radical and loyalist publications concerning these State Trials are indicative of England in the wake of the French Revolution – a society tormented by the fears of conspiracies and revolution and inspired by the opportunities of a new age of self-determination and enlightenment. Certain social concerns and political agendas of that time remain essential for peace and freedom to this day – concerns about the dissolution of social values and institutions through radical reforms on the one hand, and striving for the distribution of knowledge, democratisation, political participation and social progress on the other hand.

Almost two generations after the treason trials, the announcement of the acquittals was still fresh in the memory of one of the founding members of the London Corresponding Society – he who was the first to stand trial in 1794:

> Immediately on the words 'NOT GUILTY' being pronounced by the foreman of the worthy jury, the Session House, where the court sat, was almost rent with loud and reiterated shouts of applause. [...] like an electric shock, or the rapidity of lightning, the glad tidings spread through the whole town, and were conveyed much quicker than the regular post could travel, to the most distant parts of the island, where all ranks of people were anxiously awaiting the result of the trial (Hardy 1832: 72).[1]

Thomas Hardy, the notorious shoemaker, recorded these impressions in his autobiography when he looked back to 1794 from the year of the Great Reform Act. The treason trials of 1794 against allegedly dangerous traitors, which for many reform-

---

[1] Thomas Hardy, *Memoir of Thomas Hardy, Founder of, and Secretary to, the London Corresponding Society for Diffusing Useful Political Knowledge among the People of Great Britain and Ireland and for Promoting Parliamentary Reform, From its Establishment in Jan. 1792 until his arrest on a False Charge of High Treason On the 12th of May 1794.* Written by Himself (London: James Ridgway, 1832). It seems that Hardy took the "electric" metaphors from "Bell's Reports of the State Trials for High Treason," which was published in *A Copy of The Bill of Indictment* (London: J.Bell, 1794), 112.

ers had looked like a turning point in British history, lost political significance after 1832.

The texts presented in this anthology were embedded in the political debate of the 1790s in England and focus on the treason trials of 1794. Divided by controversial opinions over the repercussions of the French Revolution in Great Britain, the country eventually found itself in a war with its continental neighbour and divided from the inside. Whereas representatives of all political parties and social groups discussed reforms before the revolution, in later years calls for institutional changes were suspected of putting destabilizing pressure on the political order and of inciting revolution in England.

After the publication of Edmund Burke's infamous *Reflections on the Revolution in France* (1790), consensus on how to react to the revolution was lost and the supporters of reforms organized themselves into a heterogeneous movement, gathering together in so-called corresponding societies. In countless meetings, public demonstrations and ensuing publications, the members of the London Corresponding Society (founded in 1792), the Society for Constitutional Information (founded as early as 1780), the Friends to the Liberty of the Press and other organizations developed political ideas and concepts that would help to democratise political institutions from the outside. Within the parliament and the House of Lords, certain ideas of the reform movement were supported by the Whigs and by their eloquent leader, Charles James Fox[2]. More important is the fact that the Whigs tried to protect the reformers, who were prosecuted by the government of William Pitt,[3] though with very little success.

Freedom – Treason – Revolution

The title of this anthology does not suggest the chronological order of an historical process; rather, the purpose is to shed light on the various perspectives from which the political controversies of the 1790s were viewed.

"Freedom of the Press," chapter two in this volume and the first section of the anthology, illustrates the wider context of the reform movement. The breadth of this context was made possible through the public sphere created by the mass of daily

[2] Charles James Fox (1749-1806), Pitt's rival and leader of the Whigs.

[3] William Pitt the Younger (1759-1806), was Chancellor of the Exchequer at 23. He held the office of Prime Minister with one brief interval from the age of 25 until his death.

publications such as newspapers and pamphlets, which were discussed in public places, at designated meeting places and in private homes by all political and social groups in society. Freedom of the press and free speech were exercised to a high degree, though not guaranteed, as the many libel cases and even indictments for sedition and treason show. Whereas the government regarded many publications as an intolerable provocation, people who did not belong to any state institution and were thus dependent on the public sphere voiced an ambivalent attitude, as did, for example, Thelwall: "He condemns various suppressions of liberties since the 1790s, but sees overall progress because of the 'diffusion' of knowledge through the middle and lower classes."[4] The contemporary movements for the protection of a free press and for a more general political reform cannot be separated.

The next chapter, "Revolution in France and War with Great Britain," offers an impression of how the war with revolutionary France was perceived by the British public. These texts illustrate the passionate reactions to the bloodshed in a war that was regarded as either a just cause against a regime that had questioned the allegedly natural order of human societies, or an immoral fight against suppressed people who had fought for the very freedom that the British believed they had inherited through their constitutional traditions. Some of these texts reveal an astonishingly modern awareness of the senseless atrocities of war, and show sympathy for the ordinary people who suffer most.

"English Politics and the French Revolution" examines the specific repercussions on the British debate of the historical and political developments in France. Since a large variety of anthologies and studies have been published on this subject, the main focus here is on the extreme polarization of the British public regarding this issue, which was made worse by the fact that questions of how to reform the political institutions in Great Britain had been raised as early as the late 1770s under the influence of the American War of Independence. This chapter presents both loyalist and radical statements. Occasionally, fictitious narratives are presented in the form of highly conventionalised literary genres (such as Paine's fictitious last dying speech on the French guillotine).

---

[4] Michael Scrivener, "John Thelwall and the Press," in: *Romanticism, Radicalism, and the Press*, ed. by Stephen C. Behrendt (Detroit: Wayne State University Press, 1997), 120-136; here 133. See also Eckhart Hellmuth, "Criticising the Constitution; or, How to Talk about the Liberty of the Press in the 1790s," in: *Sites of Discourse – Public and Private Spheres – Legal Culture*, ed. by Uwe Böker and Julie A. Hibbard (Amsterdam: Rodopi, 2002), 199-210.

Chapters five through seven are dedicated to the high treason trials of 1794. Chapter five, "The Trials for High Treason of 1794," sheds light on the reasons and the method by which leading intellectuals and artisans of the reform societies were brought to trial upon an indictment of high treason. In chapter six, "Accounts of the Accused Reformers," some of the accused reformers' essential statements on their cases are presented in excerpt. Jeremiah Joyce (1763-1816), Thomas Holcroft (1745-1809), and Thomas Hardy (1752-1832) are included; John Horne Tooke (1736-1812) and John Thelwall (1764-1834) have been omitted: John Horne Tooke defended himself;[5] John Thelwall's defence has been published before.[6] Chapter seven, "The Legal Culture of the Trials for High Treason," presents the most interesting literature on the high treason trials as it shows how fictional and essayist literature was used to inform not only the public, but also the participants of the trials: the chief justice was admonished that the indictment was a constructive treason and therefore not covered by 25 Edward III; the jurymen were reminded that they had a duty to defend the British constitution as representatives of the people; and, after the trials, some authors tried to define the political significance of the acquittals for the public outside the court room and to raise donations for the acquitted but impoverished radicals.

Chapters eight and nine, "Radicals and Reformers" and "Loyalists and Reactionaries," include additional texts of the period of the high treason trials (from 1793 to 1796) from both the radical and the loyalist perspectives. Some of the texts are moderate; others call for violent actions against the respective political opponents.

The rare sources of the political and legal cultures of the London Treason Trials of 1794 present a variety of perspectives on a complex revolutionary period, which was dominated by the idea that a completely new chapter in European history had been opened with the events in France. Edmund Burke tried to explain this new experience in opposition to earlier times in one of his letters: "Then the greatest changes which could be rationally foreseen could have but little effect on the do-

[5] *The Trial of John Horne Tooke, on a Charge of High Treason: which began at the Old Bailey, ... November, 1794, and was concluded on Saturday the 22d, when he was acquitted* (Newcastle: Printed by M. Brown, 1794).

[6] See John Thelwall, "The Natural and Constitutional Right of Britons to Annual Parliaments, Universal Suffrage, and the Freedom of Popular Association (1795)," in: *Politics of English Jacobinism: Writings of John Thelwall*, edited with an introduction and notes by Gregory Claeys (University Park: Pennsylvania State University Press, 1995), 3-64.

mestick happiness of mankind – now no man's fireside is safe from the Effects of a political Revolution."[7]

This anthology brings together a variety of texts from both radical and loyalist authors. During the State Trials, which will be introduced in more detail in the introduction to chapter four, the political debate converged in an attempt not only to comment upon the unjustified indictment of high treason against leading members of the reform movement, but also to give these publications an interventionist status by creating what modern legal sociology calls a legal culture.

The Legal Culture of the Period before the Treason Trials

According to Lawrence Friedman, the making of law is the result of social forces, which press upon the legal system and evoke legal acts – "when legal culture converts interests into demands or permits this conversion."[8] The term "legal culture" describes "public knowledge of and attitudes and behaviour patterns toward the legal system" and the "long-term residue of social structure, representing old power and influence."[9] This definition covers two opposing perspectives, which Friedman distinguished as the external and the internal legal culture.

---

[7] Edmund Burke, *The Correspondence: January 1792 - August 1794*, vol. 7, ed. by P.J. Marshall and John A. Woods (Cambridge: Cambridge University Press, 1968), 64. For more research on Edmund Burke see F.P. Lock, *Edmund Burke* (London: Clarendon Press, 1998); Nicholas K. Robinson, *Edmund Burke. A Life in Caricature* (New Haven and London: Yale University Press, 1996); Frans De Bruyn, *The Literary Genres of Edmund Burke. The Political Uses of Literary Form* (Oxford: Clarendon Press, 1996); Robert. Zimmer, *Edmund Burke zur Einführung* (Hamburg: Junius, 1995); Tom Furniss, *Edmund Burke's Aesthetic Ideology. Language, Gender, and Political Economy in Revolution* (Cambridge: CUP, 1993); Dietmar Doering, *Die Wiederkehr der Klugheit. Edmund Burke und das "Augustan Age"* (Würzburg: Königshausen und Neumann, 1990); Stanley Ayling, *Edmund Burke* (London: John Murray, 1988); Michael Freeman, *Edmund Burke and the Critique of Political Radicalism* (Chicago: The University of Chicago Press, 1980); C.B. Macpherson, *Burke* (Oxford: Oxford University Press, 1980); Isaac Kramnick, *The Rage of Edmund Burke. Portrait of An Ambivalent Conservative* (New York: Basic Books, 1977); Jürgen Klein, "Ethik und Politik bei Edmund Burke", in: *Wolfenbütteler Studien zur Aufklärung*, ed. by Günther Schulz, 1.6 (1975), 271-303; David Cameron, *The Social Thought of Rousseau and Burke. A Comparative Study* (University of Toronto Press, 1973).

[8] Lawrence M. Friedman, *The Legal System: A Social Perspective* (New York: Russell Sage Foundation, 1975), 194; and Lawrence M. Friedman, "Transformations in American Legal Culture 1800-1985," Zeitschrift für Rechtssoziologie 6,2 (1985), 191-205; here 192-3.

[9] Friedman, *The Legal System* (1975) distinguishes "between an external and an internal legal culture. The external legal culture is the legal culture of the general population; the internal legal culture is the legal culture of those members of society who perform specialized legal tasks.

Since the legal culture of the insiders "is by no means an autonomous growth and by no means an exception to the general proposition about the primacy of society over law,"[10] the pamphlets, sermons, poems and essays on the treason trials published in the external legal culture in 1794 and 1795 could have an impact on the legal system which made the acquittals possible.

The Reform Movement of the 1790s and the Treason Trials of 1794

Did the reform movement of the 1790s present a threat to the state? On the one hand, the political aims of the artisans and intellectuals who were accused of high treason in 1794 were quite dangerous to the stability of the political order in Great Britain at a time of war with revolutionary France. On the other hand, the manner in which political goals – such as universal suffrage, annual parliaments, free press and free speech – were propagated in countless speeches, resolutions and pamphlets prepared the road to gradual democratisation in the nineteenth century.

Thomas Hardy saw the reform movement of the early 1790s justified by the time he wrote to his friend and patron, Sir Francis Burdett, himself a famous reformer of his day, on 7 March 1831:

> I congratulate you on the pleasing prospect before us [...] that great national blessing – a *Parliamentary Reform* [...] I hope the Ministers will be well supported by the *old* and *true* Reformers. Perhaps, you may smile when I tell you, that I am now, *for the first time*, in my humble measure, a supporter of Ministers. I greatly rejoice to see the great cause of Civil Liberty prospering, not only in this country, but all over Europe, and that I have lived so many years to witness it, having entered on the 80th year of my journey of life.[11]

In order to understand why the government of William Pitt decided in early 1794 to prosecute leading reformers in London, one has to go back to the trial for sedition

---

Every society has a legal culture, but only societies with legal specialists have an internal legal culture. What sets legal process in motion is demand on the system. Interests must be converted into demands; attitudes and behaviours which are part of the external legal culture must be processed to fit the requirements of the internal legal culture" (223).

[10] Friedman, *The Legal System* (1975), 194.

[11] Quoted from Alan Wharam, *The Treason Trials, 1794* (Leicester and London: Leicester University Press, 1992), 264.

against the Scottish reformers one year earlier, which encouraged the British government to do the same in London. A secret committee was appointed to examine the activities of leading members of the London Corresponding Society and the Society for Constitutional Information.[12] The Secret Committee came to the conclusion that the reformers in London had not only committed acts of sedition, but had actually committed high treason.

With the acquittal of the accused reformers in November 1794, the state failed in the end to suppress the reform movement. However, the treason trials substantially changed the public debate on reform and democratisation. By establishing a legal culture that integrated the legal discourse into a broader agenda of democratisation, the reformers had successfully participated in the process of jurisdiction.

The great success of the defence counsel (Thomas Erskine and Vicary Gibbs) could not have been achieved without the support of an intensive campaign of radicals outside the courtroom. The many texts, which were written in order to prepare, to accompany and to revise the trials, created an entire set of values and a shared identity as democrats. The purpose of these publications was to open the legal institutions for one's own interpretation of the legal status of the reform movement. The various authors objected to the government's construction of a charge of high treason and regarded their contributions to the controversy as legitimate participation in the legal process. By circulating statements from outside the legal institutions, the political, legal and fictional publications encompassed an attempt to create a democratic public sphere in which a culture of participation could be established.

In this manner, the experience of the treason trials helped to re-define the function literature played as a political activity. Literature did not comment upon political reality or educate the readers, but rather provided a language in which the highly specialized and long-winded language of the legal system was transformed into a discourse that was accessible to the public. It was a language that was intended to explain the political motives behind legal activities or to analyse the reasoning of legal experts from the point of view of various social or political interests. In this way, during the treason trials, the reform movement acquired the knowledge neces-

[12] For two comprehensive studies on the corresponding societies, see Günther Lottes, *Politische Aufklärung und plebejisches Publikum. Zur Theorie und Praxis des englischen Radikalismus im späten 18. Jahrhundert* (München: Oldenbourg, 1979) and Albert Goodwin, *The Friends of Liberty: The English Democratic Movement in the Age of the French Revolution* (London: Alan Hutchinson, 1979).

sary to participate not only in the interpretation of existing laws, but also, potentially, in the making of new ones – both to their advantage and disadvantage.

The first contribution to the legal culture of the treason trials was the publication of the report of the Secret Committee, which had been debated in the two Houses in spring 1794 and later published under the title *An Account of the Treason and Sedition* (1794). The authors of these two reports declared "that the object of these societies was to proceed in contempt of Parliament, and to assume to themselves the power of a legislature, and to introduce into the country the anarchy and confusion which has so fatally prevailed in France" (4). Pitt claimed that the constitution was in danger and that the suspension of "laws which are essentially necessary to the permanent existence of the Constitution" was inevitable (4).

In recent years, a number of editions of political literature of the 1790s have been published. These are either dedicated to individual authors or to a number of authors who wrote texts on specific historical events. Particularly, the political writings of William Godwin and John Thelwall include contributions that were published in the context of the high treason trials.[13] Claeys edited the *Political Writings of the 1790s*,[14] mainly focussing on the debate over Edmund Burke's *Reflections on the Revolution in France* and Tom Paine's *The Rights of Man.*

The anthology *Freedom – Treason – Revolution* is a compilation of mainly unpublished texts which either illustrate the political background of the 1790s or belong to the legal culture of the treason trials. Through these trials, the beginnings of a gradual development of democratic participation and the possible reform of institutions within the legal and political systems become perceivable in an exemplary way. For the most part, the anthology is made up of political and legal treatises,

---

[13] *Political and Philosophical Writings of William Godwin*; Vol. 7: Essays, ed. Mark Philp (London: William Pickering, 1993); *John Thelwall's the Peripatetic*, ed. Judith Thompson (Detroit: Wayne State University, 2001); John Thelwall, *Poems Written in Close Confinement in the Tower and Newgate, under a Charge of High Treason 1795*, ed. by Jonathan Wordsworth (Oxford: Woodstock Books, 2000); *The Politics of English Jacobinism. Writings of John Thelwall*, ed. by Gregory Claeys (University Park: Pennsylvania State University Press, 1995), and John Thelwall's "Essay, Towards a Definition of Animal Vitality," in: Nicholas Roe, *The Politics of Nature: William Wordsworth and Some Contemporaries*. 2nd ed. (Houndmills: Palgrave, 2002), 87-119.

[14] *Political Writings of the 1790s*, ed. by Gregory Claeys, 8 vols (London: Pickering and Chatto, 1995).

fictional texts, sermons, and songs relating to the treason trials.[15] This literature illustrates how both loyalist and the radical voices, presented in a variety of literary genres, not only recorded the trials, but also contributed to their course of events. The texts presented are introduced, conceptualised and annotated.

[15] Important anthologies on the political debates of the 1790s before Claeys's publication include *British Pamphleteers*; Vol. 2: *From the French Revolution to the Nineteen-Thirties*, ed. by Reginald Reynolds and A.J.P. Taylor (London: Allan Wingate, 1951), *The Debate on the French Revolution, 1789-1800*, ed. by Alfred Cobban (London: A.& C. Black, 1960), *Burke, Paine, Godwin, and the Revolution Controversy*, ed. by Marilyn Butler (Cambridge: Cambridge University Press, 1984), *Poetry and Reform: Periodical Verse from the English Democratic Press 1792-1824*, ed. by Michael Scrivener (Detroit: Wayne State University Press, 1992).

II. Freedom of the Press

The struggle for freedom of the press dates back to the seventeenth century when John Milton wrote his famous *Areopagitica* (1643), written at a time when censorship was temporarily in abeyance. Milton proclaimed the power of a free press in the following words:

> Behold now this vast City; a City of refuge, the mansion house of liberty, encompass'd and surrounded with His protection; the shop of warre hath not there more anvils and hammers waking, to fashion out the plates and instruments of armed Justice in defence of beleaguer'd Truth, then there be pens and heads there, sitting by their studious lamps, musing, searching, revolving new notions and idea's wherewith to present, as with their homage and their fealty the approaching Reformation: others as fast reading, trying all things, assenting to the force of reason and convincement.[16]

After the Restoration, the Licensing Act of 1662 (allowing censorship) was mitigated only after the Great Plague of 1664-65. After its first lapse in 1679, James II revived it in 1685. It took another ten years before censorship was eventually abolished when the Licensing Act lapsed again in 1695 after the commons had refused to renew it in 1694. John Locke, who tried to convince the Commons not to renew it, played an essential role in this process.

Freedom of the press gained new momentum in the reform movement of the late eighteenth century. The idea of the sovereignty of the people gave new significance to a free press as a means of participation and of resistance to abuse of governmental power. In the understanding of the reform movement, civil rights included freedom of conscience, trial by jury, freedom of the press, and freedom of election.[17]

---

[16] *The Complete Prose Works of John Milton*, 8 vols. (New Haven: Yale University Press; London: Oxford University Press, 1953-1982), vol. 2 (1953), 553-554; quoted in Brean S. Hammond, *Professional Imaginative Writing in England, 1670-1740, 'Hackney for Bread'* (Oxford: Clarendon Press, 1997), 28. At the beginning of the eighteenth century, authors such as Daniel Defoe and Henry Fielding fought for freedom of the press. For Defoe, see *The Best of Defoe's Review: An Anthology*, ed. by William L. Payne (New York: Columbia University Press, 1951), 73-106.

[17] See e.g. Robert Hall, "An Apology for the Freedom of the Press and for General Liberty (1793)," in: *English Radical Tradition 1763-1914*, ed. by S. MacCoby (New York: New York University Press, 1957), 60-2; for more information, see W.H. Wickwar, *The Struggle for the*

Two considerable challenges to the freedom of the press occurred as a result of the treason trials of 1794; first, when published material was used to construct an indictment for high treason; and, second, in November 1795, when the so-called "Two Gagging Acts" passed the Commons. In an "Extraordinary Meeting of the Whig Club of England, Crown and Anchor, Tavern, Nov. 11, 1795", these laws were called "a direct attack on the Freedom of the Press and of Speech – on all the rights of popular discussion, and even on the sacred right of petition."[18] The Whig Club passed a resolution demanding the preservation of the "Liberty of the Press and the Freedom of Public Discussion."[19]

The following three texts illustrate the central role of the press during the reform movement in the 1790s. Not only were reformers and radicals fascinated with the possibilities of press, but also conservative readers.

1. "Long, long live the Blessings that spring from the Press," from: *The Blessings of a Free Press, A New Song.* [London], [Dec. 31, 1792]

Let *Virgils* and *Homers*, if any such be, Sir!
Sing demi-gods, heroes, and conqu'rors and kings:
The clarion of war has no relish for me, Sir![20]
My muse never meddles with such mighty things:
With *Anacreon*, or *Horace*, by night or by day, Sir!
Of love or of wine, I could carol *sans cesse*:
But, here, a new Theme pre-engages my lay, Sir!
I sing of -- the Blessings that spring from the Press.

Freedom of the Press, 1819-1832 (London: Allen and Unwin, 1928), Peter D.G. Thomas, "John Wilkes and the Liberty of the Press (1771)," Bulletin of the Institute of Historical Research 33 (1960), 86-98, F.S. Siebert, *Freedom of the Press in England 1476-1776* (Urbana: University of Illinois Press, 1965) and Eckhart Hellmuth, "Kommunikation und Radikalismus, Loyalismus und ideologischer Pluralismus: 'Popular Politics' in England in der zweiten Hälfte des 18. Jahrhunderts," in: *Entwicklungsschwellen im 18. Jahrhundert*, ed. Karl Eibl, *Aufklärung* 14,1 (1989), 79-104.

[18] *The History of Two Acts* (London: G.G. and J. Robinson, 1796), 121.

[19] Ibid., 123. For this period also see Eckhart Hellmuth's forthcoming *"The Liberty of the Press". Zur Geschichte einer Idee im frühneuzeitlichen England* (=Veröffentlichungen des Deutschen Historischen Instituts London).

[20] This is a very stereotypical rejection of ancient heroes and the glorification of war in the decade of sensibility. See Stuart Curran, *Poetic Form and British Romanticism* (Oxford: Oxford University Press, 1986), 167.

II.

When tyranny, foster'd by dire superstition,
The world had envelop'd in Stygian night[21];
And *monarchs* and *monks*, by a strange coalition,
Half-smother'd the sparklings of *Reason* and *Right*:
Heav'n sent, in its mercy, a Faustus -- when, lo! Sir,
The darkness already begins to be less:
To the mem'ry of Faustus a bumper we owe, Sir,
For all the rare Blessings that spring from the Press.

III.

Nor Schœffer, Coberger, Frobenius, Plantinus;
Nor Aldus, nor Gryphius, nor Badius, nor Bleau;
The Stephens, Turnebus, Morell, Comelinus*[22]
Be ever forgotten by mortals below:

---

[21] A popular image in the poetry of Milton, Byron and others was the portrayal of blackness and darkness as typical of the river Styx in the underworld.

* All eminent Printers of the 15th and the 16th Centuries

[22] **Peter Schöffer (1425-1503)**, contemporary of Johannes Gutenberg, printer in Mainz between 1457 and 1503. **Anthony Koberger (Koburger, Coberger) (ca. 1445-1513)**, German printer, publisher, and bookseller. By 1480 he outstripped Schöffer at Mainz, and soon became the most successful printer in Europe. **Johannes Frobenius (1460-1527)**, inventor and printer, published a Bible in Latin in 1491 and knew Paracelsus. **Christopher Plantinus** printed the first concordance made according to the authorized Latin text of the Bible (Antwerp, 1599). This French-born Flemish printer had branch shops in Paris, Leyden, and Salamanca. **Aldus Manutius (1452-1515)**, Venetian printer, who is credited with the creation of italic type. His initiative to publish humanist texts in portable, octavo editions (e.g. Horace) had a great influence on the dissemination of ideas and was praised by Erasmus. **Sebastianus Gryphius (1493-1556)**, was a printer in Lyon and a conduit for much of the printing done in Venice at the time. Sometimes called for his birthplace **Jodocus Badius Ascensius (1462-1535)**, the French printer, born at Asche, near Brussels, taught Greek and edited classics in Lyons before he became a printer. In 1503 he went to Paris where he established the Ascensian press, which printed over 400 books, mainly Greek and Latin texts. **Willem Janzoon Blaeu/ Bleau (1571-1638)** founded the most important cartographic publishing company in the Netherlands. Blaeu depicted in about 600 maps the entire known world. When he died his sons Johan (1595-1673) and Cornelius (? -1648) continued the successful business. **Robert Estienne** (1503-1559) from Paris, also known as **Robert Stephens** or Stephanus, was the first to print the Bible divided into standard numbered verses. **Adrian Turnebus (1512-1565)**, philologist, presumably of Scottish origin, was born in Normandy and died in Paris. Little is known about Turnebus, whose work includes commentaries on the ancient classics, short treatises, and poems. Morel (in the text Morell) is the surname of several French classical scholars and printers in the 16th and 17th centuries. The author referred most likely to **Guillaume Morel (1505-1564)**, who set up a print shop in Paris and subsequently succeeded Turnebus as king's printer in 1555. **Isaac Comelinus** was a 17th-century printer.

From dust and disgrace antient Learning they drew, Sir,
And clothed her sweet form in an elegant dress:
From Nation to Nation she rapidly flew, Sir,
And scatter'd -- the Blessings that spring from the Press.

IV.
With joy, nay, with rapture, BRITANNIA received her,
Assign'd her a Fane, and made *Caxton* her priest:
Ah, how must it, afterwards, sadly have griev'd her,
When daggers were aim'd at her Favourite's breast!
Behold, in the reign of a blood-thirsty *Tudor*,
The *State* and the *Church* (as of old) coalesce.
The GODDESS to treat as a shameless intruder;
And stifle -- the Blessings that spring from the Press.

V.
But 'spite of the *State*, and the *Church* and the *Devil*,
A few faithful worshippers round her arose,
Her cause to assert, and defend her from evil;
By speaking, and writing, in verse and in prose:
The rage of a *Bonner*[23] they bravely withstood, Sir,
Bore petulant insult, oppression, distress:
Nay, scrupled not even to barter their blood, Sir,
Their blood -- for the Blessings that springs from the Press.

VI.
When *Stuarts* attempted again to dethrone her,
And shackled with fetters her innocent hands;
Upstarted a race, in defence of her honour,
Who dared to oppose such tyrannic commands.
See talents and courage unite in the strife, Sir;
See *Milton* and *Burnet*[24] encounter disgrace!

---

[23] Probably an allusion to Claudius Bonner, a working acquaintance of Elizabeth Powell, who printed a seditious pamphlet entitled *Vox Populi Vox Dei*, in order to create evidence against his employer. See Paula McDowell, *The Women of Grub Street. Press, Politics, and Gender in the London Literary Marketplace* (Oxford: Clarendon Press, 1998), 78-79.

[24] The Reverend Doctor Gilbert Burnet was King William's personal chaplain and policy adviser. The political strategist and print propagandist offered to Aphra Behn a lifelong royalist court patronage in return for a poem celebrating the coronation of William and Mary, as Martine Brownley, "Bishop Gilbert Burnet and the Vagaries of Power," in: *The Age of William III and*

See *Prynne* lose his ears,[25] and great SYDNEY his life, Sir;
Supporting the Blessings that spring from the Press.

VII.
Ev'n under a *Brunswick*,[26] I'm sorry to say, Sir,
Some daring attempts have, at seasons, been made.
Her pow'r to controul, and her friends to dismay, Sir:
And deep, at one time, was the treachery laid.
But now, when a SOV'REIGN, so good and so gracious
Possesses the crown, which may long he possess;
No minion, we trust, howsoever audacious,
Will combat the Blessings that spring from the Press.

VIII.
But should any sycophant[27] minister try, Sir,

Mary II: Power, Politics, and Patronage 1688-1702, ed. by Robert P. Maccubbin and Martha Hamilton-Phillips (Williamsburg, Va.: The College of William and Mary, 1989), 77-81, explains. Later Swift heavily criticised Burnet's support of a low woman writer and his language, as we learn from Marilyn Francus, *The Converting Imagination: Linguistic Theory and Swift's Satiric Prose* (Carbondale and Edwardsville: Southern Illinois University Press, 1994), 169-185.

[25] William Prynne (1600-1669), a Puritan barrister and pamphleteer, wrote *Histriomastix* (1633; ed. Arthur Freeman [New York: Garland, 1974]), in which he attacked the stage. William Laud held this treatise to be libellous of the Queen, who loved the theatre. Prynne's book was the first to be burned by the hangman. He was put in the pillory, where his ears were cut off, and he was branded. He was tried again in 1637, at which time what remained of his ears was cut off. The story of that trial is told in Prynne's *A New Discovery of the Prelates Tyranny* (London, 1641). Prynne was released in 1640. Later, Prynne was the prosecutor of Archbishop Laud in a case that resulted in Laud's execution.

[26] King George III.

[27] Both sides to criticise governmental corruption and the social morality of the aristocracy used this term. Edmund Burke wrote in his *Reflections on the Revolution in France*, in: *The Writings and Speeches of Edmund Burke*, ed. by Paul Langford, L. G. Mitchell, William B. Todd, vol. 8 (London: Clarendon Press, 1981), 53-293: "For though hereditary wealth and the rank which goes with it are too much idolized by creeping sycophants, and the blind abject admirers of power, they are too rashly slighted in shallow speculations of the petulant, assuming, short-sighted coxcombs of philosophy" (102-3). Paine, on the other hand, spoke in *The Rights of Man* of "the sycophancy of historians and men like Mr. Burke" (*Rights of Man, Common Sense and Other Political Writings*, ed. by Mark Philp [Oxford: Oxford University Press, 1998], 83-331; here 284) and Thelwall claimed in The Tribune, No. XXX, 140, "On the Causes of the CALAMITIES and DISTURBANCES that afflict the Nation," which had been delivered at the lecture room in the Beaufort Buildings on Sept. 25, 1795: "Citizens, let us but get rid of our placemen, our pensioners, our sycophants, our commissaries and contractors, and the old ladies who wrap themselves up in scarlet cloaks may sleep in undisturbed security" (in: Thelwall 1995: 249).

Our sacred PALLADIUM to steal or profane:
All here to her succour directly would fly, Sir;
And render his efforts and stratagems vain.
Not *Ulysses* himself, tho' for filching renow'd, Sir,
With all his duplicity, art and address,
Would, on this occasion, sufficient be found, Sir,
To pilfer the Blessings that spring from the Press.
IX.
To the MAN of the people, who ne'er was a trimmer,
To SHERIDAN, ERSKINE, BYNG, MAITLAND and GREY,[28]
And other try'd men, let us fill up a brimmer;
And crown the dear toast with a ninefold huzza!
With zeal in his heart, and a glass in his hand, Sir,
His Creed let each fautor of FREEDOM profess;
And shout, while around our PALLADIUM we stand, Sir,
"Long, long live the Blessings that spring from the Press."

---

[28] All these men were close to the reform movement and are mentioned as a group of people in Thomas Bentley's *To Lords Stanhope, Lauderdale, and Landsdowne; and to Mr. Fox, Mr. Sheridan, Mr. Grey, Mr. Byng, Mr. Erskine, Mr. Wilberforce, and all the Lords and Gentlemen generally supposed to be the Friends of Parliamentary Reform, The Friends of the Liberty of the Press, The Friends of the People, and The Friends of the Africans, &c.* (London, 22 April 1793). The playwright and Whig politician Richard Brinsley Sheridan (1751-1816) supported Fox's stand for freedom throughout the war against France. See Fintan O'Toole, *A Traitor's Kiss: The Life of Richard Brinsley Sheridan* (London: Granta Books, 1997). Thomas Erskine (1750-1823), a friend of Fox and Sheridan, was a great lawyer who was counsel for the defence in the trials of Tom Paine, Thomas Walker, Thomas Hardy and Horne Tooke. See Lloyd Paul Stryker, *For the Defense: Thomas Erskine, the Most Enlightened Liberal of His Times, 1750-1823* (Garden City, NY: Doubleday, 1949); and John Hostettler, *Thomas Erskine and Trial by Jury* (Chichester: Barry Rose Law Publishers, 1996). James Maitland (1759-1839), eighth Earl of Lauderdale, was a radical MP who strongly opposed the Treasonable Practices Bill. Maitland, Charles Grey and R.B. Sheridan were among the 39 Members of Parliament who rejected the suspension of the Habeas Corpus Act in May 1794. See *Debates on the Report of the Committee of Secrecy* (1794), 24. Charles Grey, later second Earl Grey (1764-1845), supported Fox. He was a leading member of the Society of Friends of the People. At the end of his career, he carried out his reform ideals by passing the Reform Act of 1832. In the *Debate on the Habeas Corpus Suspension Bill* (16-17 May 1794), he defended the reform movement: "What was the object of these people? 'Their ostensible object,' said the minister, 'is parliamentary reform; but their real object is the destruction of the government of the country.' How was that explained? 'By the resolutions,' said the minister, 'of these persons themselves; for they do not talk of applying to parliament, but of applying to the people for the purpose of obtaining a parliamentary reform.' If this language be criminal, said Mr. Grey, I am one of the greatest criminals. I say, that from the House of Commons I have no hope of a parliamentary reform; that I have no hope of a reform, but from the people themselves." Quoted from Cobban 1960: 336.

2. "If we possess that unimpaired, we can never be enslaved. If we lose it we cannot be free," from: *The Trial of Daniel Isaac Eaton for publishing a supposed Libel intituled Politics for the People, or, Hogs Wash: at Justice Hall in the Old Bailey, February Twenty-Fourth, 1794.* London: published by the defendant, Daniel Isaac Eaton, 1794.

Daniel Isaac Eaton (d. 1814) was one of the most notorious booksellers. Eaton was the publisher of John Gilpin's *Ghost* and the Chaunticlere allegory by John Thelwall, in which regicidal imagery is used. Eaton was prosecuted for this publication and acquitted. In the preface to his own edition of this text, Thelwall noted that Eaton had published this episode in his *Politics for the People* under the title "King Chanticleer, or the fate of Tyranny."[29] The acquittal was the third one in Eaton's career as a bookseller. Eaton's lawyer, Mr. Gurney, reminded the court of the importance of civil rights:

> No, Gentlemen, so long as we preserve those bulwarks of our constitution the Liberty of the Press, and Trial by Jury, and Juries preserve their independence, I am sure all the efforts of tyranny to obtain a footing in this Island will prove abortive.
>
> Gentlemen, This is not vain and empty declamation. The existence of every right we possess depends in the first instance upon the freedom of the press. While we profess that unimpaired, we can never be enslaved. If we possess that unimpaired, we can never be enslaved. If we lose it we cannot be free. While the press, which has been beautifully and emphatically styled "the eye of the political body," continues to inspect and watch with diligence the administration of public affairs, some hope remains that those affairs may be administered with some attention to the public interest. But if it is destroyed, or constantly harassed in the performance of its necessary functions, we may abandon ourselves to despondency and despair (51).

---

[29] Eaton had published *Thelwall's story in Politics for the People*, 2 vols. (1793-1795; rpt. New York: Greenwood Press, 1968), 102-107. Thelwall reprinted a poetic version as *John Gilpin's Ghost, or, The Warning Voice of King Chanticleer: An Historical Ballad: Written Before the Late Trials, and dedicated to the Treason-Hunters of Oakham* (London: T. Smith, 1795). See also *The Tribune* 1:165, as referred to in Thelwall 1995: xix.

3. "In Thee the gen'rous Monitor we find," from: William Pinn, *Poems on Various Subjects: in which is a Most Beautiful and Novel Description of his Majesty's Review of the Kentish Volunteers. August the First, 1799*. Chatham: Printed by C. Townson, 1800.

William Pinn wrote from a loyalist point of view. He praised the achievements of the press, which allowed one to stay informed about events in remote countries. Like reformers or radicals, he associated progress with such new forms of distributing knowledge, but he did not draw the same political conclusions.

Address to the Newspaper

PLEASING Instructor, bringing to our ken
Each act important, 'mongst the sons of men;
By thy assistance we, in little time,
May view each nation, visit ev'ry clime;
Behold the pow'r and wealth of every state;
Watch the intrigues of all the mighty great,
See their ambitious aims, and trace the cause
Of feuds domestic, or of foreign wars;
Follow their mandates to the hostile plain,
View the fierce onset, count the maim'd and slain;
Observe the victory and the lawrels won,
Share their glory, but of danger none.
Next led by Thee to contemplate the main,
Where dreadful tempests hold indignant reign;
There see the scatter'd fleet impetuous scud
O'er the rough bosom of the briny flood;
Where raging waves to lofty mountains rise,
Roar as they roll, and seem to touch the skies;
Scarce helm or sail the mariner can rule;
Tremendous elements defy controul:
With fury driven to the fearful coast,
The haven make, or, dash'd on rocks, are lost;
Whilst we in humble expectation wait
Their safe return, till you unfold their fate.

When war bursts forth, that cruel scourge to man,
When states 'gainst neighbouring states in secret plan,

Thirsting for blood and spoil from shore to shore,
When fields and seas are stain'd with human gore;
Tis then, thy province justly to display,
What dire events affect each passing day,
When the brave peasants from each hamlet torn,
In anguish deep leave relatives to mourn;
The loss of Husband, Father, Brother, Friend,
Tis thine a philanthropic aid to lend:
Point out their woes, their cares, their indigence,
And urge the public to benevolence.
When Faction to black Treason renders birth,
And base assassins dagger'd now prowl forth,
From councils dark, to plunge the murd'rous steel
Into that breast that burns for public weal,
The glorious task is thine, from fable night
To draw their foul designs to truth and light.

When potent rulers bid their heroes cease,
And deign to give their wearied subjects peace;
When commerce my expand her milky sails,
And wish no convoy but the favoring gales,
Then with a secret pleasure we peruse
The tranquil pages of the public news.

In Thee the gen'rous Monitor we find,
With silent warnings, speaking to mankind
Of strange vicissitudes, in every stage,
From helpless infancy to hoary age.

To day we learn Alphonso met his fate,
The instant he arriv'd to man's estate:
His parents' only son, of noble blood,
Who just had 'scap'd the danger of the flood,
The grand tour ended, and now quite complete
His education to engage his seat
Among the Peers, his power to display,
Or in the Privy Council bear a sway;
Hint Phebe sigh'd for, amiable and fair
Whom he ador'd, intending her to share
His every comfort, in his splendid state;

But see the hand of an unerring fate
Cuts off the thread of life, to sudden death
He leaves his Friends, his Charmer, and his breath.

And here we find another awful tale;
The sweet Priscilla, lately blithe and hale,
Pride of the age, for symmetry and mien,
Not less in beauty than the Cyprian queen,[30]
Now breaths no more; how solemn to relate,
In flames she meets her sad unhappy fate:
Drest for the Ball, conversing with delight,
On the approaching pleasures of the night,
When from the fire a spark shot to her clothes,
And in an instant the dread blaze arose;
In vain she shrieks, in vain she cries for aid,
Vain all the efforts of her frighted maid;
The raging element, the ruthless fires,
Her vitals seize, and soon the nymph expires.

For these were beauty, health, and wealth, bestow'd;
How intricate the purposes of God!
Did He, in condescention from the throne,
Upon his creatures of a day look down,
See them obnoxious to some wretched fate,
That might the peace of many ruinate,
And snatch them hence from transitory time,
To bless their souls in an immortal clime.

In the succeeding Paragraph appears
A Character who grac'd full ninety years;
Ran the good race, fought well the Christian fight,
Clos'd life's last scene with comfort and delight;
Whilst living, freely from a friendly store,
Bestow'd his bounties to the grateful poor;
Nor aught withheld his gracious God had given,
But here on earth anticipated heaven.

---

[30] Another name for Aphrodite (Venus).

Blest man! would more thy bright example choose,
How eager should we grasp the public news:
Alas! too true, where we can read of one
Like thee, we find a many are undone.

Some Bankrupts by a vain and idle life,
Some ruin'd by the Law in hateful strife;
Some votaries to gaming, some to drink,
Some victims fall in prostitution's sink
Some all their days in horrid rapine spend,
And justly meet an ignominious end.

Where dreadful rocks or shoals infest the coast,
By which the unsuspecting vessel's lost;
The beacon's plac'd to warn the future bark
To steer with caution from the fiery mark.

So you hold out the vices of the age,
And all their dire effects in love presage;
Thou kind Preceptor, offspring of the Press,
May we for Thee our Constitution bless,
And gratefully the privilege confess.

III. Revolution in France and War with Great Britain

The war against the American colonies was regarded to be the first time in English history that – in the view of many Britons – the allegedly revolutionary traditions of 1688 were betrayed. After the French Revolution, these traditions were perceived to be dangerous and were rejected. The period of reforms, which had begun in 1784 under the younger Pitt, came to an abrupt end.

After Edmund Burke's publication of *Reflections on the Revolution in France* (1790), controversy over the possible repercussions of the French revolution in Great Britain became more and more irreconcilable.[31] Burke provoked an avalanche of texts written in reply by supporters and opponents. In the ensuing struggle for reforms and even revolution, these debates were carried into the realms of literature, linguistics, science, philosophy and theology. The English responses to the French Revolution and its impact on British literature have been explored in a number of publications.[32]

---

[31] Burke 1981: 53-293. For a more accessible edition, Edmund Burke, *Reflections on the Revolution in France*, ed. L.G. Mitchell (Oxford: Oxford University Press, 1993).

[32] Paul Keen, *The Crisis of Literature in the 1790s. Print Culture and the Public Sphere* (Cambrdige: Cambrdige University Press, 1999), *Cultural Politics in the 1790s. Literature, Radicalism, and the Public Sphere*, ed. by Andrew McCann (London: Macmillan, 1999), Ian Gilmour, *Riots, Risings and Revolution: Governance and Violence in Eighteenth-Century England* (London: Hutchinson, 1992; Pimlico, 1993), Chris Jones, *Radical Sensibility: Literature and Ideas in the 1790s* (London: Routledge, 1993), *The French Revolution Debate in English Literature and Culture*, ed. by Lisa Plummer Crafton (London: Greenwood Press, 1997), *Representing the French Revolution: Literature, Historiography and Art*, ed. by James A.W. Heffernan (Hanover, NH: University Press of New England, 1992), Lynn Hunt, *The Family Romance of the French Revolution* (London: Routledge, 1992), *The French Revolution and British Popular Politics*, ed. Mark Philp (Cambridge: Cambridge University Press, 1991), David Bindman, *The Shadow of the Guillotine: Britain and the French Revolution* (London: British Museum Publications, 1989), Gregory Claeys, *Thomas Paine: Social and Political Thought* (London: Unwin Hyman, 1989), *Britain and the French Revolution, 1789-1815*, ed. by H.T. Dickinson (London: Macmillan, 1989); *The French Revolution and British Culture*, ed. by Ian Small and Ceri Crossley (Oxford: Oxford University Press, 1989), Steven Blakemore, *Burke and the Fall of Language: The French Revolution as Linguistic Event* (Hanover, NH: University Press of New England, 1988), Seamus Deane, *The French Revolution and Enlightenment in England, 1789-1832* (Cambridge, MA: Harvard University Press, 1988), Joan Landes, *Women and the Public Sphere in the Age of the French Revolution* (Ithaca: Cornell University Press, 1988), Nicholas Roe, *Wordsworth and Coleridge: The Radical Years* (Oxford: Clarendon Press, 1988), H.T. Dickinson, *British Radicalism and the French Revolution, 1789-1815* (Oxford: Blackwell, 1985), J.A. Hone, *For the Cause of Truth: Radicalism in London, 1796-1821* (Oxford: Oxford University Press, 1982), Goodwin

Richard Price (1723-1791) is remembered as the philosopher of a millenarian theory of politics. In his *Reflections*, Burke attacked Price for the political statements he had presented on 4 Nov. 1789 from the pulpit of a London meeting house. Price spoke to the members of the "Society for the Commemoration of the Revolution of Great Britain", who had met in order to celebrate the achievements of 1688. With *A Discourse on the Love of our Country*, Price was among the first intellectuals to react to the events on the continent, thus causing Edmund Burke to respond in his famous book, which precipitated a well-documented and edited pamphlet war.[33]

When the French Revolution threatened the stability of the political structures in Great Britain, the once ardent speaker against corruption and for freedom and reform changed his mind completely. Burke's *Reflections* hold the "swinish multitude" – the French followers of the Revolution – responsible for political chaos and the irreversible destruction of the political institutions of France. He accused the English Jacobin reform societies, such as the London Corresponding Society, of pursuing the same goals in Britain.

After war broke out between Britain and France in 1793, the government of William Pitt tried by all means to suppress the radical reform movement. The radicals, on the other hand, deplored the war against revolutionary France in spite of the well-known atrocities.

In his lecture "On the Moral and Political Influence of the Prospective Principle of Virtue,"[34] John Thelwall explained that he distinguished between the "*principles of the French Revolution*", which *represent* "the *triumphs of reason*" and "the *rights of man*", from the cruelties of Robespierre:

> ... daggers and guillotines are not principles. The disordered imagination of a Burke, the metaphysical phrenzy of a Windham,[35] or the artful and studied harangues of that great arithmetician Pitt, may confound things

---

1979, E.P. Thompson, *The Making of the English Working Class* (Harmondsworth: Penguin, 1968).

[33] For editions of these texts, see *The Debate on the French Revolution* (1960) and Claeys 1995.

[34] All quotations are from "On the Moral and Political Influence," in: Thelwall 1995: 95.

[35] William Windham was one of the most controversial politicians of his time. For Thomas Holcroft's "Letter to the Right Honourable William Windham on the Intemperance and Dangerous Tendency of His Public Conduct" (London, 1795), and many more letter of Windham to Burke and letters addressed to him, Cobban 1960; for more information in this book (155).

together as opposite as darkness to light, or as their darling measures to the interests of humanity and justice; but we will not be so deceived.

Thelwall emphasized that "It is not the men of France, that I glory in; it is not the execution of the King – I am an enemy to all executions!" He warned that the British government might "attempt to establish the same system of terror". Thelwall believed that "the new fangled inquisitorial system of spies and informers [...] has supplanted the constitution of Britain".

1. "The War with the French People is both Impolitic and Immoral" (1796), from: William Hodgson M.D., *The Case of W. Hodgson, now Confined in Newgate for the Payment of Two Hundred Pounds, after Having Suffered Two Years' Imprisonment on a Charge of Sedition, Considered and Compared with the Existing Laws of the Country: by himself.* London: printed for the author, and sold by D.I. Eaton and others, 1796.

William Hodgson[36] wrote the following defence in the infamous Newgate prison in February 1796. He did not ask for mercy, but for justice: he did not consider himself to be guilty; he considered himself a victim of the oppression of the opposition by the government during the war against France. He emphasized that he spoke not only as an individual, but also as one among many citizens who are "the medium through which their rights have been invaded" (*The Case of W. Hodgson*, 14). The purpose of the publication was to give his fellow citizens "the opportunity of comparing the administration of the law with its spirit". Imprisonment not only damaged the health and the financial situation of the prisoners but also brought dramatic consequences for their families as many craftsmen and shop owners went bankrupt

[36] One of the most successful publications of William Hodgson was *The Fabulator, or the Hall of Aesop, being a selection of fables in prose and verse from the most esteemed authors* (London: H.D. Symonds, 1795). Another anthology of prose texts was entitled *The Gleaner* (1800). Hodgson was convinced that by publishing, citizens exercised and extended their rights as free human beings, helping *The Commonwealth of Reason* (London, 1795) to grow. In his *Proposals for Publishing by Subscription, a Treatise called the Female Citizen, or a Historical ... Enquiry into the Right of Women*, published around 1798, he calls the struggle for women's rights part of the "general struggle for FREEDOM." Through his writing, he wanted to help in averting "that Despotism at present exercised over the FEMALE WORLD so disgraceful to Man." He found the suppression of women to be "AS SAVAGE AS IT IS SILLY, scandalous Remnants of Feudal Barbarism, and Gothic Ignorance." Hodgson advised every thinking woman to despise such men. His long list of publications includes such diverse titles as *A Critical Grammar of French and English Language* (1819) and *The Life of Napoleon Bonaparte, once Emperor of the French, who died in exile, at St. Helena* (1844).

and lost their businesses during imprisonment. Therefore, it comes as no surprise that Hodgson asks for benevolent donations in a postscript to his address.

In the following text, Hodgson refers to a connection between the war against France and the oppressive politics of the Pitt government. William Pitt, who had favoured reforms before the French Revolution, later did everything to prevent them. Hodgson drew the attention of his readers to the economic situation of Britain, claiming that war weakens the country and damages its commercial interests. He claimed it is not only personal wealth that is destroyed, but also the happiness of thousands whose relatives suffer in the war due to irresponsible politics.

I think, that the more happiness and liberty other nations enjoy, the greater portion of these blessings will result to ourselves. And for this reason I was, and still am, decidedly of the opinion, that the war with the French people, on account of changing their government, is both impolitic and immoral; and calculated to embitter the cup of felicity out of which ENGLISHMEN, in common with the rest of mankind, have an indisputable right to drink.

Of those who think that no man should be permitted to differ, with impunity from the measures of government, I would ask, What proof have ye, that the methods pursued by the minister are such, as tend to render the people happy? Let us look through the nation, and ask the commercial men, if their interest has been promoted by this war? The bankrupt list will give an unequivocal answer to this question. Ask the tender orphans, thrown ruthless on the world; will they speak of the advantages they have reaped? Ask the disconsolate widows - the grey-headed fathers, robbed of the support of their tottering age -- the sisters, who mourn the loss of brothers -- the fond mother, whose darling son has been violently forced from her maternal arms, to fight in a cause his soul detests, and who only performs the work of blood under the terrors of a mutiny act -- ask the starving poor, deprived of employ by the operation of his schemes -- or ask the tradesman -- the mechanic -- the husbandman -- the labourer, whose earnings are now inadequate to the purchase of the necessary comforts of life, owing to the multitudinous taxes levied to support his all-destructive plans; -- will any of these say, that those opinions to which he so pertinaciously adheres, have added to their quantum of happiness? Look at them! the answer is legibly written in their squalid misery. And will any man deny that these constitute a great majority of the inhabitants of these islands? As well might he affirm, that the pensioned sycophants[37] of government bear the whole expence of the war. Where then is the superiority of his opinions? [...] Yours depopulate the earth, without making those who remain happy; mine will not decrease the number of men, if they add not to their felicity (10-12).

2. "Christian Warfare Defended and Recommended," from: *A Sermon Intended to Have Been Preached Before the Vice-Chancellor, and the University at St. Mary's Church, Cambridge, on the 28th of February, 1794, the Day Appointed for a Solemn Fast.* London: printed for C. and G. Kearsley and sold by W. Page, 1794.

After the British government declared war on revolutionary France in 1793, many loyalist pamphlets in support of the decision of the government were circulated. These authors tried to appeal to the patriotic and religious sensibilities of their readers. These texts were often presented as eyewitness war reports. *A Sketch of the Campaign of 1793*[38] was a particularly successful publication, which appeared in a variety of versions. In the preface we read that "the Author has endeavoured to describe as accurately as possible the scenes to which he was himself an eye witness; and events hitherto unnoticed, except in the public Papers, will not, he trusts, be deemed uninteresting to his countrymen" (v). The purpose of this publication, however, is a political one, as is evident in the first "letter". A grenadier is described, whose ship is at anchor before Helvoetsluys in March 1793. He is drunk and hiccups "up to his Majesty" who is pleased when he hears the grenadier threatening the reformers:

"Never mind all these Jacobins, G------e,[39] but be quiet,
We'll quell them, as quick as we'd quell you a riot."
The King was delighted, and laughed out aloud;
And the fellow receiv'd three huzzas from the croud (3).

---

[37] See footnote 27.

[38] *A Sketch of the Campaign of 1793. A Poem. In Two Parts. Letters from an Officer of the Guards, on the Continent, to a Friend in Devonshire* (London: T. Rickaby, for T. Cadell, Jr., and W. Davies, Successors to Mr. Cadell, in the Strand, 1795).

[39] Probably this stands for "Gallicae" and is an allusion to Sir James Mackintosh's, MP (1765-1832) famous defence of the French Revolution, "Vindiciae Gallicae (3rd edn., 1791)," in: *Political Writings of the 1790s*, ed. by Gregory Claeys; vol. 1: *Radicalism and Reform: Responses to Burke 1790-1791* (London: William Pickering, 1995), 270-386.

A Sketch of the Campaign of 1793, is another text about the war, however, strikingly different from Hodgson's pacifist 26-page-long sermon. The author of *A Sketch* defends the war effort against revolutionary France, his rhetorics denouncing those who warn against the atrocities of war as "philanthropists" – another term for the members of the reform movement. The author condemned the murder of the royal family in France and claimed that piety and religion were "hunted down like wild beasts" (6). Thus, the author concluded that religion and the political order, ordained by God, must be defended by war. To justify his arguments, the author introduced his sermon with a quotation from Matthew 10:34: "Think not that I am come to send Peace on earth; I come not to send peace, but a sword."

In the concluding lines of his text, the author appealed to the religious sentiments of his alleged listeners and warned that the French Revolution will spread atheism across the world:

> To conclude, let us, my brethren, attend to the voice of Heaven, let us obey the injunctions of Christianity, and draw the sword afresh against this band of atheists, who, after having overthrown their own religion and government, are striving to accomplish the same throughout the world! Remember, Fellow-Christians, that the same blood-stained sword which first gained us the ascendency of our blessed religion, must not be suffered to rust in the scabbard, when that religion is attacked by armed atheists, and insidious skeptics! (25)

This warning also suggests that the British reformers had already been affected by the ideas of the French Revolution and that war was being waged not only against external, but also internal enemies. Consequently, the horrors of war are systematically played down.

> The evils of war have, in all ages, been much exaggerated, and most unjustly portrayed by a set of men, who have obtruded themselves into notice, by assuming the prostituted name of Philanthropists. Our ears are stunned with the suppositious cries of widows and orphans: our eyes are shocked with the ghastly sights which our imagination forms, of the dying and the dead, and we shrink back with horror at the ideal picture; and our hearts are wrung with anguish at the well - dissembled tale of battle scenes, which paints, with all the glow of eloquence, and with all the invention of fancy, the public and domestic afflictions ever attendant upon war. Whole countries, we are told, are depopulated and laid waste. Misery and despair, famine and pestilence succeed in dread order; the ties

of kindred and friendship are dissolved; the bands of society are loosened and broken up; the noble pride of patriotism no more swells the bosom. The sense of man's own dignity no more impels him to a vigorous struggle against oppression. The human mind loses all its nervous elasticity, and becomes supple and abject (3-4).

[...]

But these appearances of arguments against wars, shadows as they are, must be answered, though perhaps it would be but justice to these modern sophists, to answer them by actions rather than by words, a mode however which, mercy and forbearance, the characteristics of our religion, restrain us from pursuing. In the first place then, ought to be ranked the divine authority, which is to be found in so many parts of the holy scriptures, for carrying on wars in general in support of our faith and religion; and consequently justifies the present war against that horde of blasphemous infidels and rebellious republicans, who have usurped the dominion of a neighbouring country. The banditti that inhabit this "arsenal of impiety," this horrid aceldama, have either murdered, or banished from their splendid palaces, all of the virtuous and dignified orders of men, in the persons of their clergy and nobles (4-5).

3. "Many of his political opinions would astonish our countrymen, who [...] cherish their prejudices," from: ***A Tour through the Theatre of War, in the Months of November and December, 1792, and January, 1793. Interspersed with Military and Other Anecdotes. To Which is Subjoined an Exact and Authentic Account of the Death of Louis XVI. The Second Edition.*** **With the Addition of an Appendix. London: J. Bew, 1793.**

Compared to the above publications, the 155 pages of *A Tour* is more ambitious with respect to the explanations offered to reform readers. As in *A Sketch*, entertainment and propaganda are well balanced. The political message, however, is very different.

The author reports the conclusion a Frenchman drew when he analysed the reasons why a revolution broke out in his home country. What he expects from such political changes is reminiscent of Spence's agrarian reform movement. Only the "dissemination of property" allows for "proper laws of succession and other equitable means" (*A Tour*, 29). The government must carry out land reforms in order to preserve peace: "If they do not, they may, like vampires, feed for a time upon the blood of the people; but the day will come when their own will be spilt. This said the Frenchman again, has been wofully exemplified in his country, and by many a one before" (*A Tour*, 29). The author refers to two countries where property is distributed in a fashion that will not increase poverty and unrest: the United States of America and Switzerland.

In his advertisement, the author tries to defend himself against loyalist arguments that the supporters of reforms are traitors who jeopardize the public order. Rather, he tries to explore the causes of war, which he finds in social injustices and poverty – a problem that exists throughout Europe.

In this age of invidious misrepresentation and arbitrary conclusions, the Author is aware that some of the political sentiments he has manifested may expose him to censure. He therefore begs leave to make here his political profession of faith. Though a friend to the great and general principles of liberty, he is not the less an enemy to licentiousness, disorder, and cruelty; and though averse to every species of despotism, he is not the less attached to the prosperity and interest of his country, or the less inclined to give it his little support in the war. -- Were any man unjust enough to say that these latter sentiments are incompatible with one another, he would pass the severest satire on the British Government.

The author uses the authenticity of personal experiences to draw a certain picture of revolutionary France. He claims to have been a prisoner of the French army, thus emphasizing his patriotic attitude. His French enemies, however, follow rules that allow them to treat their enemies with politeness and respect rather than with nationalistic feelings of revenge.

The person who was entertaining us with these, and many a curious tale beside, proved to be a gentleman of independent fortune, and a member of the National Convention. And a noble and an excellent original he is. The simplicity of his dress is contrasted with the most easy and refined politeness, while his lessons of philosophy are delivered with a kind of childish sportiveness, that disarms envy, and conceals his superiority even from those who listen to him with admiration. Indifferent as to his own ease and accommodation, he endeavours, with the most extensive philanthropy to accommodate and gratify every body about him; and while avowing himself an atheist, he expresses his hearty regret at being so. Many of his political opinions would astonish our countrymen, who, as the respectable Burke very truly says, *cherish their prejudices*: but will it be very easy to refute them? - Of that I am no judge.

He contends, that there is a vice in the civil polity of almost every state in Europe, that is necessarily the parent of revolution, creating all the misery and crimes that afflict the great mass of mankind, and driving them to insurrection as a last resource. The government draws the money out of the pocket of the poor, to give it, under the denomination of places and pensions, to the rich. The rich avail themselves of this to accumulate property, till at last their Colossal stride reaches from province to province, and the whole land, that seems the birth-right of the community, is monopolized by a few individuals.[40] The rest of the nation is then left at their mercy (24-26).

---

[40] The criticism of monopolies started with John Wilkes, as Ian Gilmour, *Riots, Risings and Revolution: Governance and Violence in Eighteenth-Century England* (London: Hutchinson, 1992; Pimlico, 1993), explains: "By his courageous and irreverent stand against the government, Wilkes articulated the hostility of the middling and inferior sorts to the elite's monopoly of power and place and their resentment against an unfair tax system, all the greater in a time of economic trouble" (310).

[...]

Thus are they reduced to mere working automata, with neither the means nor leisure necessary to acquire instruction, or to soften their manners to social intercourse and enjoyments; and thus is the human species degraded. The evil, by a necessary progression, grows greater; for the number of rich growing smaller, in proportion as the most wealthy swallow up the rest, the demand for labour becomes less, while the competition for employment increases. A harder bargain is consequently made, till at last the point of sufferance is past; the beast of burden kicks the load off his back, turns to a beast of prey, tears every thing he meets with to pieces, and takes a blind and furious vengeance for all the oppression he has suffered. Of this, continued the Frenchman with a sigh, my country is a lamentable example.

If we want an example of what a more equitable allotment of shares would produce, let us look towards the American Unites States, and the Swiss cantons, the two most popular governments in the wide world. In these two countries, local circumstances and political institutions have discouraged the too great accumulation of landed property. In these two countries, though many are very rich, there is nobody without a small estate in possession or perspective, or without the easy means of acquiring one. The consequence is, that in the first you may sleep in peace with your doors and windows open, and that inn the second you may with equal security leave your effects on the highway. In both, the government has no standing armies, the *King has no castles*, you hear of no malcontents, and you see no beggars. Crimes and misery, in a word, are equally unheard of. It is then evidently the duty of all good governors to provide for the dissemination of property; not by an equal Agrarian law, that would leave industry without a motive, and stifle the arts at their birth; but by proper laws of succession and other equitable means. If they do not, they may, like vampires, feed for a time upon the blood of the people; but the day will come when their own will be spilt. This said the Frenchman again, has been wofully exemplified in his country, and by many a one before.

After this monopoly of landed property, the grand source of human vices and misfortunes, the greatest scourge that can afflict a people is an extensive foreign commerce. If by the nation be understood a few merchants, ship-owners, ship's husbands, brokers, bankers, manufacturers, and fiscal officers, the nation is indeed prosperous when trade is in a thriving state. But if by the nation we may be allowed to understand all those not comprised in the above description, that is to say at least nine-tenths of the community, the case is the reverse. It is self-evident that foreign commerce can only consist of exportation and importation, unless indeed where a people should merely be brokers and carriers for others. It is equally evident, that a country can only export what is produced by the labour of its inhabitants on the soil, or by their drudgery in manufactories. If then no part of what is imported comes to the share of those who drudge and toil, can it be denied, that they give up ease, plenty, and leisure, for nothing; that the necessaries of life, the enjoyments, and repose of the many, are sacrificed to feed the luxury of the few? What a noble export trade does Ireland carry on in beef, pork, butter, and flour! - Well, what does the nation at large that live in that fertile country get in return? The advantage of never tasting meat, bread, or butter; of feeding on potatoes and butter milk, and sleeping among the litter of their pigs: all which their noble landlords, while drinking French wines, and wearing French silks, assure us is *vastly* conducive to their health! - Oh! but in some other countries, those who furnish all the exports, obtain a small portion of the returns. Yes: from America a noxious and intoxicating weed, and enervating drink from Asia, and from the other parts of Europe liquid poisons, that do indeed for a moment make them forget the sacrifice they cost.

This evil is the offspring of the former; for if property were divided with any tolerable equality, a man would begin by providing amply for his support, comfort, and enjoyment; and would only suffer the surplus to be exchanged for foreign superfluities; nor would he for superfluities condemn himself to incessant labour (26-31).

The anonymous author closes his publication with an invective against those who want to oppress opposition through libel laws – and with a gesture of modesty.

It may, perhaps, be safer in this Christian land, for the man who rejoiced that there were prisons for the libellers of a Queen, to libel a whole nation, and to advice the cutting of his fellow creatures throats from generation to generation, than it is for another to inculcate charity to our neighbours, by a candid statement of facts, and demonstrable truth. But as my tour induced me to relate the things I saw, and as these things led me naturally to the reflections that accompany the mention of them, I defy reproach, and trust that my readers will show some indulgence to the hasty production of an unskilful pen.

THE END (148).

4. 'Twenty thousand meet on a plain and shed each other's blood - without the least animosity', from: *The Curses and Causes of War, Pointed out; and the Approaching Cessation of Both Determined.* Spitalfields: R. Hawes, for the Moral and Political Society, 1795.

The following text also criticises the social division between the rich and the poor. The greed of rich people causes wars, but it is the impoverished who suffer the consequences while the rich enjoy their lives unharmed. Those who sit at home and follow the battles from a safe distance speak of victories and do not respect the integrity of individual lives. The author speaks of ineffable atrocities and human tragedies, and doubts that language could ever convey the horrors of war. Only universal suffrage and annual parliament could bring "universal peace and incessant plenty" (4). The author assures his readers that the French Revolution set this process in motion throughout Europe. The pamphlet begins with two mottos:

"It is written indeed in simple language, and relates a simple tale; but it is a tale, which we dare say, few of our Readers will be able to peruse without FEELING."

The CABINET

"BLESSED ARE THE PEACE-MAKERS."

J.C. New Test.

THE Causes of War are for the most part such as must disgrace an animal pretending to Rationality. Two poor mortals, elevated with the distinction of a golden Bauble upon their heads called a crown, take offence at each other, without any reason; or with the very bad one of wishing for an opportunity of aggrandizing themselves by making reciprocal depredations. The creatures of the Court, and the leading men of the nation, who are usually under the Influence of the Court, resolve, (for it is their *Interest* - to support their Royal Master!) and are never at a loss to invent some colourable pretence, for engaging Nations in the Horrors of War. Taxes the most burthensome are levied; Soldiers are collected so as to leave a paucity of Husbandmen: Reviews and Encampments succeed: and, at last, fifteen or twenty thousand meet on a plain and madly shed each other's blood - without the least animosity of the shadow of provocation! The kings in the mean time and Grandees who have employ'd these Innocent Victims to shoot bullets at each other's heads, remain quietly at home, and amuse themselves with Balls, Hunting, and Pleasures of every species: with reading at the fire-side, and over a cup of Chocolate the dispatches from the Army, and the news in the Extraordinary Gazette. Horace very justly observes, that "whatever mad frolics enter into the heads of Kings, it is the common people, that is, the honest artisan, and the industrious tribes in the middle ranks, unoffended and unoffending, who chiefly suffer in the dreadful consequences."[41] If King of P—[42] were not at the head of some of the best troops in the Universe he would be judged more worthy to be tried and condemned at the Old-Bailey, than any shedder of blood who ever died by a halter. But the King, he is a Hero: these names fascinate us: and we enrol the butchers of mankind among their benefactors! When one considers the dreadful circumstances that attend even victories, one cannot be a little shocked at the exaltation which they occasion. When a circle of eager Politicians have met to congratulate each other on a piece of good news just arrived, every eye sparkles with delight; every voice is raised to announce the happy event. And for what is the cause of all this joy? And for what are our Widows illuminated - Bonfires kindled - Bells rung, and Feasts celebrated? We have obtained a Victory. We have left Thousands of the Enemy *dead* on the field of the battle; and only nine-hundred of our own Countrymen are slain! Charming News! It was a Glorious Battle! But before you give loose to your raptures; consider, that to every one of these nineteen hundred, Life was equally sweet to them as it is to you: that the greatest part of them, probably, were dear to their Wives, Fathers, Mothers, Sons, Daughters, Sisters, Brothers, and

---

[41] The author refers to a famous quotation from Epistel 1,2,14: "Quidquid delirant reges, plectuntur Achivi" Thanks go to my colleague Markus Janka for having pointed out this reference to me. Bryant translates: "Whenever monarchs err, the people are punished" – "*plecti* means 'to be beaten' hence in slaves' language 'to be punished' or especially to take the rap'" (Margaret Hubbard and R. G. M. Nisbet, *A Commentary on Horace* [Oxford University Press, 1989], 333). In medieval English literature this phrase was regularly quoted, see *The Political Songs of England: From the Reign of John to That of Edward II*, ed. by Thomas Wright (London: Camden Society, 1839), 33, 166, 267: "Song of the Corruptions of the Time" [MS. Harl. No. 978. fol. 105, v°. reign of Hen. III.] (27-36); "Song on the Scottish Wars" [MS. Cotton. Claudius, D. VI. fol. 182, v°; of the beginning of the fourteenth cent. (C. 1.)] (160-189), and in the reign of Edward III, "The Battle of Bannockburn" [From MS. Cotton. Titus, A. xx, fol. 68 r°]

[42] Friedrich Wilhelm II (1744-97), King of Prussia (1786-97).

Friends; all of whom are at this moment bewailing that event, which occasions your foolish and brutal Triumph!

The whole time of a War ought to be time of *General Mourning*; - a mourning of the *Heart*; a mourning much more sincere, than for the Death of any of those Princes whose cursed ambition is often the sole cause of War!

Many of the European States are entirely Military. War is their Trade. And when they have no employment at home, or near it, they let themselves out, to the best paymaster, to butcher their fellow men: not only without so much as knowing what it is about. The principal object of crowned heads, and their minions are the extention of Empires, the increase of the Revenue, or the Abridgment or Annihilation of their subjects Liberty. Plausible words are used to hide the deformity of their real principles; for, whenever a War is deemed desirable, a specious *pretext* never yet remained unfound. The most solemn treaties and engagements are violated by the Governing part of the nation, with no more scruple than oaths are broken by a chat and a villain in the walks of private Life. Does the difference of rank and situation make any difference in the authority of the crimes? If any, it renders a thousand times more criminal, than that of a thief, the villainy of those who by violating every thing sacred between nation and nation, give rise to mischiefs more dreadful in their nature; and to which no human power can say, "*Thus far shall ye proceed*, and *no farther*!" - Are not the natural and moral evils of life sufficient, but they must be rendered more acute, more numerous, and more embittered by artificial means? My heart bleeds over those complicated scenes of woe, for which no epithet can be found sufficiently descriptive! Language fails in laboring to express the horrors of *War* amidst private families - especially those who are so unfortunate as to be situated in the seat of it!

Indeed, that a whole people should tamely submit to the evils of War, because it is the will of a few selfish, ignorant, though exalted individuals, is passing strange! - But the people are led away with a false glory; they reflect not; and if they did, and even oppose, what would avail the resistance of unarmed myriads to the mandates of a government supported by standing army?

Wretched are many that bear the name of Soldiers! Formerly the Soldier was united with the Citizen, and the toil and danger of arms lasted no longer than while the enemy was upon the territory: -- The brave defender of his country returned from victory to enjoy all the blessings of a Citizen and a Freeman. Not so at this time of day. Our provisions are now transported to Foreign Countries - our Husbandmen are seduced from the plough to be beaten by their boyish Officers, and starve beneath a knapsack. Besides sixpence a day for cloaths, food, and expences, they have nothing of their own. The Soldier, deprived of the dignity of man, is chained or driven here and there like a beast, or whipped like a slave! These are the *privileges* that attend their services under the deplorable Machinations of Tyranny!!!

Yet let us not despair. The Spirit of Truth has declared that the days shall come when "the nations shall learn War no more, but beat their swords into ploughshares and their spears into pruning hooks."

For the performance of this great work, has not GOD evidently raised up and supported the FRENCH REPUBLIC - which will infallibly hasten the dissolution of POPERY and SLAVERY, and the defeat and over and overthrow of *all the Kings of the earth* that *have worshipped the beast and listed themselves under its banner*! - It is from this great and unexampled Revolution in Apostate and Degenerate Christendom, that a System of *Peace* and *Purity* shall arise. - It is with reference to this glorious state that HE who sitteth in Heaven hath sworn - "*Behold* I MAKE ALL THINGS NEW." These are the times of refreshment that have been spoken of by the mouths of all the Prophets.

As therefore Divine Providence cannot but make use of the best Means to carry its dispensations into effect, let us by closing with its gracious designs, endeavour to hasten this happy era of time, (at least in our own country) by UNITING to purge our corrupt Parliamentary Representation) and by claiming UNIVERSAL SUFFRAGE[43] and ANNUAL PARLIAMENTS with one voice. Then, and not till then, shall we experience UNIVERSAL PEACE and INCESSANT PLENTY (2-4).

---

[43] The claim of universal suffrage goes back to the first generation of reformers like John Cartwright and John Wilkes. **John Cartwright (1740-1824)** fought for parliamentary reform since 1775, and devoted his whole life to a campaign for universal suffrage, secret ballot and annual parliaments.

5. "... when he entered in such a horid guise, His Mother shriek'd," from: Robert Merry, *The Wounded Soldier, a Poem*. By Mr. M-y. London: printed for T. G. Ballard, [1795?].

Robert Merry (1755-1798), the author of *The Laurel of Liberty* (1790), was a member of the London Constitutional Society and was well acquainted with radicals such as Tooke, Joseph Priestley, John Thelwall, Thomas Holcroft, Jeremiah Joyce, and William Haley. He was married to an actress, Miss Brunton, and also knew William Godwin, whom he introduced to Mrs. Mary Robinson.

Merry belonged to a group of English poets who lived in Italy and published sentimental verse in *The Arno* (1784) and *The Florence Miscellany* (1785). He called himself "Della Crusca" after the Della-Cruscans (who had founded the *Accademia della Crusca* for linguistic purity in Florence in the 16th century). After his poetry appeared in the *World* of 29 June 1787, Merry came to England where his poetry became extremely popular. "The verses of *Della Crusca* are the most beautiful things I ever saw or read in my life," his friend Topham said on 18 November 1787.

Most of Merry's disciples who lived in the Beaufort Buildings (where Thelwall had his lecture room) became Della Cruscans. Later Merry became the object of William Gifford's satires in *The Baviad* (1791) and *The Mæviad* (1795), and of Lord Byron's in his *English Bards and Scotch Reviewers* (1809). From 1791 on, Merry played a major role in the reform movement when he organized the Friends of the Liberty of the Press together with Mackintosh, Sheridan, and others.

In his poem, Merry tells the story of a soldier who is wounded in battle in France and returns home.

The Sun was just retired, the dews of Eve,
Their glow-worm lustre scatter'd oe'r the vale;
The lonely Nightingale, began to grieve,
Telling, with many a Pause, her tend'rest table.

No clamours rude disturbed the pensive Hour,
And the young Moon, yet fearful of the Night;
Rear'd her pale crescent, o'er the burnished Tower,
That caught the parting Orb's still lingering light.

'Twas then, where peasant Footsteps marked the way,
A Wounded Soldier feebly moved along,
Nor ought regarded he the Soft'ning ray,
Nor the melodious Bird's expressive Song.

On Crutches borne, his mangled Limbs he drew,
Unsightly remnants of the Battles rage;
While Pity, in his youthful form, might view
A helpless Prematurity of Age.

Then strange contortions, lab'ring slow
He gained the summit of his native Hill,
And saw the well known Prospect spread below,
The Farm, the Cot, the Hamlet and the Mill.

In spite of Fortitude, one struggling sigh,
Shook the firm Texture of his tortured Heart,
And from his hollow and dejected Eye,
One tremb'ling Tear hung ready to depart.

How chang'd, he cried, is the fair scene to me,
Since last across this narrow Path I went:
The soaring Lark felt not superior Glee,
Nor any human Breast, more true Content.

When the fresh Hay was o'er the Meadow thrown
Amidst the Busy Throng I still appeared,
My Prowess too at Harvest Time was shewn,
While Lucy's carrol ev'ry Labour cheered.

The burning rays I scarcely seemed to feel,
If the dear Maiden near me chanc'd to rove,
Or if she deigned to share my frugal meal,
It was a rich Repast, a Feast of Love.

And when at Evening, with a Rustics' pride,
I dared the sturdiest Wrestler on the Green,
What Joy was mine! To hear her at my side,
Extol my Vigour, and my manly Mien.

Ah! Now no more the sprightly Lass shall run,
To bid me welcome from the sultry plain;
But her averted Eye my sight shall shun,
And all our cherish'd fondest Hopes be vain.

Alas! My Parents, must ye too endure,
That I should gloom for e'er your homely mirth,
Exist upon the pittance ye procure,
And make me curse the Hour that gave me birth.

O hapless Day! When at neighb'ring Wake,
The gaudy Sergeant caught my wond'ring Eye;
And as his Tongue of War and Honor spake,
I felt a wish to Conquer or to Die.

Then while he bound the Ribbands on my Brow,
He talked of Captains kind, and Generals good;
Said a whole Nation would my Fame avow,
And Bounty call'd the Purchase of my Blood.

Yet I refused that bounty, I disdained
To sell my service in a Righteous cause;
And such to my dull sense it was explain'd,
The Cause of Monarchs, Justice, and the Laws.

The Rattling Drums beat loud, the Fifes began,
My King and Country seem'd to ask my aid,
Thro' every Vein, the thrilling ardour ran,
I left my humble Cot, my Village Maid.

O hapless Day! torn from my Lucy's charms,
I thence was hurried to a Scene of Strife;
To painful Marches, and the din of Arms,
The Wreck of *Reason* and the waste of *Life*.

I loathsome Vessels, now with crowds confin'd,
Now led with Hosts to Slaughter in the Field;
Now backward driv'n, like Leaves before the Wind,
Too weak to Stand, and yet asham'd to Yield.

Till oft repeated Victories inspir'd
with tenfold Fury the indignant Foe;
Who ruthless still advanced, as we retir'd,
And laid our boasted, proudest Honors low.

Thro' frozen Desarts then compell'd to fly,
Our bravest Legions mouldered fast away;
Thousands of Wounds and Sickness left to Die,
While hov'ring Ravens mark'd them for their prey

Ah! sure Remorse their savage Hearts must rend
Whose selfish, des'prate phrenzy could decree,
That in one mass of Murder MAN should blend,
Who sent the *Slave* to fight against the *Free*.

Unequal Contest! - at fair FREEDOMS call,
The lowliest Herd glows with celestial Fire;
The rules, directs, pervades, and conquers all,
And Armies at her sacred Glance expire.

Then be this Warfare of the world accurs'd;
The Son now weeps not on the Fathers Bier;
But grey Hair'd Age, for Nature is revers'd,
Drops o'er his Children's Grave an Icy tear.

Thus having spoke, -- by varying Passions tost,
He reach'd the Threshold of his Father's shed,
Who knew not of his Fate, yet mourn'd him lost,
Amidst the Number of the unnam'd Dead.

Soon as they heard his well remember'd voice,
A ray of Rapture chas'd habitual Care;
Our Henry lives, we may again rejoice,
And Lucy sweetly blushed, for she was there.

But when he entered in such a horid guise,
His Mother shriek'd, and dropp'd upon the Floor;
His Father look'd to Heaven with streaming Eyes,
And Lucy sunk, alas! To rise no more.

O may this Tale, which agony must close,
Give deep Contrition to the self-call'd great;
And shew the Poor, how hard's the lot of those,
Who shed their Blood, for Ministers of State.

FINIS

6. "Freedom advances near," from: *A New Song, to an old Tune*, -- viz. "God save the king." [London], [November 1792]

In this radical song the British are called to support France and the revolution.

GOD save "The Rights of Man!"
Give him a heart to scan
Blessings so dear;
Let them be spread around,
Wherever Man is found,
And with the welcome sound,
Ravish his ear!

II.
See from the Universe,
Darkness and Clouds disperse;
Mankind awake!
Reason and Truth appear,
Freedom advances near,
Monarchs with terror hear,
See how they quake!

III.
Sore have we felt the stroke;
Long have we bore the yoke,
Sluggish and tame;
But now the Lion roars,
And a loud note he pours;
Spreading to distant shores,
LIBERTY's flame!

IV.
Let us France agree,
And bid THE WORLD BE FREE--
Leading the way.
Let Tyrants all conspire,
Fearless of sword and fire,
FREEDOM shall ne'er retire,
FREEDOM shall sway!

V.
Godlike, and great the strife,
Life will indeed be life,
Should we prevail.
Death, in so just a cause,
Crown us with loud applause,
And from Tyrannic laws,
Bids us -- ALL HAIL!

VI.
O'er the Germanic powr's,
Big indignation lowr's,
Ready, to fall!
Let the rude savage host,
In their long numbers boast,
FREEDOM's almighty trust,
Laughs at them all.

VII.
FAME! Let thy Trumpet sound!
Tell all the World around!
Tell each degree!
Tell Ribbands, Crowns, and Stars,
Kings, Traitors, Troops, and Wars,
Plans, Councils, Plots, and Jars,
FRENCHMEN are FREE!

VIII.
God save -- "The Rights of Man!"
Give him a heart to scan
Blessings so dear!

Let them be spread around,
Wherever Man is found,
And with the welcome sound,
Ravish his ear!

IV. English Politics and the French Revolution

For a long time, those groups in society that favoured reforms were behind Pitt, who had carried out quite a few reforms. However, when Pitt decided not to support the repeal of the Test and Corporation Acts in 1787, many – particularly the Dissenters – looked for a new political ally, finding one in Charles Fox. In the wake of the centenary of the Revolution of 1688, the first reform societies came into being. When the French Revolution broke out, it found a fairly well organised and articulate group of sympathizers in British society.

After the publication of Edmund Burke's *Reflections on the Revolution in France*, the British public was divided into those who rejected reforms as a danger to British institutions and those who believed that reforms were inevitable. The dissenters and radicals believed that unless reforms were carried out, more and more constitutional rights would be lost. Many radicals defended constitutional change as a return to the old Anglo-Saxon traditions of participation and freedom rather than as an introduction of the new ideas conceived during the American and the French Revolutions. Radicals believed that the need for reform was justified as an autochthon process reaching back to the Anglo-Saxon tradition (as opposed to Norman feudalism), or was linked to the achievements of the so-called Glorious Revolution of 1688. The opponents of political change, the loyalists, warned that the idea of "change" was imported from France and, therefore, could precipitate a revolution.

1. "Tom Paine and Priestley wou'd/ Deluge the throne with blood," from: *Sedition, Levelling, and Plundering; or the Pretended Friends of the People in Council.* London: Printed and sold by S.W. Fores, who again opened his Exhibition Room, to which he has added several Hundred old and new Subjects, [1792?].

The broadsheet "Sedition, Levelling, and Plundering" begins with the famous praise to British monarchs and continues as a loyalist propaganda song in which the radical reform movement is heavily attacked for its political intentions.

I.
GOD save great George our king[44],
Long live our noble king,
God save the king;
Send him victorious,
Happy, and glorious.
Long to reign over us,
God save the king.

II.
Old Mother Church disdains,

Th' vile Unitarian* strains,
That round her ring;
She keeps her dignity,
And scorning faction's lie,
Sings with sincerity,
God save the king.

---

[44] For the relationship of the Hanoverian King George III (1760-1820) to the radical movement, see John Brewer, "English Radicalism in the Age of George III," in: *Three British Revolutions: 1641, 1688, 1776*, ed. by J.G.A. Pocock (Princeton, NJ: Princeton University Press, 1980), 323-367. Under George III, the court became ever more "domestic and enclosed, the monarch less and less of a public figure. [...] George III lived in the snug bosom of his family, the first 'middle-class' monarch," as John Brewer, *The Pleasures of the Imagination: English Culture in the Eighteenth Century* (London: Harper and Collins, 1997), 20-21, remarks.

* It is but justice to observe, the Unitarian Dissenters only, are a Sect so restless and turbulent; the Independents and Anabaptists stand aloof from all Society with them, and are perfectly satisfied with the PRESENT FORM OF GOVERNMENT.

III.
Sedition is their creed,
Feign'd sheep, but wolves indeed,
How can we trust?
TOM PAINE[45] and PRIESTLEY wou'd
Deluge the throne with blood;
And lay the great and good,
Low in the dust.

IV.
Hist'ry, thy page unsold,
Did not their fires of old
Murder their king?
And they would overthrow,
King, Lords, and Bishops too,
And while thy gave the blow,
Loyally sing.

V.
TOM PAINE and PRIESTLEY are,
More base and desp'rate far,
Than vile Jack Cade;[46]
He for reform did cry,
They, for equality,
Wou'd stain true liberty,
With British blood.

VI.
Priestley, the TRUTH go preach,
Thy flock no ERRORS teach,
Leave such base ways;

---

[45] Thomas Paine (1737-1809), the author of *The Rights of Man* (1791-1792), and Joseph Priestley (1733-1804) became "the twin objects of intense popular and official vilification," as Colin Bonwick, *English Radicals and the American Revolution* (Chapel Hill, NC: University of North Carolina Press, 1977), 245, points out.

[46] The majority of the people who took part in Jack Cade's rebellion against Henry VI were peasants and small landowners from Kent who opposed forced labour, corruption and heavy taxation. Cade's men defeated the government troups and invaded London where they were eventually forced to yield to the king and received a pardon. Cade's rebellion became popular through Shakespeare's Henry VI.

God's word cease to pervert,
To peace thy flock exhort,
Not Liberty distort,
MEND THY LAST DAYS.

VII.
Paine! Paine! thy motley life,
Compound of frauds and strife,
Plainly declares,
Thy aim is levelling
Nobles, State, Church, and King,
Like a rogue then you'll sing
PLUNDER!!! who cares?

VIII.
O Lord our God, arise,
Scatter such enemies,
United we'll sing;
Confound their politics,
Frustrate their knavish tricks,
On thee our hopes we fix:
God save the King.

2. "Tell me then, ye sons of discontent, what are your wants?" from: *Principle and Practice Combined: or, The Wrongs of Man. An Oratorio. As it was often performed by the Jacobines of Paris, with great Applause. The Music selected from modern French Airs.* By one who feels himself a Patriot. London: J. Parsons and J. Barker, 1792.

The loyalist author of this operatic piece warns the Whigs and Tories not to underestimate the radicals' intentions. He ridicules the French and attacks radicals such as Tom Paine, whom he suspects of wanting to destroy everything British. Putting the derogatory words into the mouths of those the author wants to ridicule intensifies the satire of this piece.

Admonition to the Whig Club, by Way of Preface

The old Wigs are become lank and threadbare, do in charity give them to shoeblacks.

I ever considered the titles of Whig and Tory as names of reproach for two factions, who have disturbed the peace of these realms (iii).

Tell me then, ye sons of discontent, what are your wants? - Ye want to dip your fingers in the hive, that you may once more lick the honey; but beware, lest the labouring bee should give you a sting (iv).

Principle and Practice Combined.
Part One
Recitative
Tune: Men are born free and always continue so.

Frenchmen were born slaves, and I fear they will continue so: their old masters tax'd and deprest them; their new masters doubly tax, and compel them so fight for their own slavery.
Wonderful al-ter-a-tion! (5)
[...]
Part Two
Recitative
Tune - The law is the expression of the general will.

How shall we find words to express the general will, or volumes to contain it, when men's tempers and inclinations differ like their visages? When interest, and not reason, actuates their minds, the voice of truth sounds but feebly, and the cry of oppression is but the loud trumpet of sedition, to call the discontented to the standard of self-created tyranny.

Note: The two following Airs may be sung to any of the following tunes.

Tune 1st - No man can be accused, arrested, or held in confinement, except in cases determined by law, and according to forms thereby prescribed; they who solicit, promote, execute, or cause to be executed, any arbitrary orders, ought to be punished.

Tune 2d - Law should not establish any punishments but such as are strictly and evidently necessary: and no man should be punished but by virtue of a law established and promulgated before the offence, and legally applied.

Tune 3d - As every man is presumed innocent till his guilt is declared, whenever the detention of any one is judged indispensable, all rigour beyond what is necessary to secure his person, should be severely prohibited by law.

Air I.

FRENCH KING

Ye sons of Galliæ, say, have I wronged you?
Ye daughters of sincerity, speak your woes.

Have I shut up your children in dungeons?
Have I robbed you of the patrimony of your fathers?

Have I broken up your houses? Have I murdered your faithful servants?

Have I ruled you with the rod of tyranny? Have I held the dagger to your throats, to make you swear ingratitude to your friends?

The sight of my slaughtered friends is still in my eyes. - Hark! how they cry for protection to their helpless king!

Save them! Save them! Their crime is but loyalty - fidelity is the error for which they suffer.

Come, then, ye fortunate assassins, boast one generous act - do by me as you have done by my followers, and end this life of sorrows!

But do not slain in the sacred name of justice; mock not her awful tribunal.

Have ye no kind poniard, no death-giving cordial, that ye seek my destruction by falsehoods? that ye must tax me with treasons of your own conceptions? - Look in your own hearts, there is the font of treason! There is deep hidden guile and dark intentions! Ye talk like patriots, and yet are you climbing to power on the ruins of your country; ye forestall provisions, to make the poor desperate; ye give the peace of France to the ravage of profligates, that ye may govern your brethren; you make laws bind me, and not yourselves; you gave me a veto, and commanded the ignorant multitude to force my conscience; you abolish all law, and yet I am to suffer for imaginary offences! Blush, blush, ye hypocrites! and as you are all declared equals, confess to the whole world that ye are an host of public robbers!

Air II.

FRENCH QUEEN.

I am blistered with the tongue of slander, and the voice of ingratitude is against me.

The voice of an ungrateful people whom I sought to make mighty, when I aimed at the destruction of their enemies - an enemy whose virtues I did not know till the hour of my distress!

My crime is against them, not France; and if the generous Briton pities me, the axe of the traitor can do me no harm.

Oh, my instant victims, let me embrace you, for few are the moments we are suffered to enjoy!

Thy innocence cannot save me, because while you live the usurpers are in jeopardy.

But our monuments shall be raised in the minds of the charitable, when our enemies would wish to be forgotten.

CHORUS OF PRUSSIAN SOLDIERS.[47]

Tune - *The Manifesto.*

With slow majestic steps we entered France (and made a wondrous stir) we threatened to tear up the streets, and set the great city of Paris on her head; to roast the Jacobines and eat up the Fuellants - Ye Gods! it was a glorious fight to see, ten thousand volunteers flying before fifteen hundred Prussians - even the invincible Hector Dumourier turned pale!

---

[47] In 1792 the French armies were defeated by the Prussians at Verdun.

Then might you behold the free-born Frenchmen (like a band of imprest bedlamites)[48] marching with their shaven heads, and coatless backs, to atone for their own and their general's cowardice.

And lo, the day was come - the fate of kings and empires hung on the conflict of an hour -- surrounding nations trembled at the expectant stroke - the rival armies stood at awful distance, with defiance, glaring from their wrathful eyes - (growling like two boar-cats in a gutter, making much noise, but meaning no harm) when two of our brave commanders claimed a single combat, the purple sacrifice was brought, and Bacchus bled to satiate the son of Mars.

Whether they walk'd, or were carried to their tents, we know not, but our retreat was noble; for we measured back more miles in one day than we had advanced in a week!
Natural in-cli-na-tion.

Part Three
Tune - The first part of the rights of man

Tom Paine solo
Behold the man who has found a measure for all shapes! I can persuade a wealthy people that they are ruined, and a free people that they are enslaved - I can lace up a fat Englishman in a strait French boddice, and

[48] Mary of Bethlehem (Bedlam), a hospital for the mentally ill, belonged to the Royal Hospitals of London which had been established in Tudor times. From the 17th through the late 18th centuries, the public was allowed into Bedlam to watch the patients. "Bedlamites" is (in the terminology of the time) a term for insane people.

make him pay me for his own abuse. I am the corrector of laws, the ruler of kings, and the scourge of princes; and I am - I am - damme, I'll tell ye who I am - I am Timothy Factotum, the son of a staymaker!

Duet.
Paine and Fayette[49].
(Paine seeing Fayette looking thro' the prison gate.)

Tune - Tom Paine's letter to the National Convention[50].

PAINE.
Ha! are you there, thou arch-apostate! Thy master Louis[51] is peeping through just such another loop-hole, and if he keeps his head upon his shoulders, 't will be in compassion to his weakness, not out of respect to his kingship. Happy would you now be to enjoy the honors of me your fellow citizen.

FAYETTE.
Thy fellow! peace, pitiful animal, safely may you kick the lion now his teeth are drawn. Thou slander-monger! thou scavenger of republicans! you was only employed to do the dirty work which would soil a gentleman, to disguise verity, and inflame the minds of the ignorant. When such unskilful pilots seize the helm, 'tis time for men of honor to quit the found'ring bark, and leave the wreck to plunderers.

PAINE.
And have I wasted so much good ink upon thee? Is it for this I belied my conscience when I had declared to the world that I had found three honest men (at the same time I looked into my own heart and I could not find any thing that was honest) did I not hold you up to public fame, when I hoped you was a scoundrel! but thou (unthankful monster) hast deceived me.

---

[49] In his *Rights of Man* (1791-2), Tom Paine was full of praise for M. de la Fayette, who had fought in the American War for Independence and during the French Revolution. La Fayette had organized the national guard of the revolutionary army. See Paine, *Rights of Man* (1998), 147-50.
[50] The French National Convention held its first meeting on 21 September 1792. It abolished the monarchy and set up the republic.
[51] Louis XVI was executed on 21 January 1793.

FAYETTE.
Thy praises hurt me more than thy reproach. These chains I wear are badges of injustice, and become me better than any rank under thy rude cabal.
When my complaining country groaned with oppression, and the cry was Freedom! I drew my sword in her defensive cause: threats could not stay me, tortures were but spurs to urge me in the glorious task! I ask'd no favour, and I feared no frown, But when I saw delusion was the aim (a paltry club deter'd the Gallic senate!) power not liberty, offence and not resistance, I saw my prince (like a tamed beast of shew) dragged to command, and punished to obedience! my native loyalty sprung up by the genial warmth of my affection; I felt the emotions of a son whose father was insulted - but, alas! my arm was weak in his support, I could no longer stem the ocean of mobility, and we both sunk together!

Chorus of Furious Spirits
To an old French tune little known in England.

Despotism is gone forth as the head of armies, waving the broad ensign of liberty.

He spreads his gin in foreign countries and baits it with the salt of advantage. But when the hapless people are ensnared; 'tis vain to struggle with their bondage.

The spark of Gallic virtue is extinct, the pavements of Paris are washed with the blood of the innocent!
Justice is trodden down by the oppressive rabble, the mouth of truth is stopt by the hand of violence!

The grim wolves of famine approach to devour the wretched remains, and France now endures those miseries she has so often brought on other nations.

GRAND CHORUS
To be sung by every man according to his own tune.

Come, gentle peace, and calm our furious hearts,
Parent of ease, and nurse of genr'ous arts;

At thy approach expiring trade revives,
Safe in thy wardship splendid traffick thrives,
Thy sister Freedom joins the prosp'rous train,
(Slaughter and rapine in thy absence reign,)
Like the great sun you bid the meadows teem,
And nature glows beneath thy vivid beam! (8-18)

FINIS

3. "Bring the Gold, the Fees then bring, And you shall Loyal find us," from: *The associators, at the Crown-and-Anchor, in the Strand. A song.* [London, 1793].

According to the loyalist author of the song "The associators", radicals prefer the "Crown and Anchor", Strand. Their corrupt nature makes it easy for them to give away the interests of the poor for money, although they claim to be their advocates.

"Ye venal herd in evil hours".

THE ASSOCIATORS,
At the Crown-and-Anchor, in the Strand.

A SONG.

TUNE: - *"Come then all ye social powers."*

Ye venal herd in evil hours,
Come rally round your places,
Sinecures and Pensions ours,
By grinding poor men's faces.
Bring the Gold, the Fees then bring,
And you shall Loyal find us;
We care not whose hearts we wring:
We cast the Poor behind us.

Then for the Poor we'll never care,
Tho' on them all we fatten;
Be they hungry, sick or bare,
We still on them will batten.
Bring the Gold, the Fees then bring, &c.

Though base and vile our principles,

And British Laws we barter;
We don't dread free Britons' wills,
A Fig for their great Charter.
Bring the Gold, the Fees then bring, &c.

Since the times must alter soon,
In spight of all our sorrow;
Let's enjoy the Honey-Moon,
We dare not trust *To-morrow*.
Bring the Gold, the Fees then bring,
And you shall Loyal find us;
We care not whose hearts we wring
We cast the Poor behind us.

4. "I right made wrong, and wrong I said was right," from: *The Last Dying Words of Tom Paine, Executed at the Gullotine in France on the 1st of Sept. 1794, with A Description of the genuine Water for Converting the Jacobines. Verses on the Death of Paine, and A Dialogue between a Jacobine and the Devil.* London [1794].

This entertaining narrative belies not only English orthography (which had essentially settled by the beginning of the eighteenth century) but also Thomas Paine's biography. It presents Paine's last dying speech, delivered on the French guillotine. Paine is full of remorse and confesses to have been a liar throughout his entire life. Even the Devil does not accept the Jacobins in Hell, because they do not respect his rule.

The historical Paine came close to death when he was imprisoned in France, from 28 December 1793 to 4 November 1794 by the radicals under Robespierre, for having tried to save King Louis XVI's life. After the fall of Robespierre, he was released and readmitted to the National Convention. In prison, Paine published the first part of his *Age of Reason*, which offended the religious sensibilities of many. In 1802 he left for the United States, where he died in 1809.

Ye numerous spectators gathered around, pray give ear to my last words; I am determined to speak the Truth in these my last moments, altho' I have written, and spoke nothing but Lies all my life; and nothing can be truer than what I now say of myself, viz. that I have been always a notorious liar. I was born of mean parents, yet parents who never had the mean wicked designing principles, which have brought me to the Infamy I so richly deserve. My parents lived and died honest, I have lived a dishonest, and shameful life, and shall die like a wretch who has been the pest of society, and the interrupter of publick peace. I was bred a taylor, and it was my greatest misfortune ever to have got loose from my best friends my bodkin, and sheers, and my goose; but I had always a false pride united to my poverty, and pride, and poverty, are too often united; this pride led me to commence politician, ye upstart ignorant, self conceited coxcombs, beware how you commence politicians; and forsooth I must be so vain, as to think a taylor, had a right to write the rights of man, but this in the end you see has turned out a devilish bad plan; I was that villain in grain, that tho' I knew the goverment [sic!] of England was a good one, and not to be mended, yet I must in the true spirit of lying, tell the world I could mend the goverment [sic!] of Old England, I must pretend to write upon mending it too, oh! that instead of this I had stuck to mending an old coat, or an old pair of breeches. -- oh, ye taylors stick to you buckram and canvas, and never follow the wicked devices of me thomas paine, for my tricks have been devilish, and I am afraid, I am now going to the devil for them.

I hope then you will all take warning by my fate, shun evil and corrupt company, and be particularly careful to avoid the company of those desperate rascals the jacobines; there are some few of their damnable principles in every town and village of this kingdom: I will tell you how you may know them, they are proud and imperious like myself; they have no fortune, no reputation to lose; they, like myself, are remarkably distinguished by having empty pates, empty pockets, and black designing countenances; they, like me, wish for changes in the government, only to have an opportunity to plunder and rob their neighbours; avoid then those serpents: I here openly own that a highway robber is a far more reputable character than any of those gentry, or than myself. -- stand up for your king and constitution: this is the only way to live happily and to die comfortably: this is the way to avoide the end I am here come to, oh! that I had stuck to my stitching, and for these cursed politics had never had an itching.

Sure never was taylor so fairly done over,
Oh! done over Taylor,
Sure never was taylor so justly done over.

Now to be had at the Reformation Pump, --

The Neat and Genuine WATER for converting the Jacobines,

This Water has such effect upon them, that it makes them sing God save brave George, our king and D--- the French Convention, it must be made use of in the following manner; -- the Jacobin must be taken to the pump, and according to his age, so long he must be pumpt upon, and then drink one gallon of purging liquid; and if his disorder is not got into his bones, this will be a certain cure; for this experiment was tried on Three Jacobins the other day at Nottingham, who in a short time went away singing God save the King; many hundreds can testify the happy effects of his wonderful prescription, for it intirely eradicates evry [sic!] obscene and disaffected thought from their minds.

But if this disorder should return, or that Tom Pain's distemper has got into his Bones, he must be taken to a tan Pit and dipt three times, and then tanned and feathered; --- this is a Certain Cure when all others have failed; they then will deny the devil and all his works, and D--- Tom Paine and all his words, and then will sing, "God save Great George our King, and bless all his loyal subjects;" one of which he now is by virtue of this water, and which he now recommends to all his brother jacodins [sic!], that they may come to this purgine pump, and be purged from their iniquities, and die good loyal subeicts [sic!] to their King and country.

N.B. several hundred grose of glass bottles are wanted to bottle off some of this water, in order for exportation to Sheffield, and other places, any person who would wish to contract for the above quantity, many by applying at the change pump, any time between the hours of ten and two o'clock, where they may see the proposals. No Jacobins, will be treated with : it is expected Stourbridge and dudley will have large orders.

Verses on the Death of Paine.
Stung deep with pride, to work I set my pen,
to write the common sense and rights of man;
Falsehood I cloth'd with art in truth's attire,
In hopes to set the nations all on fire;
In which I had too great success 'tis known,
As my grim lord, king Pluto[52] yet will own.
I right made wrong, and wrong I said was right,

---

[52] Lord of the Underworld.

To push the Yankies to their utmost might;
This plan took place, thousands on all sides fell
A victim to my schemes, and craft of hell;
I valu'd not those scenes, nor slaughter's field,
So it a high lucrative post cou'd yield:
Of this I mist -- inflam'd with envious pride,
I crost the Atlantic to Europa's side;
To fam'd Britannia's land I came at last,
And like a serpint [sic!] forth my venom cast,
My books I sold, disperst the nation round,
And for some time encouragement I found:
But soon my writings lost their thin disguise,
And honest Britons opened their eyes;
The King and constitution so approv'd,
Subjects so local they could not be mov'd;
Some few there was, and those were few indeed,
Could rifle bags, and see the owners bleed:
So finding none maintain'd my cause at last,
But of the nation was the mere outcast:
Britain I left, on Gallia's land did tread,
Wherein my cause has great improvement made;
But O what work those butch'ring cut throats then
Did make with innocent and harmless men;
Women, and children, shocking to relate,
To glut themselves with blood, shar'd the same state
Here low ambition, not regarding toil,
Slew their superiors, to divide the spoil:
And, Satan like, most subtle of all brutes,
Excell'd in cruelties, beyond disputes,
But O I dread the fatal day not past,
When I must give account for all at last;
My darling writings I so much esteem'd,
Witness my crimes, guilty of death I'm deem'd:
Good people warning take by my sad fall,
Poor Tom stands charged with the blood of all.
This makes my blood to chill through every vein,
To think what will become of poor Tom Pain:
Unless grim Pluto favourable be,
Poor Tom is lost, is lost to all eternity.

A Dialogue between a Jacobine and he [sic!] Devil.

JACOBINE, -- Please your Holiness I am come to beg of you to accept me into your Kingdom.
Devil. -- Where do you come from?
Jac. -- I came from Nottingham.
Devil. -- Has there not been a riot there, what is it for?
Jac. -- O please your holiness, the Loyalists have got the better of the Jacobines, and we have lost our Fire-arms and ammunition, and pitt with crew has got the possession of the Jacobin writings, which has prevented us from putting our design into execution.
Devil. -- What is the reason you Jacobins rebel against so good a king and such a mild government.
Jac.-- We will have no King, Lords, nor Commons, nor laws but such as we will make ourselves.
Devil. -- Nor will I ever suffer such rebels as you Jacobins are to come into my Kingdom; for as you will not have a King to rule over you, I must soon expect to be dethroned and lose my head; get you gone, I hate to see the face of a Jocobine: Imps, hear, take care that you never suffer a Jacobine to come into my Kingdom.
Jac.-- O! Alas! how hard is my state, must I return back to be a laughing stock to both old and young. I will repent and go to the Reformation Pump, down on my knees and pray and sing God bless the King, my heart will then be at rest and my mind at ease (2-8).
THE END

5. "... every idea of absolute perfection in Government is chimerical," from: William Augustus Miles, *A Letter to Earl Stanhope*. London: printed for G. Nicol and J. Sewell, 1794.

William Augustus Miles was a political writer whose letter to the famous Earl of Stanhope[53] comments on Stanhope's political conduct in the wake of the French Revolution in Great Britain. Miles criticised Stanhope's support for the reformers and compared the situation in England with that in France. He feared that the revolution could be imported and accused the reformers of destabilizing the country. Miles closed his 158-page-long letter with an appeal to Stanhope to withdraw his

[53] **Charles Stanhope (1753-1816)**, the third Earl, was the brother-in-law of Pitt and supported him until he broke with him over the French Revolution. Stanhope was a strong opponent of the war with France. He was called "Citizen" Stanhope. Stanhope was also a scientist and successful inventor.

support for the reformers and to acknowledge how dangerous his attitude was to Britain.

The conduct of France is recommended to us for imitation - But what have the French done, my Lord, but change from bad to worse? Yet, deplorable as their condition is, that of ours would exceed it, if we should renounce the certainty we possess, to run after Utopian schemes of equality, as useless in speculation as they have been found dangerous in practice.

[...]

The most moderate as well as the most honest men in France had long felt and acknowledged the necessity of a reform. The abuses in the public administration had accumulated to an extent which clogged the whole machine of government; and on a nearer inspection of the evils that oppressed and retarded its progress, it was discovered that any thing short of a revolution would not correct the mischiefs, or give security to the nation for an equitable and provident government in future. The instant the salutary measure was proposed, a general ferment ensued; the entire nation set up for reformers, and every one thought himself qualified for the arduous and complicated task. Unhappily for the public interest and repose, there were men who meant to go *farther*; and though they were clamorous only for *reform*, they had resolved on the destruction of monarchy. We have also men of that description amongst us; artful and designing men, my Lord, who bellow for *reform*, but mean REVOLT, and who would go any lengths rather than relinquish their purpose. The object of the new clubs and associations which they introduced and endeavoured to establish in this country, was certainly meant to excite a ferment in the minds of the people: their object was to overawe Parliament and the Nation, and the tumult once begun, who can say where it would end, whose property would be secure, or whose life respected? (10-13).

The allegedly utopian theories of French philosophers are rejected in the following remarks. Their practicability had not been proved according to the author. By suggesting the introduction of such new ideas, the British reformers jeopardized political institutions.

I wish all good and conscientious men to reflect seriously on the blessings they enjoy at present, in this mild and happy country, and to impress on their uncorrupted minds this wholesome and indisputable truth, *that as every purpose for which men enter into society is answered under a Constitution where the* LIFE *and* PROPERTY *of the peasant are as secure, and held as sacred as those of a Prince; every idea of absolute perfection in Government is chimerical, and every assurance of its practicability not only impudent and fraudulent in the extreme, but dangerous to listen to* (34-35).

6. "Jesus Christ was a Revolutionist," from: Mark Wilks, *The Origin and Stability of the French Revolution. A sermon. Preached at St. Paul's Chapel, Norwich, July, 14, 1791.* Second edition. [Norwich?]: Printed for the Author, 1791.

The Norfolk farmer and Baptist minister Mark Wilks (1748-1819)[54] opened this 77-page-long sermon with a comparison of Jesus Christ with revolutionaries:

Jesus Christ was a Revolutionist;[55] and the Revolution he came to effect was foretold in these words. He hath sent me to proclaim liberty to the captives, and the opening of the prison to them that are bound (5).

It is not to commemorate *this* event we are now met, but the Revolution in France. An event which this moment occupies the minds of thousands and thousands; and about which the minds of men are divided; some holding it in execution and abhorrence, while others, think, wonder and admire.

Amidst this diversity of opinion, I will give it as mine, that the French Revolution is of God, and no power exists, or can exist, by which it can be overthrown.

When I say it is of God, I do not mean to insinuate, that it was effected by super-natural or miraculous interpositions, or that it is so, as was the commonwealth of Israel; all I mean is, that the hand of God, has very visibly appeased in it, and that this glorious event carries with it the most indubitable evidence of the Divine approbation.

---

[54] For Wilks' biography see Memoir of the Rev. Mark Wilks (London: F. Westley, 1821) by his daughter Sarah.

[55] In the Edinburgh Trials of 1793-94, Judge Braxfield replied to Joseph Gerrald's defence that Jesus had been a reformer: "Muckle he made o' that; he was hanget."

I am so far from attributing the Revolution to miracle, that I am persuaded, such were the causes leading to it, that God, and God only could have prevented it (7-8).

[...]

Revolution: The next ground I take in favour of the Revolution is the Revolution itself; an event unparalleled in history, and which cannot fail to raise wonder and admiration even to enthusiasm (26).

I am not one of those people in England of whom Mr. Burke so much complains, as glorying in Revolutions, as though *all Revolutions* were in themselves good. With him I think they are not; and I could tell him of Revolutions, of which to glory would be to glory in our shame. He is concern'd that a comparison should be made between the Revolution in 1688, and that strange thing called the Revolution in France, and so am I; but, I feel myself particularly hurt to hear an *Englishman*, in this enlightened age, boast of the ranks, the orders, the privileges, the franchises, the subordination, the law, the revenue, the commons, the corporations, the electors, and the Church of *England* (27-28).

[...]

What a Government is in theory, and what it is in practice, is not *every where* the same; and, I sincerely wish, the Government of England was in practice what it is in theory, there would then be little need either of Revolution or reform.

It is the introduction of a Government, of which *reason* is the *author*, and *utility* the *object*.

It is the formation of a Government, which is the work of art, and a legislative intellect, reared on the immutable basis of natural right and general happiness, which *combines all the excellencies* and *excludes* the *defects* of all the various constitutions which chance has scattered over the face of the earth. It is the restoration of millions of our fellow creatures to their natural rights, who have hitherto lived on the smiles of a tyrant, or perished at his frowns (28-31).

Wilks called the revolution the "interposition of Divine Providence; by which all the schemes of Anti-revolutionists have been frustrated..." (34). In the second part of his sermon (44-77), Wilks wrote of "the Permanence & Stability of the French Revolution":

"The idea of ETERNITY adds weight to the joys of heaven; and the term, permanent, conjoined with revolutionary, affords ten thousand anticipated pleasures, beyond the bestowment of mere present good" (45).

V. The Trials for High Treason of 1794

The work of the Committee of Secrecy in the House of Commons enabled an indictment for high treason to be filed against Thomas Hardy, John Thelwall, John Horne Tooke, Thomas Holcroft and others (*Copy of The Bill of Indictment*, 1794). The accusation of high treason would not be based on material evidence according to 25 Edward III. John Barrell has convincingly demonstrated in his recent book on the treason trials that, by the end of the eighteenth century, treason was no longer primarily considered to be an act of physical threat to the king; rather, the distinction between imagining such an act and preparing to carry out such an act had been abandoned. Therefore, Chief Justice Eyre defined treason as an "overt act" of imagining or compassing the king's death. A committee of the Society for Constitutional Information and London Corresponding Society planned to call a convention; this would later be interpreted as an overt act of imagining the king's death.[56] With respect to the report of the Secret Committee, Barrell comes to the conclusion that:

> If we read this report as creatively as the committee read the papers it had seized, we might, however, be tempted to conclude that even the committee itself suspected that what it described as the 'extravagant designs' of the reform societies were designs to which the imagination of the committee itself had contributed its share.[57]

On 6 October, the Grand Jury confirmed an indictment of twelve reformers for high treason.[58] On 28 October, Lord Chief Justice James Eyre, who presided over the nine-hour-long speech given by the attorney general, opened the trial against Thomas Hardy Sir John Scott, later Lord Eldon (1751-1838). The trial lasted an unusual eight days and the printed version of the account encompassed more than 2,000

---

[56] John Barrell, *Imagining the King's Death: Figurative Treason, Fantasies of Regicide, 1793-1796* (Oxford: Oxford University Press, 2000), 34-35.
[57] Barrell 2000: 231.
[58] See *A Copy of The Bill of Indictment* (1794) for the following names: Thomas Hardy, John Richter, Matthew Moore, John Thelwall, Richard Hodgson, John Baxter, John Horne Tooke, John August Bonney, Stewart Kyd, Jeremiah Joyce, Thomas Wardle and Thomas Holcroft.

pages.[59] The sessions began at eight o'clock in the morning and often lasted until well after midnight.[60]

In spite of Hardy's acquittal – an embarrassment for the government – three more trials took place. John Horne Tooke stood trial from 17 to 22 November. This highly educated and eloquent reformer and linguist[61] contributed much to his own defence. With Tooke's acquittal, the case for a general conspiracy had virtually collapsed; yet, a third trial – against John Thelwall – began on 1 December. Following his acquittal on 5 December, his supporters celebrated the notorious radical orator. Ten days later, John Richter and John Baxter were released from prison and the treason trials, each of which had been quite different, were concluded.[62]

1. "... the object of these societies was to proceed in contempt of Parliament," from: *Debates on the Report of the Committee of Secrecy in the House of Commons. On the 16th and 17th of May, and in the House of Lords, on the 17th and 19th and 22d of the same month, 1794.* Edinburgh: J. Robertson, [1794].

In May 1794 the report of the Committee of Secrecy in the House of Commons was debated in both Houses. The committee had taken up its work in the wake of the Edinburgh trials against leading members of the reform movement in Scotland, i.e., against Muir, Palmer, Skirving, Margarot and Gerrald. The indictments for sedition in the Scottish trials were successful for the government, which wanted to suppress

---

[59] The various accounts of the treason trials that were published in London, Edinburgh, Dublin, Newcastle and Cork is evident of the extraordinary interest the public took in the trials.

[60] Lloyd Paul Stryker, *For the Defense: Thomas Erskine, the Most Englightened Liberal of His Times, 1750 - 1823* (Garden City, NY: Doubleday, 1949), 280-306, Goodwin 1979: 343-346, and Hostettler 1996: 112-115.

[61] See Stryker 1949: 307-337, and Christina and David Bewley, *Gentleman Radical: A Life of John Horne Tooke 1736-1812* (London: Tauris Academic Studies; New York: St Martin's Press, 1998), 170-189. There are also at least four different editions of the proceedings (Tooke 1794). Tooke included his experiences of various trials in his etymological work, *The Diversions of Purley*. Cf. Christoph Houswitschka, "Der Hochverratsprozeß gegen John Horne Tooke (1794): der Sprachforscher als Verteidiger seiner Bürgerrechte," in: *Literatur, Kriminalität und Rechtskultur im 17. und 18. Jahrhundert. Tagung am 17. und 18. Juni 1994 an der Technischen Universität Dresden*, ed. by Uwe Böker and Christoph Houswitschka (Essen: Blaue Eule, 1996), 262-281.

[62] Goodwin 1979: 358 and Hostettler 1996: 125-126; see also Marcus Wood, *Radical Satire and Print Culture 1790-1822* (Oxford: Clarendon Press, 1994), 132-134. Hardy, for instance, had his head bowed down most of the time whereas Tooke, assisting Erskine, was a witty and intelligent defender of his own cause.

the reform movement. The English government feared the foundation of an English Convention and decided to accuse the most important members of the English reform societies of high treason. The authors of the report demanded that sweeping measures be taken against the opposition. Members of both Houses feared that the government of William Pitt wanted to destroy rather than to protect constitutional rights.

As the complete title suggests, this book mainly presents the voices of the parliamentary opposition to the findings of the Secret Committee. The book also contains a "*List of the Minority in both Houses of the Parliament who voted against the Suspension of the Habeas Corpus Act*". Although the title implies an obvious political bias, the actual presentation indicates an attempt to achieve some objectivity.

The report then states, that from all these things it appeared to the Committee, that the object of these societies was to proceed in contempt of Parliament, and to assume to themselves the power of a legislature, and to introduce into the country the anarchy and confusion which has so fatally prevailed in France. It states, that since the seizing of these papers some proposals had been made for providing arms, and that there had been several meetings of this Societies in the Metropolis, for the purpose, as the Committee understood, of forcibly resisting the bringing the authors and abettors of these proceedings to justice (4).

Pitt himself had warned the Parliament that the Committee had convincing evidence that the reformers were about to call together a national convention after the French model.

... an assemblage, which professed, not merely to address the House of Commons for a Parliamentary Reform, but went boldly to the professed and avowed object of superceding that House of Representatives of the People, and arrogating to itself their Legislative functions. If the House were convinced, that such a design really existed, they would see there not a minute to be lost in arming the Executive Government with such additional powers, as would enable them to stop, in the first instance, an evil, which if suffered to arrive at any head, would be productive of such infinite and extensive mischief, although ultimately unsuccessful (4-5).

An investigation in the oppositional activities of the preceding two years had resulted in alarming findings.

By these they would perceive that the Corresponding Society in disseminating throughout the kingdom certain publications, and setting on foot the plan of a General Convention, demonstrated the adoption of principles which were to be the ground of action the very moment opportunity should present itself - principles which had spread desolation and horror over a neighbouring kingdom, and nearly endangered the safety, and tranquillity of almost every state in Europe. Though they might be said, and truly so, to be insignificant and contemptible in their nature and characters, yet, when those principles were adopted, and endeavoured to be spread throughout the ignorant or discontented part of the community, it behoved them to guard against them (4-5).

Pitt justified his intention to suspend the *Habeas Corpus Act*. His words show that he constructed a reality mainly derived from the report. Its authors, however, had not found any material proof for their allegations. Thus, the assumption that the reformers were planning a conspiracy was mainly constructed from publications of the corresponding societies and, therefore, based on interpretations of texts. In his reply, the leader of the Whigs, Charles Fox, rejected such a text-based construct and the conclusions that are drawn from it.

William Pitt: In past times of danger it has been thought fitting to suspend laws which are essentially necessary to the permanent existence of the Constitution, but which it has been found equally necessary to suspend, according to the exigence of the times. At the present crisis, when treasonable attempts were prevalent in every corner of the kingdom, such a measure was, if ever, now most necessary.

Such were his decided sentiments, and not his only, but those who with him had opportunity of informing themselves of facts (8-9).

[...]

Charles Fox: But however the Report was not a mere report of these stale, ridiculous, contemptible facts; but it stated also an inference arising out of these facts. He could not arrive so readily as the Ministers at his conclusion upon these points, taking them all to be exactly as they were related. He begged leave to differ from him and from the whole of the Committee upon that subject: - thought the inference of the Committee was unfair; - he would go further, he thought that taking, for the sake of argument, the inference to be fair, that would not warrant the measure now proposed. He should not go into the question whether these persons were acting consistently or not, that was not matter for consideration now (9-10).

Charles James Fox (1749-1806) did not believe that the wish to summon a Convention is illegal. Fox sharply criticised the Edinburgh trials and called them an abuse of governmental power. Should this be repeated in England, he warned, it might mean the end of freedom (11). The situation the government was planning to create would threaten the constitution in a manner only comparable to the last Jacobite rise in 1745, when a papist army jeopardized the peace and order of the country. Joseph Jekyl (who had had a seat in Parliament since 1769 and who died in 1837) supported Fox. Jekyl pointed out that most of the material presented by the Secret Committee had been published by the conspirators before. Another speaker who contributed much to defending the reform movement in the Parliament was the dramatist Richard Brinsley Sheridan (1751-1816), who pointed out that the accusations were based upon constructions of the minds of those who had read and misinterpreted oppositional publications. Edmund Burke rejected this opinion and warned Sheridan in a cynical statement that one could step up the prosecution of oppositional newspaper articles in the future.

Charles Fox: You are going to give up the very best part of your Constitution and that which every man is entitled to do, and which I am now doing, delivering the sentiments of my heart, upon the affairs of Government for the benefit of the public, will be at an end once. May I not then say here is an end of the Constitution of England! (12)

[...]

Mr. Jekyl replied to the last speaker, and expressed his very great astonishment that the Report which had just been read contained nothing in fact or in substance that had not been published long ago, and ought to have been noticed at the time, if worthy of notice now; and if there were any reason that could be given for resisting his Hon. Friend's wish, that it might be printed, it must be that all it contained had been printed and published already (16).

[...]

He [Jekyl] then concluded his opposition to the motion by stating, that the conduct and measures of Administration for some time past had tended to put an end to public and private confidence, and destroy that happiness and harmony in society which used to be the characteristics of British subjects. *There was a general cry of question! question!* (17).

Richard Sheridan: What was to be found in the famous report of the *British Barrere*? - Shortly this - a number of copies of idle papers that had been printed, published, and circulated, some of them for the last two years, and all of them before the commencement of the last Session of Parliament. Why, he would ask, had they not been prosecuted at the time they appeared. [...] He for one believed that no such practices[63] existed in the country, and that Ministers and their friends knew this to be the case, but it was necessary for them and for their views, to keep up, or rather create, some new cause of panic to gain that continuance of power over the people, which seemed to be much the object of their wishes. He believed most firmly that this measure was founded upon a conviction on the minds of those who introduced and supported it, that no such practices existed at all, in this country, that could produce any alarm that made this proposal for putting the liberty and the propriety of all the people, of Great Britain, at the discretion of the Executive Government, a power which never had been, nor ought to be given, except in times of actual rebellion, or imminent and manifest danger, which none would be hardy enough to say was the case at present (18).

[...]

Edmund Burke: Mr. Burke made a speech of considerable length in favour of the motion. He animadverted upon Mr. Sheridan's magnanimity in despising newspaper calumnies, and never prosecuting them at the time, wishing to transfer that task to the Attorney General *ex officio*, and was afraid that this would not be much liked by those who are friends to the liberty of the press (21).

In the debate, many Members of Parliament believed that everything had to be undertaken to protect the Constitution. Mr. Dundas, who organised these new policies against the reform movement, pointed out that the *Habeas Corpus* had been suspended nine times since the Revolution of 1688, and that this had never been interpreted as an abolishment of the Constitution (36). The programme of the London Corresponding Society, however, demonstrated that they intended "the complete subversion of the constitution" by means of universal suffrage and annual parliaments (38).

[63] That is, practices of high treason.

Charles Grey[64] and Richard Sheridan reminded their colleagues that Muir and Palmer were celebrated in the streets as innocent heroes. Reforms *were* necessary (39). Sheridan concluded: "The Report of the Committee was a mere political artifice. That Committee was composed of men, in part deceiving, and in part deceived. It was equally suspicious from its manner and its precipitancy" (40). No weapons had been found, as claimed in the report (41). Charles Fox explained that the word "convention" means "meeting" and that there was no reason to call it high treason. He went on:

In short, it was a government of passion, a government in which ministers strove to lull asleep all the sober operations of the mind, and to awaken only the fears and terrors of the heart. Reform they dreaded, for reason was their enemy. [...] Their whole report was trifling and inconsequential; it told nothing which every man did not know before. [...] Then what did the report consist of? Of a collection of papers which had all been seen by the public, and which if they did contain any danger, was not a danger of to-day (50-51).

"How long would it take to eradicate these opinions from the minds of these men?" (53), asked Fox in his long reply (45-58). Fox reminded his listeners that the right of popular discussion was "a salutary and an essential privilege of the subject" (54).

And in his opinion the best security for the due maintenance of the Constitution, was in the strict and incessant vigilance of the people over Parliament itself. Meetings of the people therefore for the discussion of public objects, were not merely legal but laudable, and unless it was to be contended that there was some magic in the word Convention, which brought with it disorder, anarchy and ruin, he could perceive no just ground for demolishing the Constitution of England, merely because it was intended to hold a meeting for the purpose of obtaining a parliamentary reform (55).

Persecution "had never been successful in extirpating opposition to any system either religious or civil" (56). Later the Chancellor of the Exchequer rejected Fox's conclusions.

---

[64] See footnote 28 for information on Charles Grey.

The Chancellor of the Exchequer: What he had read from their own books,[65] he thought, proved sufficiently that it was from hypocrisy only that they made use of the parliamentary reform as a pretext for their real and mischievous designs; and the papers inserted in the report, were, in his mind, a complete answer to all who confounded them with parliamentary reformers, and likewise to those who had said that the report contained no new matter whatever (62-63).

The debate in the House of Lords (May 22, 1794) brought more passionate statements against the new laws. The leader of the aristocratic supporters of reforms, Sir Charles, Earl of Stanhope, did not want to rule out that he might possibly soon be "bastilled, he would therefore speak out while he had permission to speak at all" (75). Another important contribution against the law came from the Earl of Lauderdale. The Earl of Derby quoted Lord Thurlow: "A Noble and Learned Lord had said, that all the facts stated in the Report were highly seditious, but did not amount to Treason" (106). For the same reason, all accused reformers were acquitted in November 1794.

Earl of Stanhope: With regard to the present measure, the ground and pretence for it was the most 'impudent humbug' that ever Ministers had the audacity to state, if his ears deceived him not. It was an inference neither supported by logic, by fair reasoning or by truth of conclusion, drawn from a miserable conclusion, drawn from a miserable collection of papers, most of them published two years ago. Those papers were written by a set of men, honest in their intentions though not rich, nor high in rank. They might from defect of education have been somewhat 'inaccurate' in their expressions (a laugh from Ministers) but their intentions were clearly legal (73).

Earl of Lauderdale: He would say again, that the committee should have reported facts to the House, and not merely their opinion on facts; for in the order by which the committee was constituted, it was not expressed, as in some cases, "That they shall report the same, together with their opinion thereon, to the House (78-79).

[65] That is, the books of the reformers.

[...]

Earl of Stanhope: He ridiculed then the idea of conspiracy where every transaction had been printed in the public newspapers, and maintained that if what was now stated in the report was illegal, Government ought to have prosecuted it a long time ago (93).

[...]

Besides, he maintained that the report itself was extremely unfair, and made up entirely against all the rules of evidence; parties of their correspondence, and those the most unfavourable; were selected, and the favourable ones omitted; whereas in point of justice and by the rules of law, the whole of the books of the society should be quoted in the report, and set forth at full length, that the House might not be called upon to judge from mutilated and detached passages, but fairly and equitably from the whole context, and, for aught their Lordships could know to the contrary, the whole taken together might not only be innocent, but also a meritorious work (94).

[...]

Earl of Lauderdale: What were the materials that proved this dark and hidden conspiracy? Seditious papers, that had appeared in every newspaper in the country, and treasonable writings, that had everywhere been handed about, printed, published, and circulated for the last fourteenth months (99).

2. "There can be no government where all men live upon terms of equality," from: *An Account of the Treason and Sedition, Committed by the London Corresponding Society, the Society for Constitutional Information, the other Societies of London, Sheffield, Norwich, Manchester, Bristol, Coventry, Nottingham, Derby, Birmingham, Dublin, &c. &c. their correspondence with the Convent on and Jacobin Societies at Paris; sending Deputies to France; admitting Barrere, Roland, and St. André, into the Society for Constitutional Information; also a dangerous letter to Mr. Sheridan, Chairman of the Society, calling themselves the Friends of the People; and The Whole of the Two Reports, Presented to the Hon. House of Commons, by The Secret Committee.* [London]: Printed for J. Downes, No. 240, Temple-Bar, Strand, [1794].

In this collection of material on the activities of the reform movement and their interpretation by the government, the case is prepared for the indictment that was brought against the leading members of corresponding societies. From the following excerpts, one can see that the public was informed and manipulated not only by the radicals, but also by those who were loyal to the government.

The anonymous author of the following popularised excursion into political philosophy tries to convince his readers that a republican constitution cannot work in a country the size of Great Britain.

Authentic Narrative &c.

The very word society implicates the idea of order; but as no order can exist where there is no controlling power, there can be no government where all men live upon terms of equality (10).

[...]

A monarchial government is exclusively suited to large and populous nations, because such only are enabled to provide for the expences of monarchy. The republican form is better for the expences of monarchy. The republican form is better suited to small and poor countries, because it is administered with less expence. In the former, there is unity of power, which constitutes the perfection of government; and it also includes secrecy and promptitude, without which great and complicated affairs cannot be successfully conducted. Aristocracy is necessary in a republic; drawing together the authorities that otherwise would be without union, excluding the tyranny that results from the arbitrary will of a people governing themselves. Pure democracy will always produce an inconsistent and ineffectual government, because it neither admits of union of opinions, nor of prudence, promptitude, nor secrecy; and includes in itself principles that beget disorders among, and are entirely subversive of the happiness of the people. Whether ancient or modern, all the known republics have been meliorated by aristocracy. We must not even except Athens, which was devoid of success and splendour. [...] The extent of our commerce, our wealth, our luxuries, the civilization of our manners, in a word, all the enjoyments on which are founded the splendour and happiness of our age, re-opposed to the establishment of a republic (14-15).

[...]

Liberty does not necessarily demand a republican government. England is a proof, that a people may be free under a monarch. Liberty consists in being free from obedience to all laws but those that the people themselves have made. The law is the sanctuary in which the sovereignty resides; and kings, or other magistrates to whom the executive power is delegated, being subject to the law, the people are so free as they can be consistently with their happiness. Such are the bounds of true liberty, and all beyond is anarchy. [...] The reader will be but too plainly convinced that a very daring conspiracy was formed for the subversion of the constitution of this country, and for establishing in the place thereof a system of anarchy, similar to that adopted in France. But providentially this destructive scheme was discovered in time to be completely defeated by the wholesome provisions of legislature (16).

The Second Report tried to prove that the reformers had purchased weapons for an uprising using the Loyal Lambeth Association as a cover.

It appears, that although this armed society bore the name of the Loyal Lambeth Association, none of the members belonging to it were of the parish of Lambeth, excepting the original proposer of the association, who was a member of the London Corresponding Society. The admission of persons who were afterwards members of the association was objected to at first, because they did not belong to the London Corresponding Society; but on promise that they would become members of the London Corresponding Society, they were admitted into this armed association (51).

[...]

Having thus stated the points which the committee have thought it material separately to lay before the house, they will now proceed to those particulars which will give a full and distinct view of the rise, progress, and nature of the general design, with which the facts already stated are essentially connected; for this purpose your committee will state in their report the points which appear most worthy of attention, inserting in the Appendix a more particular statement of the several proceedings to which they refer. In doing this it will be necessary to advert to transactions, some of which took place at an early period, and have already attracted, observation; but which it is nevertheless material to insert in the order in which they took place, because they are highly important in explaining more recent proceedings, and giving a connected view of the whole system.

The period from which it appears to your committee material to trace in this view the proceedings of the Society for Constitutional Information, is that of the publication of the pamphlet so well known under the title of 'Rights of Man', by Thomas Paine (54).

3. "Each day's Publication will be sold for One Shilling," from: *A Copy of The Bill of Indictment Found Against Thomas Hardy, Thomas Holcroft, John Horne Tooke, John Richter, John Augustus Bonney, Matthew Moore, Stewart Kyd, John Thelwall, Jeremiah Joyce, Richard Hodgson, Thomas Wardle, John Baxter For High Treason with A List of the Grand and Petty Jurors, and the Names of the Witnesses, Who Have been Subpœned on the Part of the Crown*. London: J. Bell, 1794.

John Bell was a bookseller, printer, typefounder, newspaper publisher and bookbinder. He was one of the most successful booksellers of his period. He brought out *The Poets of Great Britain* (109 volumes between 1777 and 1782), published Shakespeare (1774) and *British Theatre* (21 volumes from 1776 to 1778), all small format cheap editions. From 1787 to 1803 he was bookseller to the Prince of Wales. He was also the publisher of several newspapers: proprietor of *Morning Post* since 1772, printer and publisher of *World* (1787-1789), founder and publisher of *The Oracle* (1 June 1789) (see below), printer and publisher of *Bell's Weekly Messenger* (since 1796). Bell was indicted for libels several times and went bankrupt twice (1793 and 1797).[66]

---

[66] Cf. Stanley Morison, *John Bell, 1745-1831: Bookseller, Printer, Publisher, Typefounder, Journalist, &tc.* With a new introduction by Nicolas Barker (New York: Garland, 1981).

This publication begins with the "Bill of Indictment" (1-7), the list of "Petty Jurors" (8-10), and the "List of Witnesses" (11-14). In the following Advertisement, Bell promised his readers: "The Approaching Trials for High Treason will undoubtedly involve the Greatest Political Considerations that were ever agitated before a Judicial Tribunal." The advertisement shows how much attention these State Trials had gained and how much interest the public took in the professionalism and reliability of their publication. It is explained that:

Mr. Bell, of the British Library, Strand, had therefore engaged a number of Parliamentary Reporters and Short-Hand Writers to report the Trials at Large, including the Pleading of Counsel, the Charges to the Jury, and the Defences of the Different Prisoners.

In order to give these Reporters to the Public with celerity equal to the accuracy, Mr. Bell has made an extensive Printing Arrangement, that will enable him to Publish the Proceedings of the trials at large, complete, to the conclusion of the Sitting of each Day, in such a manner as will give the most perfect account at Twelve O'Clock Each Succeeding Day.

Each day's Publication will be sold for One Shilling, which may be had of all the Booksellers and Newsmen in Town; and may be also forward by the Penny-Post through every district, to such persons as choose to give orders for that purpose.

The enquiry must be made particularly for Bell's Reports of The State Trials for High Treason.

N.B. A correct Copy of the Bills of Indictment, of The Grand and Petty Jurory, and also a List of all Witnesses, on the part of the Crown, who have had notice to attend the Trials, is now published, price Six Pence, as Introductory to the Report of the Trials, and may be had as above.

The whole will be handsomely printed in Royal Octave, and may be bound as a Volume when finished.

The ORACLE will contain each day as ample an account of the Trials as can be given within the circumscribed Limits of a Newspaper.

British Library, Strand,

Oct. 22, 1794 (n.p.)

Bell printed the "Lord Chief Justice's Charge to the Grand Jury" (i-xi),[67] in which the notorious definition of high treason from 25 Edward III is quoted, though it was completely re-defined by the Attorney General:[68] "These overt acts involve in them two distinct considerations: 1st, The matter of fact of which they consist; in the next place, the relation of that fact to the design" (ii). The "Charge to the Grand Jury" is followed by a report of "Holcroft's Surrender" (xii-xv) and Bell's "Reports of the State Trials for High Treason" (1-112).

The following reformers were brought to trial upon an indictment of treason:

Thomas Hardy, late of Westminster, in the County of Middlesex, Shoemaker

John Horne Tooke, late of Wimbledon, in county of Surrey, Clerk.

John Augustus Bonney, late of the Parish of St. Giles in the Fields, in the County of Middlesex aforesaid, Gentleman.

Stewart Kyd, late of London, Esq.
Jeremiah Joyce, of the Parish of Saint-Mary-le Bonne, otherwise Marybonne, in the County of Middlesex aforesaid, Gentleman.
Thomas Holcroft, late of the Parish of Saint-Mary-le Bonne, otherwise Marybonne, in the County of Middlesex aforesaid, Gentleman.
John Richter, late of Westminster, in the said County of Middlesex, Gentleman.
John Thelwall, late of Westminster, in the County of Middlesex aforesaid, Gentleman.
John Baxter, late of the Parish of Saint Leonard, Shoreditch, in the county of Middlesex aforesaid, labourer.

---

[67] Sir James Eyre, "The Charge Delivered by The Right Honourable Sir James Eyre, Lord Chief Justice of His Majesty's Court of Common Plea and one of the Commissioners Named a Special Commission of Oyer and Terminer, Issued under the Great Seal of Great Britain, To Enquire of Certain High Treasons, and Misprisons of Treason, within the County of Middlesex, To the Grand Jury, October 2, 1794," in: *Uncollected Writings*, ed. Jack W. Marken and Burton R. Pollin (Gainesville: Scholar's Fascimiles, 1968), 129-143.
[68] See the chapter on "The Charge to the Grand Jury" in Barrell 2000: 285-317.

The three other persons included in the same Indictment, viz. Thomas Wardle, Matthew Moore, and Richard Hodgson, have not yet been apprehended (11).

The ultimate acquittal of the accused reformers is commented upon by Bell in the following, final words of his report:

In a short time afterwards the jury entered the Court, and the Judges were sent for, and the Foreman of the Jury pronounced the verdict - NOT GUILTY.

The Persons present for a few moments forgot themselves, and were applauding the verdict, but desisted from their acclamations when silence was ordered in the Court.

The Lord President thanked the Jury for the pains and attention they bestowed in the discharge of their arduous duty [...] The Prisoner, in a very laconic manner, thanked the Jury, on behalf of himself and his country, for their impartial decision.

The Lord President asked if there was any detainer against him; and being answered in the negative, he ordered him to be discharged, and the Court adjourned to Monday Se'nnight.

As soon as the verdict was pronounced, Mr. Erskine's countenance expressed the gladness of his heart. He immediately ran to the shops of the Old Bailey, and proclaimed that there was a verdict of acquittal. The intelligence was conveyed with electrical rapidity, and in a few moments the air was filled with the shouts of the multitude.

Mr. Kirby, the Keeper of Newgate, with his usual prudence, conveyed the Prisoner through his house privately, and, on entering the coach Mr. Hardy ordered the coachman to drive with all velocity. The multitude was soon apprised of the deception, and, pursuing the carriage, dismissed the horses in the Strand from their duty, and took charge of the vehicles themselves. They paraded him through many of the streets round Pall Mall and St. James's-street, through Piccadilly, and left him, as we hear, at the house of his brother-in-law, Mr. Vaughan, in Lancaster Court, Strand; where the first object of his attention was the tomb of his wife, who was buried in St. Martin's church-yard (112).

VI. The Accounts of the Accused Reformers

Different publishers in England, Scotland and Ireland published all the state trials in a variety of versions. This shows the great interest people took in these accounts. The following excerpts give an impression of how the reformers themselves reacted to the indictment brought against them and to the abuses they had to suffer during their imprisonment. Whereas Jeremiah Joyce described the hardships of imprisonment, others put a stronger emphasis on the legal aspects of the charge to the Grand Jury. Apart from John Horne Tooke, who participated in the effort of defending his interests in court, none of the others accused of high treason had the opportunity to defend themselves – either because the chief justice did not allow it, as in the case of Thelwall, or because further trials never took place, as in the cases of Thomas Holcroft and Jeremiah Joyce. These accounts were published after release from prison in order to defend oneself against the charges, as well as to respond to all those who claimed that the acquittals were not justified.

Thelwall complained in *The Natural and Constitutional Right of Britons [...]; being a vindication of the motives and political conduct of J. Thelwall* that there were members in both houses who regarded the accused as "white-washed felons" and who believed that the acquittals did not free them from "the imputation of moral guilt."[1] On the one hand, Thelwall asked how representatives of the state could possibly behave so, "outraging, in such a manner, that dearest and most sacred of all the institutions in this Country" (63). On the other hand, Thelwall admitted that he had shown "intemperance of youth", though insisting that he had not committed any crimes against the State. In this way, Thelwall and Justice Macdonald managed to establish a limited dialogue with the public and the political establishment.

One hoped that these publications would bring some profit that would compensate the financial losses caused by months of imprisonment. Thus, George Dyer quoted Holcroft's and Joyce's accounts in his *Dissertation of the Theory and Practice of Benevolence* (London 1795; see ch. 7, text 9).

1. "It is our business to pursue what is right," from: Jeremiah Joyce, *A Sermon Preached on Sunday, February the 23d, 1794. By Jeremiah Joyce, twenty-three Weeks a close Prisoner in the Tower of London, to which is added an appendix, containing an account of the author's arrest for "treasonable practices" his examination before his Majesty's most honourable Privy Council; his commitment to the Tower, and subsequent treatment.* London: printed for the author, and sold by J. Ridgway; H. D. Symonds; and D. Holt, Newark, 1794.

Jeremiah Joyce (1763-1816) wrote the following sermon in prison.[69] The appendix (33-48) gives Joyce's account of the trial itself. Joyce justified his work in the reform movement, writing that Jesus had always been his teacher:

> ... his zeal and fidelity in public life; - his attachment to his friends; - his forbearance towards his and enemies; - and his universal benevolence and philanthropy may challenge the minutest attention. [...]
>
> At the period when the following discourse was delivered, the aspect of the times rendered it not altogether improbable, that the zeal and fortitude of his friends to freedom, and to truth, might soon be brought to the test.
>
> For without alluding to that eagerness which persons of certain descriptions have manifested in suppressing the spirit of free inquiry, once the boast of Englishmen; or to the severe and even unexampled punishments which have been inflicted upon those who have dared to exercise it as their right, there were reasons sufficiently strong to awaken the serious deliberation of every human being (xi-xii).

After the accusation of treason, Joyce was even more convinced that he had done the right thing:

[69] Other reformers who published what they had written in prison are John Horne Tooke, *Prison Diary (16 May - 22 November, 1794)*, ed. by A.V. Beedell and A.D. Harvey (Leeds: Leeds Philosophical and Literary Society, 1995); John Thelwall, *Poems Written in Close Confinement* (1795), and "The Prison Diary of John Augustus Bonney" was published by Nicholas Roe, *The Politics of Nature: William Wordsworth and Some Contemporaries*. 2nd ed. (Houndmills: Palgrave, 2002), 120-140.

I can recollect no political effort of my life which can create in my breast one moment's uneasiness: not one, which, in the sincerity of my soul, I do not approve. The exertions of active life afford no small consolation, in the gloomy solitude of a prison. The pleasure of having endeavoured to live for one's country, no reverse of circumstances can ever obliterate. In humble submission, therefore, to the will of the Governor of the universe, I wait the vent of an approaching public trial at the bar of my country (xiv-xv).

[...]

Whether Life, or Death be before me, in either case, I doubt not, but that the vent will be beneficial to the world. For this, and not for myself alone, I received my original existence; to this end I have endeavoured to live; and for the sake of this, I hope, if called upon, I can cheerfully lay down my life.

Oct. 23, 1794,

Being the twenty-third Week of my close imprisonment in the Tower of London.

Joyce offered philosophical explanations for his political convictions, comparing the world with a machine:

Does the mechanic begin to form his machine without first understanding the effects its intended to produce? If he did not comprehend the purposes for which it was designed, how could he discern the causes necessary to its existence? He must not only know all the various parts which will make up the whole piece, but must perfectly understand their exact proportions. He will also foresee, and provide for the principal defects to which his machine may, in the course of time, be liable, and, by a proper division and arrangement of its several parts, so construct it, that it may be repaired at the least expence of time and labour. And if his operations be tolerably perfect, he will set such a limit to his labour, as shall enable him to effect in a given work, the greatest advantages with fewest inconveniences. To attain, however, this degree of excellence, it is evident that he must possess fore-knowledge in a limited degree, which, when considered universally, constitutes an attribute of Jehova (5-6).

Joyce regarded himself as a martyr:

Should it be our lot to suffer, in any respect, for the cause of truth, it will be well for us if we can enjoy the consolation of conscious integrity; if we have the happiness of knowing that we have been actuated by no sinister motives, but have in all our aims directed us to the advancement of the general good (26).

[...]

That the termination will be favourable to the progress of civil and moral improvement is an expectation we have a right to form. But we have no reason to believe, or even to hope, that such improvement can be accomplished without many a sacrifice on the part of those who are willing to stand in the foremost ranks of opposition to the baneful influence or error (28).

[...]

It may be reserved for us to follow them in singular, or even severer trials; if so, may we in that day enjoy the consolation which is only to be derived from an approving conscience. -- May we at all times adapt our minds to the situation we are called to fill (29-30).

In the appendix, Jeremiah Joyce tells of his examination before his Majesty's Most Honourable PRIVY COUNCIL, May 14, 1794. This examination lasted 45 minutes; Joyce, however, refused to answer most of the questions of Mr. Fawkener, the Clerk of the Council. Dundas and Pitt tried to convince him that he should answer their questions because he should not look down upon the institutions of the state:

Mr. Dundas: You had better leave the institution to take care of itself, and consider whether it will not be wise in you to answer the questions which are put to you.

Mr. Pitt: Mr. Joyce must know that every good subject will object to no question, which does not tend to criminate himself (37).

Pitt admonished Joyce that answering questions was not problematic if he were not guilty. Joyce replied: "I am sorry for it; but I do not think it right to set a precedent of an accused man answering any questions. This is my only reason" (38). Joyce remained adamant, explained his rights and showed no regret, even after months in prison:

A close imprisonment of six months has not induced me to regret my conduct before the Privy Council. To submit to a series of interrogatories where there is no specific charge, nor even accusation, is tamely to surrender a right, which no power can wrest from the meanest individual. Many illustrious characters have cheerfully suffered every oppression rather than be the means of introducing a system by which arbitrary governments are sustained.

Several of my fellow prisoners refused to interrogate upon the same principle. There is no apology necessary for introducing in this place the examination of Mr. Bonney, a gentleman of professional and irreproachable character; of manners the most mild and inoffensive; firmly attached to the constitution of the country, and against whom it were impossible to adduce even a suspicion of violence, much less a charge of TREASON (39).

John Augustus Bonney[70] (1763-1813) also refused to answer any questions in his Examination (39-40), giving the following explanation, which emphasized the call for democratisation:

Mr. Bonney: Sir, you will give me leave to make a few observations. I believe I shall be able to shorten our business very much. It is now twenty-four hours since I was taken from my family upon a warrant, which I protest I do not clearly understand. I am ordered by it to be apprehended for Treasonable Practices. What these words mean I cannot exactly make out. There are two explanations which it has struck my mind may be applied to them -- Treasonable Practices may be intended to mean the practice of Treason -- namely, Treason itself -- or it may mean Seditious Practices, which must tend to Treason; -- it is immaterial to me at present which of these two, in the explanation you put upon the words,

---

[70] Bonney was a solicitor and defended several reformers, such as John Horne Tooke in 1790, and the publishers J.S. Jordan in 1792 and Isaac Eaton in 1794.

for my answer to the charge is the same in both cases. I declare to you, Sir, I declare to you; my Lords, who are appointed to sit here and guard the welfare of your Country, and to God; that I have never been guilty of any Treasonable Practices; that I do not know of any; for if I did, and had not revealed them, I know I should have been equally guilty; nor have I have been ever present at any Treasonable Practices whatever. You have now, my Lords, my most solemn assertion against the charge against me; for upon the face of the warrant there is no appearance of any other evidence to support the charge. It is not stated in the warrant by whom I am charged; or that there is any charge at all against me. Your Lordships have indeed other means of evidence; my Papers are in your hands, but they, I believe, can testify nothing against me. You may have had witnesses before you, but if they have alleged this charge, they must be false witnesses. It is for you, however, to consider what weight is to be given to their testimony, and we are then at issue. If your Lordships are in possession of any evidence which can justify my committing me, I entreat your Lordships to do it; if, on the other hand, you have no such evidence, I require, I demand, of your Lordships to discharge me (40).

Being imprisoned in the Tower of London, Joyce had to endure the curses of passers-by:

The epithets of Jacobin, Democrat, King-Killer, with others, in the most disgusting and indecent language, were very liberally applied. This, however, gradually subsided, when instead of outrage, the spectators evidently appeared to consider me rather an object of pity (43).

Joyce believed that the freedoms which had been established by William of Orange had become "unfashionable". He obtained his political education at home – he remembered very well how infuriated his parents had been when they learnt of the suppression of freedom in the American colonies during the War of Independence (1775-1783):

To these principles, as those upon which all just government is founded, I have never scrupled to avow an open attachment; - an attachment which is not the effect of sudden impressions, but the consequence of instructions which I imbibed in early youth. I can remember nothing of earlier date than the honest indignation of a late highly respected parent, against the measures taken to enslave our brethren across the Atlantic. From him I learned to consider the cause of America, as the cause of MAN (44).

[...]

To the sound of Freedom's voice my heart always vibrated; and, imagining that he constitution of my country was built upon the generous Principles of Liberty, and that this was still the land for free inquiry, I never hesitated to avow with frankness and boldness, all my political opinions.

What I felt myself, I thought it my duty to make others feel; I endeavoured, therefore, to diffuse constitutional knowledge among my fellow citizens. And the more effectually to do this, I joined the Society of Constitutional Information, the publications of which had been put into my hands, and to the principles of which I most cordially assented (45).

Burke had polarized the political culture in the country to a great extent:

I was reserved for the author of the "Reflections", to vilify and calumniate the principle, which delights in the diffusion of the blessings of knowledge, among the lower, and more numerous ranks of society. Perverted must be his mind, who can suppose a man less fitted for the duties of life, by being able to comprehend the rights to which he has a claim. In every situation, he who knows what, and where his interest is, will be careful to pursue and promote it, by every mean in his power. Let him feel the importance and advantages which result from the Laws and Constitution of his country, and he will have the strongest motives to obey the one, and defend the other. Let him but exercise his reason and understanding, in matters of national concern, and he will enjoy a satisfaction in submitting to the authority of the Law. Instead of opposing, he will respect and venerate the powers which hold the reins of government, as necessary to secure general happiness.

A diffusion of Knowledge, then, appears to be an object of the utmost importance, in securing the stability of all good governments.

[...]

An impartial investigation by a Jury of the Country will, I doubt not, do ample justice to both [Joyce and the SCI].

As this narrative is drawn up previously, and intended for publication immediately after, my trial, I have endeavoured to render it as free as possible from any observations which might tend to bias the public opinion:

The facts are stated without comment. Many circumstances are omitted, which tended to aggravate the rigour of close imprisonment; being anxious only to exhibit the general outlines of those steps which have been taken in the present Prosecutions for High Treason.

Oct. 21, 1794 (46-47).

At the end of the appendix, Joyce described, in a note dated 23 November 1794, the reactions of the public when the acquittal became known:

The burst of exclamation that took place in the Court, upon this verdict, and which the judges neither tried to repress or reprove, was the signal of acquittal to the multitudes without.

A sympathetic shout broke from the mass of the people, which was caught and echoed to every part of the metropolis in an instant. No telegraphe - no artificial organ could convey the news with the electrical velocity of their enthusiasm.[71] It was known at the remotest corners of the town in a minute after the event, and the satisfaction was as general, as the interest which was felt in the cause (48).

[71] The speed with which the news of the acquittal spread across the country is symbolic of the sovereignty of the people. The word "telegraph" was imported from France in 1792. In the *Annual Register* for the year 1794, this invention is described: "A number of posts are erected at convenient distances; and on each is fixed a transverse beam with two moveable arms, the beam itself being also moveable. The different forms which the machine is capable of assuming is 16, and these represent the telegraphic alphabet" (394).

2. "It may be the language of the law, but surely common sense revolts at it," from: Thomas Holcroft, *A Narrative of Facts, relating to a Prosecution for High Treason; including the Address to the Jury, which the Court Refused to Hear; with letters to the Attorney General, Lord Chief Justice Eyre, Mr. Serjeant Adair, the Honourable Thomas Erskine, and Vicary Gibbs, Esq. and the defence the author had prepared, if he had been brought to trial.* London: printed for H. D. Symonds, 1795.

The circumstances under which Thomas Holcroft was imprisoned were most exceptional and have been described in detail by Barrell (2000: 315-316). Justice Eyre tried to prevent Holcroft from surrendering himself: "Eyre was apparently warning Holcroft that if he surrendered to the warrant he would compromise his claim of innocence, by acknowledging a resemblance between himself and the 'false traitor' named in the indictment. 'I do not know you,' Eyre continued, 'and therefore it is impossible for me to know whether you are the person stated in the indictment" (315). It took some time before Holcroft got Eyre's point. He was, nevertheless, eventually arrested and sent to Newgate.

After Thelwall's acquittal, the Attorney General, Sir John Scott, the later Lord Eldon (1751-1838), decided not to prosecute Holcroft. Holcroft's acquittal was accompanied with a refusal to allow him to vindicate himself in court. This resulted in open letters to Scott, Eyre, and Adair, which Holcroft published in the *Narrative of Facts*.

In contrast to Thelwall, Holcroft had been denied the right to vindicate himself – such actions ought to be "properly timed," he was told by the Chief Justice: "At present, you are not called upon to say anything; and you have no right to detain the court by a long speech" (72). When Holcroft insisted, he was admonished by Eyre: "You stood indicted by your Country; and no man, who happens to stand in that situation, ought to complain of injustice; because he accuses his country of injustice, when he makes that complaint" (73). Eyre reminded him that it was he who had brought himself into custody through his own voluntary surrender (*ibid.*).

In this publication, Holcroft presented his view of the events of 1794 and explained why he joined the Constitutional Society in 1792:

I ardently applied myself to the study of man, and the means of promoting his welfare and lessening his evils, as connected with political institutes.

[...] The chief of these principles are, that man is happy in proportion as he is truly informed; that his ignorance is not a fault but a misfortune, because his quantity of knowledge is inevitably the result of the circumstances under which he exists; that to be angry with him therefore, to treat him unkindly, and to punish him, is criminal; in other words, is erroneous; that to instruct him, and while instructing to convince him of the benevolence of the teacher's intentions, is the only way to cure him of his mistakes and diminish the commission of crimes; that, in proportion as he advances in the knowledge of facts, he will increase the means of happiness; and that, as facts are unlimited in number and variety but still are subject to certain unvarying laws, the increase of his happiness is likewise certain, yet unlimited.

Being convinced that these are indubitable truths, I necessarily became the opponent of all violence, and a determined friend to the publication of truth; since by that alone the well-being of man can be promoted (3-4).

Holcroft described the public persecution with which the reform movement had to cope. People attacked them in the public: "if it were not entirely accommodating, the peaceable citizen, after being entrapped, was insulted and turned, nay frequently kicked, out of tap-rooms, coffee-houses, and public places" (9). All supporters of the reform movement, including booksellers, ballad singers and many other artists, were accused of being enemies of the state. Holcroft accused the government of having caused brutality by publishing propaganda against them (13-14).

Holcroft described the political situation early in 1794. The work of the Secret Committee, to which Edmund Burke belonged (17), had invented a dubious conspiracy theory (19).

Surely, said I, this age has more general information, and therefore more virtue, more wisdom, than the past. There cannot be another meal-tub plot. No Titus Oates[72] could now impose his execrable fictions on mankind. Yet, what am I to think? (19-20).

---

[72] Titus Oates (1649-1705) was the Anglican priest who fabricated the "Popish plot". By the mid-1670s, he had infiltrated catholic counsels in order to learn their secrets. In 1677 he became catholic himself. In 1678 he claimed to have uncovered a conspiracy to overturn the Anglican establishment. Anti-catholic feelings increased and caused the Exclusion crisis. Oates's accusations resulted in the execution of 35 Catholics. From 1681 on, his credibility waned, and in 1685 he was tried for perjury and condemned to life imprisonment. He was pardoned in 1689. See also

[...]

a fatal and a mighty blow was aimed at the very essence of social well-being, and nothing but the fortitude of the individuals accused, and the understanding which I still believed existed in the nation, could avert the danger. This narrative is a history of my own motives, and conduct; written in order that I may be justified to the world, and may not lose that utility of which the loss of the world's esteem would deprive me (21-22).

Holcroft quoted from a letter he had sent to his children in Devonshire on 30 September 1794. He did not know whether the authorities had intercepted this letter, in which he asked his children not to worry about their father's indictment (22-25). Holcroft visited Justice Eyre and offered to deliver himself to the authorities, because he did not believe he was guilty of high treason.

My Lord, being informed that a bill of High Treason has been preferred against me, Thomas Holcroft, by his Majesty's Attorney General, and returned a true bill by a Grand Jury of these realms, I come to surrender myself to this court, and my country, to be put upon my trial; that, if I am a guilty man, the whole extent of my guilt may become notorious; and, if innocent, that the rectitude of my principles and conduct may be no less public (29).

Eyre warned Holcroft that he would have to arrest him as soon as he revealed his identity: "I would not wish to take advantage of your coming forward in person..." (31). After some negotiations, Holcroft surrendered himself to the authorities (33). The authorities, however, could not accept Holcroft's surrender and insisted on an official arrest in his home (36-37). In Newgate he was allowed to move about freely, a privilege that was not granted to the other prisoners (38):

To defend myself by shewing the falsehood of the accusations was a duty; but it was a duty which at this moment I knew not how to discharge: I had no documents, nor could I tell of what I was accused (39).

The accusations were incomprehensible to Holcroft.

Eberhard Späth, "Die Enthüllungen von Titus Oates: Fiktion als Mittel der Politik," in: *Literatur, Kriminalität und Rechtskultur im 17. und 18. Jahrhundert: Tagung am 17. und 18. Juni 1994 an der Technischen Universität Dresden*, ed. Uwe Böker and Christoph Houswitschka (Essen: Blaue Eule, 1996), 241-261.

There was not a specific statement of any action of mine; but affirmations concerning the collective actions of twelve men, together with other unknown conspirators, which, respecting myself at least, I knew to be totally and without exception false (41-42).

Holcroft set a plan of defence for himself, which he submitted to his lawyers, Thomas Erskine and Vicary Gibbs (42-45). He strongly emphasized the fact that he refrained from the use of any violence because he was a "democrat" (43). He protested against the indictment and the list of witnesses (46-48).

I conceive that the Indictment is most unjust, and flagitious. It combined heterogeneous actions, meetings, accusations, and persons, that ought all to have been kept free from confusion. [...] Indeed, the conduct of no two individuals ever was or ever can be confounded (46).

Holcroft wrote about the trial against Thomas Hardy.

The whole power of the Government was directed against Thomas Hardy; in his fate seemed involved the fate of the nation, and the verdict of Not Guilty appeared to have burst its bonds, and to have released it from inconceivable miseries, and ages of impending slavery. The acclamations of the Old Bailey reverberated from the farthest shores of Scotland, and the whole people felt the enthusiastic transports of recovered freedom (48-49).

Holcroft was never allowed to read his defence in court. Therefore, he published it after his acquittal.

I hoped that so much respect, at least, would have been paid to justice as that I should have been permitted to state a few facts, in the open court, concerning myself; by which means they would have best been circulated through the kingdom (50).

Holcroft emphasized that he was an "adversary of all force, in all possible cases". William Sharp confirmed that Holcroft had rejected the use of violence in London Corresponding Society meetings (53-55).[73] Sharp called Holcroft a kind of "Natural

[73] Blake's friend and fellow-engraver, William Sharp (1749-1824), illustrated for the *Novelists Magazine* and various books, and produced plates after old masters and contemporary artists such as West, Trumbull and Reynolds. He was a member of the SCI. Sharp was also apprehended for

Quaker [...] [who] did not believe in the secret impulses of the spirit, like the Quakers" (56). Another witness, Mr. Symmonds, stated that Holcroft (together with Tooke) had rejected the term "convention" and had suggested "meeting" in order to avoid misunderstandings (56).

Holcroft rejected the concept of "constructive treason" (63) and expected compensation for the damage that was caused to his reputation (68). Holcroft was imprisoned for eight weeks (69). On 1 December 1794, Holcroft, Bonney, Kyd, and Joyce were acquitted and released from prison (71).

In a letter published separately and addressed to Lord Chief Justice Eyre (98-114), Holcroft justified the publication of his defence speech (98) and expressed that he did not understand why Eyre did not want to allow him to publish it after the trial: "Was it to warn, or to intimidate, that you advised me to take care of publishing my sentiments, on my own case?" (101).

I attribute no malice to you, but some mistakes; and those mistakes are rendered dangerous by the talents you possess, and the station you fill. I admire your faculties, because they are comprehensive. I censure your errors, because they are baneful. I know that, if I had the power to convince you that they are errors, you would commit them no more; and, if I want that power, who or what am I to accuse; except the mutual want of the means of making ourselves intelligible; that is, our mutual ignorance? Let us both therefore sincerely and cordially exert ourselves to forget persons, and inquire into facts (99-100).

[...]

My lord, contrary to custom is one thing; indulgence is another. The forms of courts may be regulated by custom; and to those, whether just or unjust, having accepted the high office you hold, you may think proper to conform. But what does indulgence mean? That too must either be just or unjust. If it mean a just action, surely a just action is no indulgence. If it mean an unjust action, it scarcely can be characterized by a word by which, if it have any precise meaning, seems to incline to the side of be-

---

treasonable practices in 1794, but not indicted after he being forced to give evidence for the Crown, as Barrell points out (2000: 368). See also Marilyn Butler, *Romantics, Rebels and Reactionaries: English Literature and its Background 1760-1830* (New York and Oxford: Oxford University Press, 1982), 43.

nevolence. It is no fault of mine, my lord, that the world has long been amusing itself with words, instead of truth (101-102).

Did this dumb acquittal leave me wholly unsuspected? I can solemnly assure your lordship it did not. Since my release from prison, I daily meet men, who used to approach me with smiles and friendship, who now avert their eyes, and either from dislike or timidity shun my acquaintance. I state a fact, not a complaint (104).

Holcroft closed his letter to Eyre with an admonition that the court had used unacceptable language and legal fictions.

It may be the language of the law, but surely common sense revolts at it. What, is it impossible for my country to be mistaken? And of what does this country consist? Of three-and-twenty men, nominated by the officers of the Crown, composing what is called a grant jury, instructed by the crown [...] I have heard national prejudices too frequently repeated; but I never heard an assertion so violent as this, except from the mouth of lawyers, uttering the fictions of law. Ignorant as I am of these fictions, till this period I was ignorant that this was one of them. I had heard that the king could do no wrong; but never before knew that his subjects were equally infallible (107).

In another letter to the "Honourable Thomas Erskine; and Vicary Gibbs, Esquire" (118-127), Holcroft thanked his lawyers for having succeeded under exceptionally difficult circumstances.

The nature of the accusation was still more confounding. It was a mass of heterogeneous facts, vague but perplexing assertions, and tedious and stupefying readings and recapitulations. It is now proved, that there was nothing treasonable in them: but their artful and benumbing effects you had to destroy, or freedom had to fall (121).

[...]

He then will most cordially join me, when I affirm that the intrepidity with which you encountered an embattled host of Crown layers, whose angry brows were dark as Erebus[74], whenever the Bench above them de-

[74] Erebus, the son of Chaos, embodied primordial darkness. Later Erebus is also identified with the Infernal Region below the earth. Erebus is often used metaphorically for Hades itself.

cided that the practice of the courts was in favour, was such as I believe no pleader in the kingdom could have equalled; that the acumen with which you examined witnesses, Spies I mean and informers, extracting truth from the black recesses of audacious falshood, wrestling it forth and dragging it to light, was no less admirable; that the discrimination with which you detected and exposed, even without wounding, the prevarications not of hired ruffians but of infatuated and prejudiced men, drew applause even from your adversaries; and that, by your knowledge of the human heart, you so managed the witnesses for the Crown as to make these very witnesses prove the injustices and the falshood of the charges brought against your clients (122-123).

Holcroft praised Erskine's "almost super-human energy": "Sir, you saved a nation; and a nation's love, will follow you to the grave; and there rest, in everlastingly fond remembrance, over your ashes" (124). Few lawyers would have taken the risk of defending alleged traitors.

You toiled for a nobler purpose than to render your children the future satraps of despotism. Lighted by the torch of Liberty, you saw the worshippers of Mammon forging their own shackles. With a mind too elastic, too independent, too comprehensive to stoop thus basely, the sight inspired you with increasing fortitude; and you met the select legion of all the Inns and Halls, marshalled against you in dreadful array (125-126).

In the appendix to his defence, Holcroft is concerned with the political purpose of the accusations, which blame the reformers for having destroyed peace in England, thus provoking feelings of hatred in the public: "... such unjust decisions tend to increase that unrelenting animosity, that savage hatred, which already rages in the public mind" (4). In the following lines, Holcroft tried to define crime in order to prove that the government's repression is in itself criminal, and aims to prevent people from learning and understanding.

Although crime always destroys the fragile fabric of interests within a society (6f.), it is the criminal who suffers most in the end:

Since therefore the selfish criminal commits greatest injury against himself, whom he intended to benefit, and the disinterested criminal is in like manner acting under mistake, it follows that all crime is error of the understanding.

Crime therefore is ignorance: which is the absence or want of knowledge. Consequently, and this is one of the most important of truths, knowledge is the sole means by which crime can be prevented.

If this reasoning be just, it follows that to attempt to prevent crime by coercion is an error of the understanding: or, in other words, is itself also crime.

This may be elucidated by an inquiry into the nature and consequences of punishment: which is one of the most important branches of coercion.

Punishment is the infliction of pain and disgrace; generally speaking, either by the permission or at the instigation of society; sometimes purposing to reform the criminal, and at others not; for criminals are frequently put to death; but always with an intent to prevent crime (7-9).

[...]

Had punishment been an effectual means for preventing crime, as soon as punishment had been begun crime must have been on the decrease.

This effect however is not produced; for men continue, from the introduction of punishment to the present hour, to be imprisoned, pilloried, whipped, and hanged.

Fear, falshood, revenge, and desperation are the vices which punishment produces; and even revenge and desperation are not so destructive as fear and falshood.

Fear confuses, distracts, and debilitates the mind. To prevent crime, we must communicate knowledge.

[...]

When a man, from the perversity of his understanding, has committed his first crime, he is immediately sent to prison, according to law: that is, Law dooms him to the society of men, whose understanding are in a still more perverted state than his own. Law, which is emphatically stiled the wisdom of ages, does this! How would common-sense act? Common-sense would instantly consign the criminal to the superintendence and admonition of the wisest and most virtuous men the nation could boast. Men capable of great crimes are, almost without exception, men of extraordinary energy and enterprize; and such men, thus benevolently treated and instructed, would become as active and indefatigable, in good, as they had been daring and restless in evil (11).

Holcroft – like Dyer – hoped to contribute to the development of a benevolent attitude among his fellow citizens.

"Oh could I but worthily treat the grand system of Benevolence for which I contend, could I but call to your recollection the innumerable facts, with which you are all acquainted, that demonstrate its power of increasing the happiness of man, I should then indeed rejoice at the opportunity now afforded me (15-16).

The legal system reacts to crime rather than encouraging people to act in a benevolent manner; thus, it is unable to develop benevolence: "Benevolence is the very opposite of crime: it is just intention carried into effect" (18). Holcroft called the high treason trials "an experiment on the perplexities which Statute Law, Precedent Law, and Constructive Law so amply afford" (18). In contrast to the legal system, Holcroft emphasized, "Benevolence has been my system" (23).

So voluminous and complex is law that no learned professor in this court, in this kingdom, or that ever existed, can remember its contents: so perplexed are its precepts that they are for ever varying: and so self-contradictory are its precedents that they have destroyed all certainty: and advocates the most able, judges the most upright, and juries the most conscientious, when once entangled in its intricacies, are in continual anger of exonerating the vicious, and condemning the guiltless (18).

In contrast to the legal system, Holcroft emphasized: "Benevolence has been my system" (23). Holcroft criticised Pitt (36-40) and the corruption of parliament (41-44):

To put the matter in a still more shocking point of view, we thus are taught that our wise and humane representatives will pass act after act, to take away the fortunes, liberties, and lives of their constituents; but not one to correct that abominable corruption for which, if men could deserve hanging, - No, no: I will not finish my sentence. Men cannot deserve death. They deserve our aid, our instruction, our love. And, if so, must not humanity blush at the sanguinary pages, which these impeccable legislators, each time they meet, consult how they may render more sanguinary? (48-49)

Holcroft believed that the political consequence of such a corrupted system must be social destruction: "The remedy is at hand; gentle, gradual, and peaceful reform. But they will neither take nor administer the necessary medicine. No: to offer them the sanative draught is Treason!" (51). Even when threatened with death, he would never cease to warn his fellow citizens of the dangers to their civil rights.

Beware of the hundred and sixty-two! Beware of the Oligarchy! Beware of gore-streaming Civil War! Have pity on the people, have pity on yourselves, and REFORM! And, if this be treason, welcome DEATH! I am ready (52-53).

[...]

What are the effects produced by the institutes of which men are at present so tenacious? Why, these institutes confine the poor to continual labour; by which they are wholly deprived of leisure. These institutes fix them in a degree of want, that precludes them the benefit of common necessaries. These institutes impel them to seek relief from their miseries in that forgetfulness which inebriety promotes. These institutes stimulate them to pilfer, by robbing them of the enjoyments in which their lawgivers riot. These institutes teach them selfishness, by convincing them that, if they do not hoard, they must starve. These institutes incalculate and habituate them to revenge, by inflicting punishment and violence, as the only mode which these institutes know of correcting mistake (57-58).

[...]

To rob man of knowledge is to be guilty of the worst of crimes; and of this crime I boldly accuse our lawgivers, our non-reforming representatives, our oligarchical one hundred and sixty-two (59).

The entire legal system is built upon repression and controlled by spies (61). It does not encourage people to improve:

This calumniating instrument deforms the sweet aspect of a well spent life [...] It practices acknowledged falshoods, which its fabricators call fictions; and, plunging its object in a torrent of legal venom, then leaves the poor suffocated wretch to escape and purify himself as he can (67).

At the end of his defence, Holcroft drew the following conclusion:

Gentlemen, though I hold it impossible for any human being to merit so offensive a punishment, yet, as I am afraid I am singular in this opinion, I do not mean to appeal to your humanity, but to your justice; and, if I am a traitor, if I have compassed or imagined the death of the King, if you have any sort of proof that can justify such a verdict to your own consciences, then pronounce me Guilty; and let my members be cut off, my bowels burnt, my head severed from the trunk, and my body divided into four quarters and sent to be at the King's disposal: for it matters little to me whether it be the King's and the hangman's, or the vultures' and the wolves' (78-79).

3. "When the Ministers had made an effort to support their false accusations of High Treason," from: Thomas Hardy, *Memoir of Thomas Hardy, Founder of, and Secretary to, the London Corresponding Society for Diffusing Useful Political Knowledge among the People of Great Britain and Ireland and for Promoting Parliamentary Reform, From its Establishment in Jan. 1792 until his arrest on a False Charge of High Treason On the 12th of May 1794*. Written by Himself. London: James Ridgway, 1832.

This lower-middle-class autobiography was written in the third person to show solidarity with all people of Hardy's social background. It was published by David Vincent in *Testaments of Radicalism* (London, 1977), 31-102. In the appendix to his autobiography (98-127 in the original) Hardy had published many letters which Vincent did not include calling them "fragmentary and repetitious" (28). The following two excerpts from letters were read at the public anniversaries of the acquittal of 1794. They introduce the reader to Hardy's thoughts on the origins of the reform movement – the wish to improve the diffusion of knowledge. In the second excerpt, which was also taken from a letter to a friend, Hardy described the political situation in which the government organized the treason trials in order to suppress this new spirit of knowledge and participation of the uneducated classes.

Although we were, at first, but few in number, and humble in situation and circumstances, yet we wished to consider how to remedy the many defects and abuses which had crept into the administration of Government: and in prosecuting our enquiries, we soon discovered, that gross ignorance, and prejudice, in the bulk of the nation, was the greatest obstacle to the obtaining redress. Therefore, our honest hope was to have a well regulated, and orderly Society formed, for the purpose of dispelling that ignorance, and prejudice, as far as possible, and to instill into their minds, by means of the printing press, in a legal and constitutional way, as sense of their rights as freemen, and of their duty to themselves, and their posterity, as good citizens, and hereditary guardians of the liberties transmitted to them by their forefathers (Letter to a Friend written in 1799 and read on 5 November 1824, the 30th anniversary of Hardy's acquittal) (104).

When the Ministers had made an effort to support their false accusations of High Treason against those innocent men, and did succeed, they wickedly, and impudently perverted the clearest truths, to explain away their assertions in support of the infamous doctrine of constructive treason; but they were completely foiled in that also, by the prompt decision of three separate, discerning, and honest juries, who pronounced the accusation of falsehood; and, in a manly way, declared that no treason did exist. Such was the happy result of the important trials. When we look back a few years, from 1790, and forward ten or twelve years, we have but a gloomy picture to view of hundreds of our worthy fellow country-men, who were persecuted, prosecuted, imprisoned in distant prisons, far from their families and friends, and some banished to foreign climes, for merely declaring openly, and honestly, their political principles, and opinions of the mal-administration of the Government; and suggesting, and recommending a different, more advantageous, and just administration of public affairs, which every free-born Briton is justly entitled to do. [...] The consequences of such cruelty, was a warm discussion of the great political question, whether this nation was really to be what it professed, and gloried in, a free country, or to be ruled by sheer despotism? The discussion became more and more animated by the friends of liberty, and the supporters of arbitrary power; and that powerful engine, the printing press, was actively employed on both sides (Letter read on 5 November 1829) (114).

VII. The Legal Culture of the Trials for High Treason

Many published statements on the trials for high treason did not originate from within the legal institutions such as the accounts of the State Trials, but were published by interested observers. Such outside observers warned the public that a success for the government would carry consequences not only for the accused reformers, but also for civil freedoms. Others tried to support the government in its effort to control the reform movement and to stop their alleged conspiracy. One of the most famous contributors to the cause of the opposition, who exerted considerable influence on the trials even before they began, was William Godwin. He published a letter in the *Morning Chronicle* "To Such Persons as may be appointed to serve upon Juries for the Trial of Seditious and Treasonable Words,"[75] and, even more important, "Cursory Strictures on a Charge Delivered by Lord Chief Justice Eyre to the Grand Jury, October 2, 1794."[76] Hazlitt spoke of the "legendary status" of this article.[77] Godwin also published "A Reply to an Answer to Cursory Strictures, Supposed to be Wrote vs Judge Buller, by the Author of Cursory Strictures."[78] The following texts have never become as legendary as Godwin's, but might also have contributed to the acquittal of the accused reformers.

---

[75] In Godwin 1968: 123-127; William Godwin, "Letter 5: To such persons as may be appointed to serve upon juries for the trial of seditious and treasonable words," in: *Political and Philosophical Writings of William Godwin: Political Writings II*, ed. Mark Philp and Austin Gee (London: William Pickering, 1993), 24-27; also in [Eyre, Sir James], "The Charge Delivered by The Right Honourable Sir James Eyre, Lord Chief Justice of His Majesty's Court of Common Plea and one of the Commissioners Named a Special Commission of Oyer and Terminer, Issued under the Great Seal of Great Britain, To Enquire of Certain High Treasons, and Misprisons of Treason, within the County of Middlesex, To the Grand Jury, October 2, 1794," in: Godwin 1993: 67-76. Randa Helfield, "Constructive Treason and Godwin's Treasonous Constructions," *Mosaic: A Journal for the Interdisciplinary Study of Literature*, 28:2 (1995), 43-62, for information on Godwin's Strictures.

[76] In: Godwin 1968: 145-175; also William Godwin, *Cursory strictures on a charge delivered by Lord Chief Justice Eyre to the Grand Jury, October 2, 1794* (London, 1794), [Cup.407.c.23]; also William Godwin, "Cursory Strictures on the Charge delivered by Lord Chief Justice Eyre to the Grand Jury, October 2, 1794. First Published in the *Morning Chronicle* October 21," in: Godwin 1993: 77-105.

[77] Pamela Clemit, *The Godwinian Novel.The Rational Fictions of Godwin, Brockden Brown, Mary Shelley* (Oxford: Clarendon Press, 1993), 37.

[78] Godwin 1993: 115-121; and, for Buller (1746-1800), see [Sir Francis Buller], "Answer to Cursory Strictures on a Charge delivered by Lord Chief Justice Eyre to the Grand Jury, October 2, 1794. By Lord Chief Justice Eyre. Said to be Written by Judge Thumb. In the Ministerial Paper Called the Times, October 25, 1794," in: Godwin 1993: 107-113.

1. "What is the proper definition of a juryman, by the laws of England, in the case of high-treason?" from: *A Calm Inquiry into the Office and Duties of Jurymen in Cases of High-Treason: with Seasonable Remarks. Earnestly Recommended to their Attention in the Present Crisis*. London: Printed for J.S. Jordan, 1794.

A Calm Inquiry is a 51-page-long pamphlet; its anonymous author is concerned with the treason trials and "the mode in which they shall be conducted". It would be of greatest importance for the future of the English Constitution, as he warned (1). The author explained the two opposing attitudes toward the people indicted for high treason. Whereas the government and their supporters regarded them as traitors who prepared a revolution as in France, the others spoke of "judicial terror" and saw the "freedom of discussion" – which English people were so proud of– to be in danger (v). The author did not want to enter into "the examination of these opinions" (ibid.), and pretended not to take sides. The following excerpts demonstrate that the author did not want to exaggerate the situation, and that he also did not see the constitution, as a whole, to be in danger. However, he believed he was obligated to remind the jurors of their constitutional rights and responsibilities. He makes the jurors the heroes of the trials.

Introduction

THERE are few subjects, at this very interesting crisis, on which the public mind has been more agitated than the question of the Trials now commenced for HIGH-TREASON. They present, indeed, the strongest claim to attention, since in the decisions to which they shall give rise, and the mode in which they shall be conducted, the most important interests of the constitution are involved.

With respect to the object of those trials, and the characters of the parties implicated in their issue, opinion is widely divided. There are some who conceive that a deep and dangerous conspiracy has for some time been going on in this country, for a purpose no less detestable than to overturn the established government, and introduce into this island a revolution similar to what has lately taken place in a neighbouring state; that of this conspiracy the prisoners have been the chief contrivers, and the most active promoters; and that it is necessary that they should fall victims to the justice of the law, in order that the constitution, whose destruction they had planned, may derive strength and stability from the salutary exertion of its vengeance, and others, by their fate, be deterred from engaging in like attempts. Some again there are of the opinion, that these men have in no instance stept beyond the strict limits of the construction; that they have only availed themselves of that freedom of discussion which is the undoubted privilege of every British subject; and that they are now brought forward as the victims of a system of false alarm, originating from those in power, artfully fomented for political purposes, and which would be apt to lose its effect on the public mind if not kept alive by the influence of judicial terror.

Into the examination of these opinions I shall not at present enter. I must own, however, that I have never been so strongly infected with a spirit of alarm, as to apprehend that the British constitution was much in danger, from a tendency to disaffection on the part of its subjects, or the effects of any internal machinations; neither can I easily be persuaded, that here exist British ministers so devoid of feeling, so lost to all principle, as to be prepared coolly to sacrifice the lives of innocent men, for the vile purpose of public delusion; much less that they can be so absurd as to expect to find British jurymen the easy dupes of their infamous arts, or the convenient tools of their inhuman policy. But it appeared to me extremely material, amidst the agitation of the public mind, and the division of public sentiment, that jurymen should be reminded of the nature and extent of the functions to which they are called by their country, and exhorted, on a question of such magnitude and importance, not to trust out of their own hands the sacred power with which they are invested by the constitution. From the result of the short inquiry now submitted to their attention, I trust it will appear to the readers, as well as to me, that the regulations of the British constitution, as they apply to the case of the persons to be tried, are at once wise and merciful, calculated to give effect to the operations of justice and to guard against the encroachments of oppression.

The member of no society, and the adherent of no party, the interest I take in the event of their trials, arises merely from my sympathy with the case of twelve men exposed to suffer as traitors, and my desire that they should enjoy the benefit of that fair and impartial trial to which, by the law of England, they are entitled.

Sorry, indeed, should I be, that the British constitution, which has so well provided for its security, by affording equal protection to all its subjects, should ever be attempted to be defended on false principles, or its interests separated from those of justice and humanity. From these it must derive its permanence and stability, the form its brightest ornament and firmest support: for while the steady and impartial administration of justice is necessary to render it formidable to its enemies, the mild and benignant spirit of humanity, can alone ensure its reign in the hearts of its subjects (iii-viii).

Excerpts (from the main text)

In an inquiry of this sort, the first question to be asked is, What is the proper description of a juryman, by the laws of England, in the case of high-treason? By the express words of the statute, he ought to be a person of the same condition with those whom he is to try: the reason of this is evident. As the charge is of a nature so delicate and important, it is proper that the jurors should be qualified in every respect to enter into the feelings of the persons accused, and be likewise bound to provide for their interests as if they were their own. This description, *that they shall be persons of their own condition*, applies particularly to the situation of jurymen as contrasted with that of a judge. The jurymen are twelve, supposed to be equals and neighbours of the persons accused, chosen indifferently, and superior to all suspicion,* without any interest, except that of justice, and without any partiality, except (where the circumstances are such as incline them) to the side of mercy. Whereas the judge is one in a situation remote from that of the party accused, and therefore not so capable of entering into his feelings; and in consequence of his connection with the crown, from which he derives his appointment, liable to be influenced by undue or corrupt motives• (9-10).

---

* 4 Black. *Com.* page 350.

• 4 Black. *Com.* page 349 [= Sir William Blackstone (1723-1780), *Commentaries on the Laws of England: A Facsimile of the First Edition of 1765-1769*, 4 vols. (Chicago: University of Chicago Press, 1979). Bonwick points out that this definitive commentary on English law was criticised by reformers such as Major John Cartwright (1740-1824): "Sir William Blackstone had failed to distinguish between laws and constitution in his Commentaries" (1977: 238-239) because it had been composed before the American Revolution. "On that occasion, a people had systematically gone through the Lockean process of formulating a contractual structure of government; no similar attempt had been made before" (239). Later, Jeremy Bentham (1748-1832) attacked Blackstone "on account of his reverence for precedent and tradition, and his 'ungenerous antipathy' to-

[...]

The next question to be asked is, What is the legitimate province of the jury? 'A jury of twelve men are by our laws the only proper judges of the whole matter in issue before them,'* and that as well of the law as of the fact.♣ And herein consists the grand distinction between civil and criminal cases. In civil cases the jury are bound to abide in their decision by the law as explained by the judge, their province is solely to find the fact, which itself is decisive; the intention is not at all looked to. And in such cases it is to be recollected, that the court have the power of setting the verdict aside if found contrary to the law. But in criminal trials it is exactly the reverse; the jury have the case entirely in their own hands, and are to form their judgment upon the whole of it, not only the act alledged to be criminal, but the motive of the person accused, and the intention, with which it was committed; the intention, as has been remarked, is the very pith of the cause. They are not to listen to the mere dicta of a judge, who shall in such an instance interpose with his opinion, or suffer themselves to be in the smallest degree influenced by what may appear to be his sentiments of the matter; but they are to decide for themselves, on the whole of the transaction, and from their own full and unbiassed [sic!] investigation of all the accompanying circumstances, to find their verdict, innocent or guilty. The jury are to consider themselves as invested with the solemn function of judging of the hearts of the persons accused. In the discharge of so awful a trust, they are bound to have recourse to every means of investigation; and they cannot answer to their own consciences if they find a verdict guilty, upon any other grounds than a full, clear, and unequivocal conviction of the wicked and malicious intentions of the party before them (11-13).

---

wards legal reform," as James Sambrook explains in *The Eighteenth Century: The Intellectual and Cultural Context of English Literature 1700-1789* (London: Longman, 1993), 114].

* 4th Coke's Institutes, 84. [= Sir Edward Coke, The First Part of the Institutes of the Laws of England, or, a Commentary upon Littleton: Not the Name of the Author Only, but of the Law Itself. *Revised and Corrected With Additions of Notes, References, and Proper Tables, by Francis Hargrave and Charles Butler, Esqrs. Of Lincoln's Inn, Including also The Notes of Lord Chief Justice Hale and Lord Chancellor Nottingham; and An Analysis of Littleton, written by an unknown Hand in 1658-9. By Charles Butler, Esq.* 18th ed. Corrected. (London: J. & W.T. Clarke, 1823; rpt Lawbook Exchange, 2000). Sir Edward Coke (1552-1634) (often pronounced and spelled Cooke) published the first part of this commentary on Sir Thomas Littleton's (1422-1481) *Treatise on Tenures* in 1628].

♣ Vide Libel. Bill.

This was particularly true for high treason, because it represented "the highest civil crime" according to Blackstone. However, the legal definition of high treason did not allow for much interpretation:

It is peculiarly fortunate for the subject, and is to be considered as one of the chief excellencies of our criminal code, that the crime of high-treason, so penal in its consequences, is clearly and unequivocally defined by the statute of 25th EDWARD III which is to be regarded as the great land-mark of treason; the jury are by it freed from all the intricacy or doubt, and are therefore in danger of being led into a violation of their duty, either by mistake or misconstruction. This statute, both in the spirit and the letter, is so plain and intelligible, that it cannot easily be mistaken, or unintentionally misconstrued.

And this a circumstance the more peculiarly fortunate, as it has at different periods of our history been attempted to be done away or set aside, by the introduction of constructive and extravagant treasons; it becomes, therefore, indispensably necessary that the jury should not only completely comprehend the general principle recognized by the legislature, but resort likewise to the precise words adopted by them in penning the statute (13-14).

The author quoted from Blackstone (9th ed., 1783: vol. 4, 75, 76, 83) the entire passage concerning 25th Edward III and explained its meaning to a general public. According to Blackstone, it had always been extremely difficult to prove high treason. There had only been a few periods in English history when "the spirit of inventing new and strange treasons" prevailed; for example, in the case of Henry IV and Queen Mary, and, particularly, during the bloody government of Henry VIII (19). In the period after Mary, one returned to 25th Edward III (20). The author warns the jurors:

... that when under a profligate reign, corrupt judges have presumed to misinterpret the original statute, in order to build upon it constructive treasons; and in consequence of such representations and other undue influence, juries have been induced to bring in a verdict guilty: the purest patriots whom England ever saw, have suffered as traitors on the scaffold: impartial posterity have reversed the sentence, and have transferred the imputation of infamy from the memory of the undeserving sufferers, to that of the judge and jury (22-23).

Such sentences had always been revised by later generations (23). In the case of the indicted reformers, the jurors had to remember, "that any case of constructive treason, not directly specified in that statute, cannot constitutionally be brought forward without a distinct and express interference of the legislature" (23). It was no surprise that the conclusions of this *Calm Inquiry* were not as impartial as the author pretended to be in the opening lines:

They [the jurymen] in fact represent the country, with whose interest they are intrusted, and they cannot give confidence either to the crown or the judge, without betraying the rights of the subject, and surrendering the constitution itself (26-27).

[...]

A charge of treason, it is to be recollected, has frequently been made an engine of political craft in the hands of designing men, and brought forward to serve a particular purpose, or ruin an innocent or meritorious individual (29).[79]

[...]

The danger which I conceive, in the present moment, most to be dreaded, is, that our fears for the constitution should induce us to take improper means of insuring its safety, and that we, as is commonly the case in the hour of excessive alarm, should endanger the very blessing we so much prize, by our too great anxiety to preserve it (35).

[...]

It [the bill of indictment] contains not, as has been usual in such indictments, a brief and simple recital of one great act of treason, but a variety of complicated charges, built upon one another. Among these charges I find that of meeting in order to concert the plan of a convention, of appointing delegates for the purpose, and of exhorting others by writings and pamphlets, to adopt the same measure (38).

[...]

---

[79] The author quoted Blackstone (1783: vol. 4, 11), who warns that the death penalty is "a matter that requires the greatest deliberation ... for life is the immediate gift of God to man" (30).

There have likewise, in all periods of our history, existed speculative and ingenious men, who have amused themselves in the retirement of their closets with forming theoretical plans of government, and who, thinking too favourably of human nature, have looked forward to an æra of ideal perfection in society, which experience has hitherto shewn to be sufficiently remote: but it never has been found that these men, have been dangerous members of the community, or that though from system, they were the admirers of visionary republic, they were not, at the same time, in their practice, very peaceable subjects of a limited monarchy (41).

The author of the *Calm Inquiry* pointed out that the Convention was not traitorous since the reformers had demanded what many members of the highest ranks of politics (among them Pitt) had described as necessary before the French Revolution (39). The assassination of the King would not serve the aims of the reformers because it would raise the population's anger and revenge (45). This would be "insanity" (46). In the concluding remarks, the focus is not on the question of guilt alone, but on the question of civil liberties. In what manner would the constitution – especially the freedoms of 1688 – be damaged if the reformers were found guilty in spite of the existing laws?

When I consider the importance of the question involved in the issue of these trials; a question which to me, indeed appears the most important that has occurred since the æra of the revolution, 1688, I must own that my mind is considerably agitated. It is not merely a question whether twelve men shall be legally condemned or acquitted, interesting as that consideration must be to every friend of justice and humanity, but whether the British constitution itself shall be preserved its true principles (48-49).

[...]

Sure I am, that every honest juryman, and every true friend of the constitution, will concur with me in the sentiment, that whatever be the degree of their guilt, if it be of a nature which does not clearly come under the description of high-treason, by the statute of EDWARD III, infinitely better were it that they should be acquitted, than that the British constitution should suffer violation in order to bring them to punishment (50-51).

The treason trials became a political and publishing event even before they began. On the last page of the *Calm Inquiry*, the account of the treason trials were announced in the version of Manoah Sibly, the "Short-Hand-Writer to the City of London"; i.e., the official professional in this business:

The public will please to observe, that Mr. Sibly being the regular, official, Short-Hand Writer at the Old Bailey, his Account of these very interesting Trials may be depended upon for Accuracy and Precision: they will therefore be careful to ask for Sibly's Account of the Trials. Printed for J.S. Jordan.

2. "Let Freedom's fair name/ Each bosom enflame," from: *Trial by Jury, A New Song*. London.

The author of this song praises the institution of the trial by jury, which was regarded as an Anglo-Saxon tradition that had survived Norman feudalism. Such participation, which did not exist in the political institutions, contributed to the protection of freedom by the people. The author summarized this political message in the first stanza of his song: "The sum of my lay/ Is Blest be the Day/ That a Trial by Jury remains." The chorus repeats this. In the following stanzas, we learn, the jury can avert all possible dangers to the constitution. The victory of the jury is then praised as an achievement that will be remembered by future generations.

II.
Let Ministers sly,
Their stratagems try,
To forge for a Citizen chains;
With joy in our hearts,
We laugh at their arts,
While a *Trial by Jury* remains.
Cho. With joy, &c.

III.
Let treacherous spies,
In a Patriot's disguise,
For Britons uncautious lay trains:
The mask is too thin
To cover their sin,
While a *Trial by Jury* remains.
Cho. The mask, &c.

IV.
Let lawyers perplex
The question, and vex,
Their labour is lost and their pains;
While *Erskine* is by
Their quirks to decry,
And a *Trial by Jury* remains.
Cho. While, &c.

[...]

VII.
Let Freedom's fair name
Each bosom enflame
That fetters and slav'ry disdains;
If Freedom be lost,
No more may we boast,
That a *Trial by Jury* remains.
Cho. If Freedom, &c.

VIII.
That Freedom to save,
All dangers we'll brave,
And spend the last drop in our veins;
That our children may say,
"O blest be the day
That a *Trial by Jury* remains."
Cho. That our, &c.

3. "All tyrants dead, and heav'n born LIBERTY," from: *A friend to the distressed Patriots. On the Death of Mrs. Hardy, Wife of Mr. Thomas Hardy, of Piccadilly; Imprisoned in the Tower for High Treason. She expired in Child-bed on Wednesday, August 27, 1794, and declared in her last moments, that she died a martyr to the sufferings of her husband.* London: J. Smith and J. Burks, 1794.

The four-page-long poem originally sold for one penny. Vincent wrote of it's author, Citizen Lee: "The death of his wife in childbirth following the attack on his house while he was in prison awaiting trial for high treason elevated his emotional life from the private to the public sphere" (Vincent 1977: 16). Hardy also published the poem in his *Memoir* (Vincent 1977: 62-63), writing: "The author, Citizen Lee, went to America, in 1796, and died soon after. He wrote many beautiful poems, which have been published in several volumes. Free for ever be the land which afforded an asylum and a grave to the patriot bard!" (61). The Methodist radical poet and publisher Richard Lee, later 'Citizen' Lee, was a millenarian. He believed that God had made the French Revolution in order to destroy the Catholic Church. According to Barrell, "Lee was the most daring, the most seditious, and arguably the most prolific of all the popular radical booksellers trading in London in 1795. [...] Few of his pamphlets are longer than eight pages, or a single folded sheet. Lee was aiming at the very bottom of the market."[80] After the elegy "On the Death of Mrs. Hardy", Lee wrote "The Tribute of Civic Gratitude; a Congratulatory Address to Thomas Hardy", celebrating the acquittal of the founder of the London Corresponding Society.

Exalted hero! glory of my verse;
THY WEIHGTY SUFFERINGS!
would the muse rehearse!
With melting lays obtain the listening ear,
And draw from Pity's eye, the pearly tear.
I see thee, fetter'd in tyrannic chains,
Thy spirit laden with a thousand pains;
Yet heedless to the mighty load of woe,
No plaint is heard, no tears are seen to flow;
The pleasing hope of bringing SLAVES RELIEF,

[80] Barrell 2000: 608; see same for more titles on Lee, especially Jon Mee, "The Strange Case of Richard 'Citizen' Lee: Poetry, Popular Radicalism, and Enthusiasm in the 1790s," in: *Radicalism in British Literary Culture*, ed. Timothy Morton and Nigel Smith (Cambridge: Cambridge University Press, 2002), 151-166.

Inspires thy gen'rous soul, and lulls thy grief.
On Heav'n reclining, still thou hop'st to see
All tyrants dead, and heav'n born LIBERTY
Her gentle sway extending all around,
Each human forehead with her LAURELS crown'd!
But why art thou enchain'd what hellish might,
Presum'd to rob thee, of thy dearest right?
To rob the world; so good a man confin'd,
He suffers not alone, but all mankind!
'Twas TYRANNY's FELL DEED; his haggard eyes,
Saw truth in thee, reflected from the skies;
Bright as the morning planet, with her light,
Chasing the shadows of retreating night;
And trembled lest the SECRETS should be known,
That are in HELL conceal'd, and prop his Throne,
With the strong energy of fear imprest,
Thee, SON OF HEAV'N! his iron hands arrest;
Grasp not alone the common joys of life,
But ev'n the brightest gem, THY LOVING WIFE!
Inhuman monster! smiling at the smart,
That nature shot thro' each united heart.
BEHOLD THE SCENE, the piercing scene appear!
Imagination drops a pitying tear.
Bereft of thee, thy tender partner pines,
Thinks of thy state, and dangers new divines;
'Till in her bosom black despair conceives,
Nor beam of hope the pungent pain relieves;
Tho' thy misfortunes all her efforts claim,
The hand of nature bears upon her frame:
Feeble, and unassisted, hear her cry,
"For thee O husband! 'Tis for thee I die!"
The martyr falls - Angelic guides convey,
The spirit to the climes of endless day.
Ah! now the cruel tidings reach thine ear,
Thy dauntless courage melts into a fear:
Thy joints relax, thy fearful face grows wan,
And all the stoic softens into man.
For one soft moment, other care resign'd,
Ev'n LIBERTY, her image fills thy mind;
Yet in the cause thy soul unmov'd remains,

And from th' OPPRESSOR's ROD new vigor gains,
How great thy sufferings! how amazing great
Thy patience, future poets shall relate!
Man shall record with gratitude thy name,
The winds from pole to pole, shall waft thy fame,
And (if the muse her object may pursue,
And set futurity to moral view;)
Ere thou rejoicing yield'st thy fleeting breath,
Thy wife to follow thro the paths of death.
FREEDOM SHALL REIGN! from earth thou shalt arise,
And bear the tidings to th' impatient skies!
And will ye deign to hear my mean applause,
Ye friends of man, and pillars of the cause!
Who firm as rocks, amid the storm have stood,
And dar'd all dangers for the public good;
Ye, who with HARDY NOW are doom'd to feel,
The lawless vengeance of ambitious zeal!
How wou'd my heart with gen'rous rapture glow,
Could my weak strain alleviate your woe;
Inspire some noble bosom, to a deed,
Humanity and Nature's dictates plead,
TO PITY YOUR MISFORTUNES; and impart
His needful succour, - Every feeling heart,
Eager must yield the strongest aid it can,
To *prop* the *cause* of *God*, of *Angel* and of *Man*!

A FRIEND TO THE DISTRESSED PATRIOTS

FINIS

N.B. The profits arising from this Poem, will be appropriated to the benefit of wives and families of persons imprisoned by the suspension of the Habeas Corpus Act

4. "Boast, BRITAIN, thy JURIES! thy glory!" from: Morganwyg Iolo, *Trial by jury. The Grand Palladium of BRITISH LIBERTY. A song, sung at the Crown and Anchor, Feb. 4 1795, in celebration of the late trials for High Treason, and Triumphant Acquittals of Thomas Hardy, John Horne Tooke, and John Thelwall; and in honour of their Counsel Thomas Erskine, and Vicary Gibbs.* By Edward Williams, "author of Poems, Lyric and Pastoral, lately published" [London, 1795].

Morganwyg Iolo is the bardic name of Edward Williams (1746-1826). Erskine is mentioned in this poem by name, but none of the defendants are, as Barrell points out. There were many more encomiums to Erskine in the months following the acquittals. In the eyes of many radicals and reformers, Erskine and Gibbs were national heroes who had not only saved the lives of the accused reformers, but had also protected the constitution (see Barrell 2000: 403-404).

HERE, Brothers, we meet in th'abundance of joy,
Prepar'd with our festival strain,
The storms, tho' severe, did but little annoy,
Their thunders exploded in vain:
See how firmly the mountain sustains ev'ry shock,
Tho' lightenings fly, raging, around,
And INNOCENCE, like an immoveable rock,
Is ever invincible found.

Come hither! ye *Spies* and *Informers of State*!
With Consciences offer'd for sale;
Come hither! and all your atchievements relate!
Whilst Ridicule joys in the tale!
Or will ye, disgrac'd, to your PERJURER throng,
Nor *Memory* wish to possess;
Then haste! gnash your fangs! whilst we call for the song
Of Triumph's exulting excess!

Th' ASSERTORS OF TRUTH that were trampl'd awhile,
That *Villainy* fiercely pursued,
Claim the song of our gladness -- true Sons of our Isle,
With virtues gigantic endued.
What joy to the world! these to MAN and his CAUSE,
The JURIES OF BRITAIN restor'd:
Our JURIES -- our themes of eternal Applause!

Let their names be for ever ador'd.

Boast, BRITAIN, thy JURIES! thy glory! thy plan!*
They treat the *stern Tyrant* with scorn!
O! bid them descend, the best Guardians of Man,
To millions of ages unborn:
Far and wide as the light, of true FREEDOM the soul,
Be thy BLEST INSTITUTION proclaim'd;
With ERSKINE, with GIBBS, on Eternity's roll,
In the language of Glory be nam'd.

---

* The Principle of Trial by Jury originated in Britain.

5. "ERSKINE and GIBBS! whose names, to Nature dear,/ Ages unborn may gratefully revere", from: William Hayley, *The National Advocates, a poem. Affectionately inscribed to the Honourable Thomas Erskine and Vicary Gibbs, Esquire.* London: J. Debrett, 1795.

"ERSKINE and GIBBS!" was also written in praise of the achievements of Thomas Erskine and Vicary Gibbs in the defence of Thomas Hardy, Horne Tooke and others. The poem, which is some 448 verses long, strictly avoided any compromising statements about the defendants. Even the two lawyers are mentioned only once at the end of the poem. William Hayley (1745-1820) published this epic poem, which ran to 33 pages, with the radical publisher J. Debrett in London. With a piece published in Thelwall's *Imperial Magazine* in January of 1790, Hayley had contributed to a controversy on the function of literature. Hayley also wrote an ode, which he dedicated to John Howard, Esq. F.R.S., author of "The State of English and Foreign Prisons".

In an "Essay on History; in Three Epistles to Edward Gibbon, Esq.", which was published in 1780 by J. Dudley, Hayley uses the metaphor of mining history for gems of the "tragic Muse":

> O History! whose pregnant mines impart
> Unfailing treasures to poetic art;
> The Epic gem, and those of darker hues,

Whose trembling lustre decks the tragic Muse
(Hayley 1780: Vs. 193-96).

In the case of the poem dedicated to the "National Advocates", it is "spirits divine" who observe the fortunate outcome of the treason trials on "Britain's favour'd isle", where the "sound of joy" can be heard in the "crowded streets" of London:

The National Advocates.

SPIRITS divine! who, pleas'd at Nature's birth,
Took your kind station round the recent earth
To watch the world, in viewless state sublime,
A guardian each of each allotted clime --
Ye, who with pity have had cause to melt,
And anguish, such as angels feel, have felt,
To witness evils that ye most abhor,
The fiend-like phrensy of insatiate war,
Leagues without justice, without glory strife,
And mad profusion of envenom'd life;
Though crimes, from which your hallow'd optics shrink,
Hurry the vex'd globe to perdition's brink,
Ye will not yet your guilty charge abjure,
And fly from evils that ye fail to cure --
No, Ye have heard from Britain's favour'd isle,
Sounds to excite a troubled Seraph's smile,
And draw to earth, on just protection's plan,
Pure spirits, friendly to the weal of man.
The sound of joy that town to town repeats,
Circling from London and her crowded streets,
As Echo guides it, with exulting hand,
To every confine of th' enfranchis'd land, --
That sound of joy was not the frantic roar
Of martial triumph pamper'd high with gore,
That giving murder a gigantic frame,
Rears the grim idol deck'd with Glory's name,
When sanguinary man, with impious pride,
In false devotion real guilt to hide,
With inconsistence not to Pagans known,
Presents preposterous thanks to Mercy's throne,

For having tainted both the earth and air,
With blood that Heaven commanded him to spare. --
The sound of joy, this sympathetic song
Would with fond zeal to distant time prolong,
Spoke not of war, but peace's nobler palm;
In civic tempests it announc'd a calm;
Assuring Britain, in her worst alarm,
That Law's bright ægis blazes on her arm;
That round her sons the snares of legal death
Burst at the hallow'd touch of Virtue's breath.
Ye nameless powers, who Reason's voice inspire,
Who give to Eloquence her patriot fire;
Ye, who when man, in fields of spotless fame,
Strains noble faculties with noblest aim,
Haste to refresh him true honour's goal
With eulogy, the music of the soul;
Grant in this verse such lucid praise to live,
As only Truth, fair child of Light, can give,
They only merit, who, of spirit clear,
And, deaf to int'rest, as exempt from fear,
Exert, while Power's presumptuous claims they scan,
Celestial gifts in aid of suffering man;
Shew splendid talents sanctified by worth,
And made a blessing to th'admiring earth: --
To you, entitled to the world's applause,
Fraternal advocates in Freedom's cause: --
To you, whom Friendship with fond pride unites,
With all the lustres of her ancient rites,
Of equal probity and varied powers,
In arduous duty's spirit-trying hours,
Each to the other a benignant star,
The Scipio and the Lælius of the bar: --
To you, illustrious friends, whose legal fame
Shall last, while Law herself, a sacred name,
Holds her primæval right, her blest employ,
Parent of peace, and cherisher of joy: --
To you I offer, nor will you refuse,
You, who as Freedom's child caress the Muse,
Tribute, no power commands, no treasures buy,
Pure as the tear of joy in true Love's eye;

Verse undebas'd by adulation's art,
Fresh from the fountain of a feeling heart,
That scorns all Party rage of either side,
Faction's fierce spleen, and Pow'r's suspicious pride,
And, loving England, that her laws display
The blest beneficence of temperate sway,
Honours her advocates, whose truth and zeal
Stand the firm pillars of the public weal: --
Yes, ye brave pleaders in a cause, whose weight
Press'd on the vitals of a panting State,
'Twas not alone the being of a few
Black with false guilt, in dim suspicion's view,
Whose lives, in deference to minds so rare,
Justice consign'd to your defensive care:
'Twas Britain's honour, 'twas her noblest wealth,
The very essence of the public health,
For which your patriot eloquence display'd
Those matchless powers, that bold yet temperate aid,
Which Themis[81] sanctioned with a sacred smile,
And rightful joy convuls'd her rescued isle.
Whence is the gen'rous pride, a test of worth,
That makes a Briton glory in his birth?
Not that this country, Nature's favour'd isle,
Is fenc'd by commerce with a golden pile;
And can impel, with rich temptation's flood,
Poor continental kings to trade in blood,
Though reaping, as their fruit of martial care,
Discomfiture, disgrace, dismay, despair:
No: he exults that in his native land,

[81] Themis was the Titanid-goddess of custom, assemblies and right order. She presided over the feasts of the gods on Olympos. She was also one of Zeus' most trusted advisers, an oracular goddess.

Hearts by the warmth of Liberty expand;
And Intellect, a tree that loves the light,
Shoots like a cedar of imperial height;
While fearless Freedom, with an eagle's ken,
Searching the soul of measures and of men,
Alike contemns, in their unmasking hour,
The dupe of Party, and the slave of Power;
And celebrates, what here she still can find,
True public virtue in a potent mind.
When a sick nation, like a feverish child,
Sinks in a panick, wayward, dark and wild;
From fear to fear in blind confusion runs,
Mistakes for foreign imps her genuine sons;
Calls Loyalty a Traitor, Truth a Liar,
And Freedom's vital warmth Sedition's fire:
When rampant Power, beyond Ixion[82] proud,
Impregnates with chimeras every cloud,
Blest be the minds, whose virtuous labours serve
To save their darkling country's visual nerve;
While fancied plots and shadowy perils fly
Distemper's film, that dimm'd the nation's eye,
Who, with recover'd sight, exults to see
It is not treason, still to wish her free.
Reason may smile, if sophistry would show
A faithful subject is a treacherous foe;
And those, who strike at vices in the State,
Must mean a Monarch's fall, and seek his fate;
As if corruption were the vital spring
Of that effulgent mortal styl'd a King.
Unguarded Poet, in his troubled time,
Beware, cries Caution, how you rant in rhime,
Lest you should find there's treason in the metre,
That deems a Monarch a mere earthly creature.

---

[82] Ixion was the king of the Lapiths in Thessaly. He is chiefly known as the first human to shed kindred blood. This occurred when Ixion invited his father-in-law, Deioneus, to come and collect the price that Ixion owed him for his bride. Upon his arrival, Deioneus fell into a pit filled with burning coals Ixion had camouflaged. Because this was a crime new to the human race, nobody could purify Ixion and he wandered an exile. Zeus took pity on him and decided to purify Ixion. See Pindar, *Pythian Odes* II. 21-48 and Homer, *Iliad* XIV. 317-318.

With rational respect, not stupid awe,
As the just offspring and the guard of law,
The voice of England, her creative voice,
Hails in a King the ruler of her choice.
And Nature here, as if inclin'd to claim
Immortal rev'rence for the regal name,
Bade Alfred's virtues to the world evince
How rightfully we prize a Patriot Prince:
Model of Kings! in a benighted age,
All that adorns the Hero and the Sage;
Lycurgus, Cæsar, Antonine in one,
With all their talents, of their errors none:
Thou, whose pure spirit to thy subjects taught,
The Sons of England should be free as thought:
Thy arm preserv'd, and thy more potent mind,
With sapient aid, establish'd or refin'd,
For scenes more perilous than martial strife,
Our guardian Juries, as the friends of life!
With fond delight, and with parental love,
Thy people's Father! from the realms above,
Thy sainted spirit may exult to see,
That people guarding what they owe to thee:
Law's soundest buckler, Freedom's brightest dower,
Shielding bold Truth from irritable Power.
Ye Great, whose souls to genuine glory spring,
With such ambition as becomes a king,
Mark how true greatness may in ev'ry clime
Command unceasing life thro' distant time!
Gifts, that Beneficence, on Wisdom's plan,
Confers to meliorate the lot of man.
Live unimpair'd, unconscious of decay,
While Pride's ignoble pageants pass away.
The heart of Alfred still our love excites,
He lives, he breathes in ev'ry Jury's rights!
Though of his line no Prince upholds the name,
He still exists the favourite of Fame!
Though following kings, of ampler pomp and power,
Finish'd in fume their transitory hour:
Tudors of hot, and Stuarts of cold blood,
Have sunk like wrecks in a tempestuous flood:

For, at the will of Heaven's Almighty Sire,
Palaces fall, and dynasties expire. --
The noble Line, that, with Religion's smile,
Freedom invited to this far-fam'd Isle;
Whom Honour wasted on his golden wings
To this his fav'rite throne, and cried: "Be Kings!
Rule with mild sway whom Force shall ne'er enslave,
And long may Virtue guard what Freedom gave!" --
This Line, that boasts the purest claim to power,
May sail -- Avert, just Heav'n! their final hour;
And keep them as they keep their regal vow! --
Yet they may fail, and mortals know not how:
But if - in times no living eye can see,
Distant, far distant may that period be!
If England must perceive with fond regret
The star of Brunswick is for ever set;
A George with Alfred may this glory share,
That Law's pure current was his sov'reign care:
If from great Alfred's reign free Juries flow,
The independent Judge to George we owe.
Mild Sov'reign! doom'd, in life's tumultuous dream,
To feel of bliss and woe each wide extreme,
Justice could well thy youthful care engage,
May Heaven make Peace an idol of thy age!
O bid this wheel of War revolve no more,
This frantic lottery of guilt and gore!
Where, when Truth weighs the profit and the pain,
None but the Fiends of desolation gain.
Let not false policy, to Nature blind,
And deaf to Reason pleading for mankind,
Precipitately urge a barb'rous war,
That Equity and Truth alike abhor,
As weak in conduct, as devoid of right;
And boding certain ill in ever'y light:
Speed as it may, each opposite event
Freedom must fear, Humanity lament.
No, cry the advocates for lasting strife,
Let us be prodigal of wealth and life;
Let Britain's treasure round the globe be hurl'd,
Long let her subsidise the regal world;

Rather than see the Gallic rage advance,
And madd'ning Europe ape the crimes of France!
England, brave nation, of an honest mind,
Yet often dup'd as credulously blind:
Too apt, when artifice obstructs thy view,
To shrink from fancied ills, and scorn the true;
Learn, when thy neighbour of superb pretence,
Whose feelings are too quick for sober sense;
Learn, when assuming France, by Folly led,
Might best awaken thy judicious dread:
Not in the hour when, spurning base controul,
She pluck'd the iron from her wounded soul;
Not in the hour when Indignation's arm
O'erthrew her proud Bastile, as with a charm,
And gave to festive Joy the vacant space,
Nobly disburthen'd of Earth's dark disgrace:
No - in her ancient calm, her nerveless hour
Of tame submission to despotic power,
France might excite more reasonable fear,
Than all her armies in their first career;
For, when Tyranny's cold grasp she lay,
And strove to smile her sense of wrongs away,
On her soft breast a specious Fiend she nurs'd,
Of all insinuating fiends the worst:
Pleas'd to empoison nations with her breath,
And sow the viewless seeds of public death;
To deaden virtue, to dispirit joy,
And all the energies of life destroy.
For in the minds that, fearful of deceit,
Slowly embrace this fascinating cheat,
Reason, self-puzzled, loses all its skill,
To mark th'eternal bounds of good and ill;
To them Religion's sweet seraphic face
Appears the sickly mask of sour grimace:
Man, her dear charge, they deem a moving clod,
And, deaf to the paternal voice of God,
Despite the gift his gracious power bestow'd,
Feeling existence a lethargic load.
Whence sprung the fiend, whose tyrannous controul
Thus robs of every joy the palsied soul?

Born to avenge what Greece endur'd from Rome,
Amidst an attic garden's baneful bloom
Rose the fair pest, in beauty and in power
And new Pandora! wretchedness her dower:
Sweet was the wreath of fading flowers she wore,
And gay* Philosophy the name she bore

Two kindred forms, where'er she moves, are seen,
The sure attendants of their potent Queen:
First, bloated Indolence, whose cheeks disclose
The sickly colours of the wither'd rose;
Whose languid arm scarce bears the light employ,
To lift the bubbling cup of mimic joy;
Whose lips deride, with a contemptuous sneer,
Firm Virtue struggling in Contention's sphere.
Behind her, Apathy, whose half-glaz'd eyes
Ne'er melt with love, or sparkle with surprise;
Whose touch, more cold than Terror's icy breath,
Shoots through the wither'd heart petrific Death.
With these, her ministers, to Rome she fled,
And struck the nerve of Roman vigour dead;
The tow'ring Eagle fell her palsified prey,
And dying Freedom curs'd her baleful sway.
Awhile she sat with Triumph's flag unfurl'd,
The laughing Vict'ress of the Roman world;
In pomp Circean, there she joy'd to shine;
Her cave the palace, Emperors her swine!
But soon her nerveless slaves, unfit for war,
Sunk into dust before the sons of Thor;
The Sorceress fell, with all her feeble charms,
Crush'd by the brave barbarians' massive arms.
Through many an age she lay in lifeless trance,
But wak'd to wider ill in servile France;

* The doctrine of Epicurus is ever ruinous to society; it had its rise when Greece was declining, and perhaps hastened its dissolution, as also that of Rome. It is now propagated in France and England, and seems likely to produce the same effect in both. GRAY's *Works*, 4to. page 202

Gallia's proud Genius, who by force in vain
Had toil'd to forge an universal chain,
Tried o'er the earth his empire to extend,
By the smooth arts of this insidious friend;
Snare Virtue's sons by Pleasure syren form,
And sap those bulwarks that he fail'd to storm.
Brave generous Britons, who have less to fear
From open enmity's uplifted spear,
Beware this smiling pestilence, and know
In French Philosophy your deadliest foe!
O for that warning lyre, whose solemn swell
Loudly proclaim'd th' advancing Lord of Hell,
When first that prime Artificer of Ill
Leap'd with light bound o'er Eden's highest hill! --
For not more hostile to those happy bowers,
Came the fierce Chief of Falsehood's treach'rous Powers,
Than the gay Syren, fraught with impious guile,
To the frank virtues of this fearless Isle.
Yet vain such warning! -- As a welcome guest,
Deluded Britain met the smiling pest;
And oh how wide new scenes of woe extend,
Since the base stranger grew her bosom friend!
Vain Dissipation, in her wild abyss,
O'erwhelms the temp'rate guards of genuine bliss:
No more Fidelity, with Seraph's power,
Spreads her firm wing around the nuptial bower,
That heirs of Truth, of Virtue, Health, and Grace
May spring to life from Passion's pure embrace;
Prepar'd to cherish with affection fond
Each private duty, and each public bond:
No more Content, and Gratitude, whose light
Turns Earth to Paradise in mental sight,
Through dark'ning scenes bewilder'd Reason guide,
And make Humility more strong than Pride:
To French Philosophy these fall a prey,
And Life's prime blessings are all laugh'd away: --
Nay, Life itself! For, when the Sophist tribes
With the keen stroke of their sarcastic gibes
Have cut the cordage, for our safety given,
By which the anchor'd spirit rests on Heaven --

What gulphs the vessel of the Mind o'erwhelm,
When spleenful Phrensy has usurp'd the helm!
Have we not seen a France-taught Sophist here
To impious Suicide a refuge rear,
And give, with argument's delusive air,
A treach'rous sanction to her mad despair?
Tempestuous England! Though we oft surmise,
The heavy vapours of thy varying skies
Breed in our sadden'd frames the mental strife,
Where fancy sickens with disgust of life:
Not all thy fogs, however damp and dense,
Can fix such langour on our loaded sense,
As false Philosophers by stealth impart,
To the cold fibres of the hard'ning heart;
When their base maxims on our spirit steal,
And quench our native flames of love and zeal.
No, though around us exhalations run,
That seem to smother the enfeebled Sun;
True English minds, that English still admire,
And feel the genuine glow of patriot fire,
Defy the storm from southern caves releas'd,
And the raw vapours of blighting East.
Within themselves an antidote they bear
Gainst all the dark caprices of the air;
'Tis fervent gratitude, and fond esteem
For names still bright with Public Virtue's beam;
'Tis gen'rous pride, of reason the result,
That makes a Briton in his birth exult,
As the compatriot of minds, whose worth
Has giv'n such splendour to his speck of earth;
That, while o'er other realms in Slavery's chain,
An heavy mental twilight seem'd to reign,
Here, and here only, with meridian ray
Glow'd the full warmth of intellectual day;
And generous thoughts, that no damp winds controul,
Form the pure climate of the healthy soul.
"Aye, in old time, cries Age-engender'd Spleen,
Such England was! -- but mark her alter'd scene:
See Lux'ry torrents like a hot lava shoot,
With'ring all Genius, killing Virtue's root;

Nor leaving ought unblasted by their fire,
That Sense can praise, or Honesty admire."
This fretful humour of the fancied Sage
Has in each polish'd æra spent its rage;
While credulous Simplicity, aghast,
Has heard of present shame, and glory past;
Of nerveless bodies, of enfeebled minds,
And every ill that sickly Fancy finds;
When all's inverted that her optics see,
And nothing is, but what has ceas'd to be.
But come, Historic Truth, whose hand enrolls
Each splendid record of exalted souls;
Come, Moral Fiction, o'er whose mimic glass
Bright pageants of ideal merit pass:
Come hand in hand, fair friends to Virtue, come,
And strike this murmuring detraction dumb!
Say, in each group your blended scenes unfold,
Keen Admiration can no names behold,
That claim in public love a nobler part,
Or win more honour from the upright heart,
Than you, ye Legal Heroes of my song,
As dear to fancy, as in reason strong;
Who, in despite of mental toil and pain,
That seem to threaten the o'er-burden'd brain,
Breath'd the pure soul of manly eloquence,
Simple in language, liberal in sense;
And, with intrepid Virtue's guardian care,
Rescued the Captives tangled in the snare
Of blood-hound spies, whose prostituted mind
Toil'd to create the guilt it could not find.
No: proud Antiquity's departed host,
Whose shadowy marvels Learning loves to boast,
Shew not, in civic glory's favourite days,
Pleaders more worthy of a People's praise.
When by rapt Greece Demosthenes was heard,
And thunder seem'd less potent than his word;
The stormy passions of revenge and ire
Ting'd his bright language with intemp'rate fire:
When Tully, destin'd to the Grecian's doom,
Pour'd forth philippics to applauding Rome;

Personal hate, with patriot virtue warm,
Gave force and fury to his verbal storm.
These heroes of the hot forensic scene
Blended with public zeal their private spleen: --
Not so the Pleaders who this verse inspire,
Who merit pæans, from a nobler lyre:
As free from virulence, as void of fear,
In conduct graceful, and in motive clear,
They paid just homage to presiding Law,
With manly deference, and decent awe.
No selfish pride, in which light minds rejoice,
Rais'd to victorious sway their temp'rate voice:
But England's welfare, on their heart imprest,
Pure public virtue, glowing in their breast,
Arm'd their just souls with intellectual force,
To check Authority's vindictive course,
And turn Delusion's tide in Danger's hour,
Reckless of frowns from Prejudice and Power.
ERSKINE and GIBBS! whose names, to Nature dear,
Ages unborn may gratefully revere:
While this memorial of your worth I raise,
And firmly credit what I fondly praise;
One hateful truth shall Mem'ry dare suggest,
Grav'd on the deep recesses of her breast:
Rudely she teaches, from her ample range,
That Public Virtue is most apt to change.
The faithful hand, that these frank lines supplied,
Ne'er lavish'd incense by the heart belied;
But, with fond zeal to court in joyous youth
A public idol of imagin'd truth,
Has oft discarded an unfinish'd task,
Finding Apostacy in Virtue's mask;
For ere my fingers could the garland weave,
Like that our hapless Father twin'd for Eve,
It dropp'd, and all its faded roses shed,
Scorning to garnish an Apostate's head.
But may this civic wreath, in eager haste
Form'd of wild flowers, by Merit's smile be grac'd!
For lives preserv'd unquestionably due,
(The nameless donor proves the tribute true;)

Bays from Sincerity's obscure retreat
May cherish Virtue in Contention's heat.
Ye, to whom England owes a pleasing debt,
That English gratitude should ne'er forget;
Thus Freedom prays, to recompense your care,
Deign, righteous Heav'n! to ratify the pray'r:
"Live my firm aids to life's serenest end,
Friends to each other, each the people's friend;
Live beyond life of Briton's glory part,
Enshrin'd for ever in the public heart!"

FINIS

6. "Has not the cry of treason! treason! been vociferated through every part of our distracted island?" from: Mark Wilks, *Athaliah; or the Tocsin sounded by modern alarmists: two collection sermons, towards defraying the expense of the defendants in the late trials for high treason: preached on the nineteenth of April, 1795, in St. Paul's Chapel.* Norwich, [1795].

The Norfolk farmer and Baptist minister Mark Wilks (1748-1819) needed 106 pages for his fierce attack of the government's charge to the Grand Jury of high treason. Wilks accused the government of alarmism and used a typological structure to compare Pitt and his supporters to biblical personalities. His intent was to demonstrate that their behaviour was more a habitual reaction of powerful people to certain situations than a legitimate reaction to a unique threat to the state.

Preface

The following Sermons being wholly political, some may object to their being preached on the Sabbath Day - Let such remember, the design was to do good, and that the great Christian LAW-GIVER asserts, "It is lawful to do good on the Sabbath Day."

M. WILKS

NORWICH,
20th April, 1795

Introduction

After an absence of two thousand six hundred and seventy-three years,

ATHALIAH

visits her deserted orb; the end of her coming is revealed in the title-page of this pamphlet.

On Sunday last she shewed herself twice to crowded assemblies in this city, and we are happy to say, with good effect. Her appearance procured WANTON ALARMISTS general abhorrence, and by exciting compassion, obtained injured innocence considerable relief. Some of her successors having most iniquitously brought Thomas Hardy and his fellow sufferers into a series of trouble, and involved them and their friends in a debt of more than 4000l. She is now commissioned to take a tour through the kingdom of their assistance, and is authorized to inform the public, that subscriptions for their relief are received by ...[83]

Wilks tells the biblical story of Athaliah, suggesting a typological connection between this narrative and the events of 1794:

Sermon 2 KINGS, XI.14 TREASON! TREASON!

Tell me, citizens, have we among us, no *infamous calumniators*, [...] Has not the ghost of Athaliah lately haunted the pulpit, the bar, the senate, the court; and has not the cry of *Treason*! *treason*! been vociferated through every part of our distracted island by the worst of characters?

It is a notion commonly received among divines, that the old testament abounds with types; accordingly, any one disposed to indulge his fancy might suppose Athaliah a type of modern alarmists. -- Typical writers always run parallels between the type and the anti-type -- and according to this mode they would point out at least a threefold resemblance in the present picture (6-8).

[...]

[83] It follows a list mainly of printers and book-sellers.

In this country the type and anti-type exactly agree. The mildest thing we can say of modern alarmists, is, that they have been influenced by a spirit of error. They, like Athaliah, have been sounding the tocsin and raising a cry *Treason*! *treason*! without the slightest evidence to justify the horrid imputation.

So far the cases are similar; but as all parallel cases admit of some disparity, a trifling dissimilarity will be met with here. -- Athaliah complained of treason, but did not attempt to prove any; our *alarmists* have complained, and have exerted all their power, and strained every nerve to substantiate their complaint; but, thanks to heaven, without the least effect.

In the public eye, the arguments aduced to criminate certain societies, and those virtuous individuals for whom I am about to beg, are so *idle* and *futile* as scarcely worthy an attempt to refute. -- What are they?

1. The adoption of French phrases.
2. The distribution of seditious pamphlets.
3. Addresses sent to the Jacobins and the French convention.
4. The joy and grief manifested at the victories and defeats of the French.
5. A determination to call a convention.
6. A resolution to watch parliament, and not to apply to it for redress of grievances.
7. The message from the king, the report of the secret committee, and the addresses and votes of both houses of parliament.

Isaiah condemns those who watch for iniquity, and who make a man an offender for a word. - How applicable is this censure to those persons, who charge virtuous citizens with treasonable designs, because they adopt French phrases! (8-10).

[...]

And what, is it a crime for Britons, so noted in all countries for their attachment to liberty, to love the friends of freedom, and to approve the principles and conduct of brave heroes fighting under her glorious banner? [...] But the word that has inspired the most dread in a British senate, and the adoption of which appears most criminal, is that of 'CITIZEN - CITIZEN!! How *terrific*! how *inauspicious*! how *inimical* to the interests of all nations, and subversive of all good government!! (11-12)

[...]

The distribution of pamphlets is another fact on which our antitypical alarmists rest the charge of a treasonable conspiracy. -- What! are we in Hanover? No. -- To the immortal honour of the elector of Hanover, the government of that electorate is more lenient and tolerant. -- There, indeed, an ordinance was published, Dec. 19th, 1794, by order of George the Third, by the Grace of God, King of Britain, FRANCE, and Ireland, Defender of the Faith, and so forth; commanding antiquarians, librarians, and readers in public societies, to deliver to the police office complete catalogues of their books and pamphlets before they should be lent or read; and in case of *non compliance*, a fine of from six to twenty-six rix-dollars to be paid by the offender; and all suspicious books and pamphlets to be seized by an officer of the police.

Now, though this act was considered by some as militating against the liberty of the subject, it does not attempt to construe the sale or circulation of books and pamphlets into the crime of high treason. - And will any man dare to say, that the laws are more sanguinary in England than in Germany? If the offence of political inquiry, and of circulating pamphlets, can be atoned for in Hanover, by a few rix-dollars, shall it be punished in England with imprisonment and death?

Besides, the circulation of a book, by no means proves an *approbation* of its *principles*. Have not bishops, and the inferior clergy, combined to circulate the Bible in foreign countries, at the very time their conduct has been hostile to its contents?

Is every man who *buys*, *lends*, *gives away*, *recommends*, or any how circulates the testament, a *Christian*? As the removal of every evil within the reach of an enlightened and heroic people; as the improvement of social order, and the alleviation of miseries of the civil condition of men. It is, in my opinion, impossible to judge of a man's principles, either by the books he reads or circulates. The only fair conclusion that can be drawn from the circulation of books, is, that those who circulate them, wish to promote a spirit of inquiry.

May the angry seas lift their waves, and deluge *that country*, and wash away the stains of *that government*, where it is a crime to hazard an opinion, to sow the seeds of knowledge, and to fan the sparks of political inquiry, by the circulation of books!

Since we have been at war with France, since the treasonable correspondence bill has passed into a law, I should suppose any man worth of punishment, who should dare to correspond directly of indirectly with that republic. But to construe congratulation into treason, at a time when there was no law to prohibit such an intercourse; at a time when the two nations were in a state of perfect amity and friendship; when the individuals in both countries were emulous to excel in friendship; when English officers were fighting under the banners of French freedom against German despot; when an English face was respected in every place and company in France, and when almost all the individuals in this country were enthusiastic admirers of the French revolution; when it was considered as a downfall of tyranny, despotism, superstition, and oppression; as the removal of every evil within the reach of an enlightened and heroic people; as the improvement of social order, and the alleviation of miseries of the civil condition of men (15-19).

[...]

But though this correspondence was represented by a noble lord as evidence of a treasonable conspiracy, with the most apparent solemnity, I have not the most distant idea of his *sincerity* at the time; but consider him as playing the hypocrite with the nation, with the sole view of exciting alarm. - The *period* when the accusation was brought forth, furnishes sufficient reason for doubting the sincerity of the accuser. - Every body knows that earl Stanhope, and the late Dr. Price, conducted a correspondence on the part of the revolution society of London with the national assembly of France, and many patriotic societies of that country, as early as 1789. Letters on political subjects *to* and *from* societies at Paris, Alais, Arras, Auxerre, Amiens, Bourdeaux, Brest, Bayonne, Bourges, Bergerac, Calais, Chalon, Cressey, Cherburgh, Chartres, Cognac, Dijon, Grenoble, Havre, Liste, L'Orient, Marseilles, Nates, Orleans, Pontoise, Rouen, Rennes, Strasburg, Toulouse, Versailles [...][84] and many other places, were made as public in this country as the press could render them.

The Manchester address, signed T. Cooper and J. Watt, and that from the constitutional society in London, signed J. Cartwright and D. Adams, were sent in the month of April, 1792. These with the answers of Carra, &c. were printed in almost every newspaper, and handed about in every part of the kingdom, and yet the government never proclaims their treason-

[84] Wilks mentions the names of 30 cities.

able tendency till May 22d, 1794. - This extensive correspondence with the national convention, the Jacobin and other societies in France, must have been known by our government several years; and criminal, why do they all, this interval, preserve an acquiescent silence? (20-22).

[...]

A determination to call a convention, is another thing which has induced the ghost of Athaliah to raise a cry of *Treason*! *treason*! (25)

Wilks defends the right to call a convention by referring to the ancient constitution of Alfred the Great:

In favour of conventions we may not only adduce the plea of legality, but of *custom* and *precedent*. -- In the glorious days of the immortal Alfred, conventions were held in the highest esteem; and Salisbury plain was the grand theatre where the national convention met to revive the laws (27).

Wilks also refers to other conventions which had been called without being fought by the state. He asks the rhetorical question of how often Charles Fox had boasted in Parliament of belonging to "a convention of delegates, instituted to promote a reform in parliament" (28). Wilks believed that as long as these meetings were organized in a legal and peaceful manner, one should hail the event.

Therefore, to impute treasonable purposes to virtuous citizens, *merely* for forming a design to do what had been done *over* and *over*, without the least censure from the executive government, is an act of *absurdity too gross* to admit of any excuse (28).

[...]

Let crown lawyers say what they will, and judges consign to the halter and axe whom they please, I will give it as my opinion, that till societies are formed in all parts of the kingdom, to investigate the theory and practice of government; till there is some grand bond of union between those societies; till the great bulk of the nation has some legal and powerful control over the constituted authorities, we shall never see golden days fruitful of golden deeds!

A resolution to watch parliament, and not to apply to it any more for a redress of grievances, is another thing which excites the cry of *Treason*!

treason! - [...] To suppose parliament above the inspection of the people, *is to err* (29-30).

Wilks insisted that the people have a right to take part in the election of MPs, who are their "trustees", and to have means by which to evaluate them in order to determine whether they should be re-elected (31). Wilks advised his readers to record notes on MPs' conduct as representatives. Such evaluation should be accepted without suspecting "the horrid crime of treason" (32).

In fine, that parliament should object to being watched, and should construe the people's vigilance into treason, seems strange! (32)

[...]

Methinks I now hear Athaliah or her antitype exclaim, What, traitor! will you attempt to exculpate these wretches? will you dare to appear the advocate of men, whose treasonable purposes and wicked machinations have been proclaimed as on the house top: first, by the king's message; secondly, by the reports of the secret committee, and thirdly, by the votes and addresses of both houses of parliament? (33)

It is not high treason to assume that ministers and the bureaucrats might go wrong (34). These suspicions show how important it was that the Grand Jury successfully defended the rights of the people:

In opposition to every thing insinuated in the king's message, to every thing advanced in both houses of parliament, and adduced in evidence by suborned vagabonds, I ask, what says an English jury? Methinks I hear the clerk of the arraigns call out, Thomas Hardy, hold up your hand. Turning to the jury, I hear him inquire, Gentlemen of the jury, is the prisoner guilty of the treason whereof he is charged, or not guilty?

Hear, Englishman, hear with transport! hear with grateful thankfulness to God! hear the foreman of the jury, as the mouth of all, give the lie to the lip of flander, and rescue innocence from the jaws of death, by the just and inevitable reply of NOT GUILTY!!!

Yes, gentlemen of the jury, we appeal to YOU to attest the innocence of the men we love (34-35).

Wilks asked why the representatives of the government "bellowed treason without a shade of proof" (36). He offered what he believes are the true reasons for the charge to the Grand Jury.

Ministers well knew the dangerous predicament in which they stood; they had weakly, and as some thought wickedly, involved the nation in a most disastrous war; every day plunged them deeper and deeper in the fatality, which they had brought upon their country; they saw no hopes of extricating the nation from it with honour, nor of proceeding in it with success, and they dreaded all reflection of the subject! they knew that if the alarm should be suspended for a moment, and that if men had time and leisure for the exercise of their understandings, the war, and the principles on which it was undertaken, would be scrutinized and discussed (39-40).

[...]

Danton, Robespierre, Marat, and Santerre, were the cursed Athaliahs, who, by spreading false alarms among a too irritable and credulous people, led their furies to this scene of slaughter (44).

Wilks condemns spies and informers, whom Swift called "the most accursed prostitutes and most abandoned wretches" (46):

Humanity and reason teach us, how much better it is to prevent crimes than to punish them; but tyrants have no humanity, and to the voice of reason they are always deaf! (54)

[...]

Having heard the voice of scripture, let us now attend to the oracle of facts.

Facts say, what our children's children will think incredible, that *Thomas Hardy, J.H. Tooke, J. Thelwall, T. Holcroft, J.A. Bonney, S. Kid, J. Joyce, J. Richter, and J. Baxter*, in the year 1794, were tried for the same offence imputed to the Son of God; that this charge was attempted to be substantiated by the very same kind of evidence, the oaths of spies and informers; and, that had it not been for the combined talents of Erskine and Gibbs, the wisdom and virtue of faithful jurors, the interposition of a gracious God, these sheep, designed for the slaughter, would have died the victims of intolerant knaves! (56-57).

[...]

Facts tell us, spies are devils! and reason tells us, if there be a God that judgeth in the earth, these court emissaries, these base hirelings, who sell themselves to work wickedness, may expect judgment without mercy, as their certain doom! (59).

[...]

"Let us live down calumny and soul reproach; and while we are called Anarchists, Jacobins, Republicans, and Revolutionists, let the legality of our conduct, the goodness of our morals, the utility of our lives, and sweetness of our temper, give all our slandering foes the lie, convince them of our indissoluble attachment to the NATION, the LAW, and the King.

Where is Palmer and Muir? Where is Skirving and Margarot? Where is Winterbotham, Ridgway, and Holt?

And but for the jurisprudence of this country, the just decision of an incorruptible jury, the superintendant care of God, I might have called, Hardy! Tooke! Thelwall! Holcroft! Richter! Joyce! Bonney! Kid! where are you? and have had no answer. Yes, I might have interrogated *myself*, with a Where am I? and have found myself on a Newgate drop!!!"

Second Sermon. 2 Kings, XI. 14

Like in the first sermon the topic is "Treason! treason!" (60-62).

[...]

Methinks I now hear you say, Why cull your evidence from a history eighteenth centuries old? Why not come nearer home? Does not the history of our time, and the history of the last year, furnish sufficient proof that the best men England knows, have been charged, and unjustly charged, with the foulest crimes Englishmen could perpetrate and commit? Just reproof, I had lost sight of that indictment which charges T. Hardy, J.H. Tooke, J. Bonney, S. Kidd, J. Joyce, T. Holcroft, J. Thelwall, J. Richter, J. Baxter, &c. with a crime, which the right hon. Sir James Eyre, in his charge to the grand jury, states to be the highest crime which can be committed, and which is punished with a severity, which nothing but the *Salus Populi* can justify.

Let me observe, that to be moved and seduced by instigations of the devil, wholly to withdraw our cordial love and true obedience from our sovereign lord the king to strive to stir up, move, and excite rebellion and war against his majesty, - to subvert the government, to depose our sovereign lord the king from the royal state, title, power, and government of this kingdom, and to bring, and put our said lord the king to death, *would be bad indeed*! And did I suppose Hardy and his colleagues had conspired to overthrow the whole government of this country, to pull down and subvert from its very foundation that glorious fabric, which it has been the work of ages to erect, and which has been cemented with the best blood of our ancestors; did I suppose they intended to involve in the general wreck, the *wisest*, *mildest*, RICHEST, and most patriotic king, that ever *cut* a *figure* in history; though Judge Eyre talks of the severity of the law in such cases, I should think no punishment too severe to be inflicted on such traitors. Happy for them, a jury of their country has pronounced them innocent; and I believe, had the indictment charged them with stealing of a sow and pigs from his majesty's farm at Windsor, and had called that a treason, it would not have appeared more ridiculous in the public eye. So far from these persons being capable of such deeds, I believe *them*, and all the societies in this kingdom, implicated in the same charge, to be the most virtuous characters; and I now call in the king's message, the reports of the secret committee, the addresses of both houses of parliament, the suspension of the Habeas Corpus act, the defamation and abuse of sage senators, the infamous indictment presented by a grand jury, the harangues of crown lawyers, and the depositions of perjured spies, to prove that the worst of crimes are sometimes imputed to the best of men (71-74).

Wilks praised the characters of the accused reformers. He leaves no doubt that he supported their efforts to reform the government, calling them "the salvation of their country".

Whatever may be our civil or religious creed, whether we believe with

Socinus[85] or Athanasius[86], whether in politics we think with Sidney[87] or Jeffries[88], without morality we are bad men; but shew me a man of *gospel morals*, and you shew me a man who excites my love: a man high in the estimation of God himself, and who ought to be respected by the human race.

Pray is Thomas Hardy, that ringleader of conspirators and king-killers, a moral man? *He is*; it is *sworn* he is; it is sworn by *many*. - It is sworn, not by spies and perjured vagabonds, *but by the men who revere an oath*.

Yes, the judge himself reminds the jury, that no man, perhaps, ever called such a number of respectable witnesses to his moral character, and

---

[85] Founder of an Antitrinitarian sect; the Socinians derive their name from two natives of Siena, Lelio Sozzini (1525-62) and his nephew Fausto Sozinni (1539-1604). The Socinians rejected authority and insisted on the free use of reason, but they did not reject revelation. Cf. J. Toulmin, *Memoirs of the Lift, Character and Sentiments of Faustus Socinus* (London, 1777). Toulmin was a well-known author of sermons and religious tracts who wrote for a considerable Dissenting audience. His *Life of Socinus* had 332 subscribers. Rosemary Sweet, *The Writing of Urban Histories in Eighteenth-Century England* (Oxford: Clarendon Press, 1997), 221.

[86] Cf. Thomas Paine wrote in his notorious *The Age of Reason*, ed. by Philip S. Foner (Secaucus, N.J.: Citadel Press, 1998), 180, about the New Testament: "We know from history that one of the principal leaders of this church, Athanasius, lived at the time the New Testament was formed; and we know also, from the absurd jargon he left us under the name of a creed, the character of the men who formed the New Testament; and we know also from the same history that the authenticity of the books of which it is composed was denied at the time. It was upon the vote of such as Athanasius, that the Testament was decreed to be the word of God." William Godwin wrote in the sixth book of the *Enquiry Concerning Political Justice*, in: Godwin 1993, "that the stupendous miracles of Moses and Christ were never really performed; that the dogmas of the Athanasian creed are erroneous" (Vol. III, 331).

[87] The Whig leader Algernon Sidney (1622-83), after whom Thelwall named his eldest son, was executed for high treason, but exonerated in 1688 after the Glorious Revolution. He is the author of the *Discourses concerning Government*, ed. by Thomas G. West (Indianapolis: Liberty Classics, 1990), which Thomas Jefferson regarded as important as the writings of John Locke - both leading sources for the philosophic foundations of liberty and human rights. Reformers regarded Sidney as a martyr. See J. Carswell, *The Porcupine: The Life of Algernon Sidney* (London: John Murray, 1989) and A.C.Houston, *Algernon Sidney and the Republican Heritage in England and America* (Princeton University Press: Princeton, New Jersey, 1991).

[88] Judge George Jeffries (1648-89) condemned Algernon Sidney to death as an accomplice in the Rye House Plot (1683), a conspiracy to assassinate Charles II of England and his brother James, duke of York (later James II), as they passed by Rumbold's Rye House in Hertfordshire. However, the king did not make the journey. The plot was revealed and the great Whig leaders Lord William Russell and Algernon Sidney were executed although the actual conspirators were only minor figures.

that in this respect he stood unimpeachable. Is John Horne Tooke a moral man? Dr. Beadon, bishop of Gloucester, has sworn he is. - The bishop has known him forty years, and on many occasions, a friendly and intimate connexion has taken place between them, and he voted for his obtaining the degree of B.A. because he knew him to be qualified, as being a man of *knowledge*, *morals*, and *regular conduct*. The last of these armed traitors, who went through the formality of a trial, was poor *Thelwall*! And here let it suffice to observe, that the evidence to his character, and the manner in which that evidence was given, was so affecting as to drown spectators in a flood of tears. Had the characters of Bonney, Kidd, Joyce, Holcroft, Richter, and Baxter, been brought to the test; had they been weighed in the balances of the Old Bailey; or, to express myself in other words, *had they been tried*, there is every reason to believe, they would have *come forth as gold* (74-76).

Wilks also wrote about the good reputation of the accused reformers:

... they are composed of the excellent of the earth; whose enlightened judgment, restrained passions, love of virtue, and moral rectitude together with the reproach under which they lie, warrants the assertion, that the worst of crimes are sometimes imputed to the best of men (76-77).

Wilks criticised William Windham (1750-1810), who was one of the most fervent opponents of the French Revolution and of reforms in England. Windham was a Foxite Whig who took Burke as his political guide. He became Secretary of War in 1794. He was notorious for the strange variety of his opinions and for the reactions he provoked. Reformers such as Holcroft, Joyce and Thelwall regarded him as a corrupt politician. Wilks mentioned this in his sermon (80). Wilks' criticism, however, focussed on Windham's war politics against France, which mainly gained support from "flannel waistcoat manufacturers" (81). Wilks reminded his readers that the reformers' release from prison did not cause any unrest or trouble in the public. There were no Levellers, rioters or anarchists among them (85).

Having argued in favour of these *insulted patriots*, the morality of their conduct and their goodness of heart, a goodness of heart manifest in all their public transactions, we might now examine the object of their pursuits, whether it has been the overthrow of government and the introduction of licentious anarchy, or whether it has been a reform in the commons house of parliament.

That a reform in parliament has been the alpha and omega, the first and the last, the beginning and the end, and the all in all, at which they had aimed, is reduced to certainty, and set beyond the shadow of a doubt by *innumerable oaths* in a court of justice (86-87).

Wilks called the reformers "England's truest friends" (87) for wanting to reform the Parliament (88). These reforms, however, had to be forced upon the "*state functionaries*, on whose perfection so much depends" (90). Wilks listed a number of Members of Parliament who were in favour of reforms before they had been corrupted and paralysed by the institutions they served. He mentions Burke, Grenville and Pitt, but also Fox and Sheridan, who had supported reforms and had defended the accused reformers in 1794. The fact that he also included the "founding father" of the reform movement in the 1770s, John Wilkes, shows how radical Mark Wilks must have been in his political opinions.

How are they mighty fallen!" is a lamentation applicable to some of them, though some of them, as Peter expresses it, have hearts exercised with covetous practices, once they had their golden days, fruitful of golden deeds! Then they held meetings, drew up resolutions, formed committees, headed conventions, and laboured day and night, in parliament and out of it, to procure reform. What says the conduct of these gentlemen, these virtuous, zealous, and wise reformers? That a reform in parliament is a desirable attainment and what every Englishman is bound to pursue (91).

Wilks explained why reforms are so necessary and quoted the "Declaration of those Rights of the Commonalty of Great Britain, without which they cannot be free" (92). Wilks demanded universal suffrage and annual parliaments (94) in order to do away with the old system and its growing number of rotten boroughs. Wilks's included lists of facts and detailed statistics to justify his arguments (95-99).

This we may, must, and will say, without a moment's hesitation, that *salvation* and *reformation* are inseparably connected, and that incorrigible obstinacy and relentless perseverance in chicanery and corruption, must ere long involve the government and nation in inevitable ruin! Tell me, citizens, tell me, what is the end of the government? Tell me, you servants of the state, you national deputies, for what purposes have you been appointed to offices of honour, emolument, and trust? What is the end of civil institutions, and the design of all the various branches of legislation and executive government? Is it not the happiness of the people? If so, let me ask another question, - Is the nation really happy? Ah, sirs, facts those stubborn things which yield to no contradiction, the sacred oracle of facts, the authenticity of which no infidel disputes, tell us the contrary, and demonstrate beyond all the power of theory and speculation the absolute necessity of speedy reform (99-100).

Wilks described social changes in the country, the migration from the country to the cities, and the depopulation of entire areas. He detailed a list of the costs of the wars which had taken place in the eighteenth century: "In a little more than one century, has it not cost this nation more than four hundred millions to butcher and destroy the human race?" (101). Wilks described the nature of the political system of Great Britain as a "war system" (103). Therefore, the formerly accused and now acquitted reformers had tried to reform the country for legitimate reason. A reformed Parliament ...

... would render the press free, the laws simple, judges unbiassed, and English juries independent; would retrench needless places and pensions, reduce immoderate salaries, diminish taxes, and make the poor happy, and have acted up to these views, have they done right or wrong? Have they deserved the foulest censure, or the praise, thanks, and admiration of a whole nation? (104)

Wilks asked for donations to help the released prisoners find re-establish themselves in business, having suffered tremendous economic damage during their imprisonment.

As you may have been informed by public advertisment that collections would be made here to-day for the use of the reputed traitors, perhaps you may now expect to hear me beg.

Beg! what, beg for patriots! for zealous, innocent, suffering patriots! for citizens, who have been dragged from all their dear enjoyments, thrust, under loads of odium and disgrace, into dens and dungeons, built for the confinement of the basest villains. Shall I beg for men, while acting for the good of their country and striving to preserve all the orders of the state, have had their trade hurt, their fame wounded, and their lives endangered by hireling emissaries and vile alarmists! Beg! did I say, God forbid! no, I will not so disgrace my country, disgrace your patriotism, disgrace the cause of liberty and freedom throughout the world, as to beg for men, who have been suffering for that cause, and who have a claim on our exertions, our humanity, our love, our all!

Citizens, let it suffice to observe, that as four thousand pounds are wanted to defray the expence of the late trials, I expect to see a patriotic emulation fire your souls, and a general contention take place, who shall be first to give and give most.

Finis (105-106).

7. "May the People ever keep a watchful eye," from: Charles Stanhope, Earl Stanhope. *Substance of Earl Stanhope's speech, delivered from the Chair, at a meeting of Citizens, at the Crown and Anchor, on the 4th of February 1795 to celebrate the happy event of the late trials for supposed High Treason; and published at the request of the Meeting; and the Toasts together with an appendix by Earl Stanhope respecting the trial by jury.* London: J. Burks, J. Smith, and T. Spence, [1795].

Shortly after the acquittals of the accused reformers, the celebration of these events through song and drink became popular among the supporters of the reform movement. In the course of the following decades, this custom created continuity by passing on knowledge of the 1790s reform movement to younger generations of reformers at the beginning of the nineteenth century. At such celebrations, reformers would sing new political songs to old tunes, for example, or would drink toasts to their shared cause. Earl Stanhope's speech took place in one of the first gatherings to celebrate the victory of the democratic cause.

Toasts for the Dinner to celebrate the event of the Late Trials for High Treason.

1. Trail by Jury, and may the People ever keep a watchful eye over every attempt to undermine that *invaluable* Right.
2. *Thomas Hardy, John Horne Tooke, John Thelwall, and the innocence of "acquitted Felons."*
3. Long Life and immortal Reputation to those Jurors, who, by their Verdict, have defeated the doctrine of Constructive Treason.
4. Thomas Erskine and Vicary Gibbs.
5. The assistant Counsel, and the meritorious Attornies of the 'acquitted Felons.'

6. The Speedy Abolition of the *Spy-Trade*.
7. May the present Ministers never experience a *Nine-Day's Trial*.
8. The Liberty of the Press, that Palladium of the people's rights.
9. The Habeas Corpus Act, and may personal Liberty never again be violated on false pretences, and thanks to *Richard Brinsley Sheridan*, for his manly opposition to its Suspension.
10. The unalienable Rights of the People.
11. A free and equal Representation of the People as the only effectual Security of all their Rights.
12. May every people, who are only *virtually* represented, be likewise only *virtually* taxed.
13. The "*Swinish Multitude*," and may the honest Hogs never cease to grunt, until their wrongs be righted.
14. A Speedy Peace, and thanks to the honest Minority of *One* in the House of Lords, for the motion, debate, and protest against interfering against the *internal* Government of France.
15. The force of Argument against the Argument of Force.
16. May the Authors of unjust War be its Victims.
17. May Foreign Mercenaries never pollute the Soil of Britain.
18. May New taxes cease to be the Ministerial "*Order of the Day*."
19. May we never engage in Wars to unpopular as to require the Aid of *Crimping*.
20. The Millions of Great Britain, and may their Voice soon silence those who maintain, that a House of Commons ought *not* to speak the Voice of the People.
21. The cause of Liberty throughout the world.
22. The brave *Koseiusko*[89]and the unfortunate Patriots of *Poland*.
23. May the Benefit, of the Criminal law of England be extended to Scotland, and Trial by Jury to all Nations.
24. May the Admirers of the Criminal law of Scotland *monopolize* its Benefits.
25. May Responsibility in Ministers soon be the Practice, as well as the Theory of the Constitution.
26. The Friends of Parliamentary Reform throughout Great Britain, and may they never appear to countenance the proposition of Mr. Pitt, "that this is *not a time* when reform ought to be pursued."

---

[89] Andrzei Kosciuszko (1746-1817) was a Polish national hero who had led the insurrection in 1794 and was defeated. In 1795, for the third time, Poland was partitioned by Russia, Prussia, and Austria.

27. The PRESENT Lord Mayor of London, and thanks to him for his Constitutional Conduct during the late Trials (2).

Substance of Earl Stanhope's Speech.

Stanhope, whom Thelwall compared with Kosciuszko,[90] distinguished between "visionary Plots" and "Plots real and substantial" in order to emphasize the political character of the treason trials. The former type of plots was invented to curb "the Liberties of the PEOPLE".

Citizens,

We have seen certain ministerial Prints, filled with foul Calumny, against the Men who (according to the Laws of their Country) were to be put upon their Trial. We have seen also circulated, throughout the nation, with malicious and wicked Industry, Pamphlets and Hand-Bills without number, in order to *prejudice* the Minds of the Public, against the Men accused: and (what was peculiarly base, and unjust) even to *prejudice* if possible the Minds of the Jurymen who were to try them for their *Lives*.

Citizens,

We have heard maintained, of late, Doctrines *novel* in this country; but, not more novel, than unconstitutional, and dangerous. We have been told of the existence of strange Laws, which, however, are *not* to be found amongst our statutes, nor in any Book of onr [sic!] Common law whatever. We have witnessed Maxims having been advanced, and Principles having been supported, which I believe, were never before heard of; at least, never before heard of, in a *free* Country; and which Maxims could never have taken root, but in the Heads, or in the Hearts of *despotic Tories*.

---

[90] See Thelwall 1995: 204: "Kosciusko, like Stanhope, was an aristocrat only by birth: he could perceive that the peasantry are the life, the soul, the existence of society."

Citizens,

We have seen Men, supposed to have been guilty of separate and *distinct Overt Acts of Treason,* included in one and the same Indictment, and charged *all* together, in the very *same* words, with the very *same* offences (3-4).

Stanhope objected that the jurors had been elected from 200 people so that the prisoners would not have enough time to exercise their right to have the potential jurors checked. He also complained that 200 witnesses were heard – he had heard that someone had talked about a "Cloud of Witnesses" which was expected to cause confusion (5) – and that there was no way to check whether the witnesses of the government were spies (4). Stanhope proposed that the accused reformers were systematically denounced in defiance of the English law:

"Every Man is deemed INNOCENT, until he is PROVED to be guilty." And it is another equally well known Maxim of the Law of England, that "No Man CAN be proved to be guilty, until that important Stage of the Proceedings, when he is heard in his defence" (5).

Stanhope rejects the interpretation – voiced during the trials – that the use of the term "Citizen" meant "*a kind of Indication of an EVIL Intent*!" (7). He quoted Blackstone, who used the word "Citizen" in the sense of "the Inhabitants at large" (7). An entire section of Stanhope's speech is dedicated to the emergence of civilization made possible by the printing press. The barbarism which existed in Europe prior to the invention of the printing press is demonstrated by the fact that people of that time who could write were acquitted, the so-called "Benefit of Clergy". This right had been abused in recent times:

It is an Act of Parliament to give to *Peers*, and also to *Lords* of Parliament (that is to say to give to *Peers*, and also to the Right Reverend *Bishops*,) what is called the 'Benefit of Clergy;' which benefit of Clergy is now in certain Cafes given to *everyone* but which, previously to the passing of that Act, was confined to those *who could read*.

Now, that Act of Parliament [...] enacts; that if any *Peer* or *Lord of Parliament* shall be guilty of *Housebreaking, Horse stealing*, or Highway-Robbery, such *Peer* or *Lord* of Parliament shall have his Clergy '*though he cannot read*' (7-8).

For Stanhope, this is "gross, and almost brutish Barbarism":

The invaluable ART OF PRINTING has dispelled that former Darkness; and, like a new *Luminary* enlightens the whole Horizon. The *gloomy Night of Ignorance* is past. The pure unsullied *Light of Reason* is NOW so much diffused, that it is no longer in the power of *Tyranny* to destroy it. And I believe, and hope, that glorious *intellectual Light* will, shortly, shine forth on Europe, with *meredian* Splendor.

Citizens

The Art of Printing (that most useful and unparalled Invention) is however, as nothing, without *that*, which alone can give it energy and effect: you need not to be told, that I mean, the sacred LIBERTY OF THE PRESS, that *Palladium* of the people's Rights

Citizens,

But, even the *Liberty of the Press* itself, is totally insecure, without that Fortress of the People, by which alone it is defended a preserved; namely, the TRIAL BY JURY, that Citadel of the Constitution (9).

Stanhope listed all the essential elements of the constitution, claiming the constitution would be nothing but a broken pipe without them: "a fair, free and equal Representation of the People, in the Common's House of Parliament"; "Annual Parliament"; *Habeas Corpus* Act; Liberty of the press; Trial by Jury" (9). He emphasized that jurors should be financially independent from the State (9).

Erskine criticised the method by which the Attorney General constructed the charge of treason from a number of books and pamphlets. Crucial quotations had not been checked properly as was common in a libel case. The accused reformers were confronted:

... with having maliciously and traiterously composed, and caused to be composed, "DIVERS *Books, Pamphlets* and *Writings*" (without reciting any one of the Words therein contained, and even without mentioning the Title of any one of such Books, Pamphlets or Writings.) And they were also charged, with having maliciously, and traiterously published, and caused to be published "DIVERS *other Books, Pamphlets* and *Writings*," and so forth! So that, there is NO Book, or number of Books, in any the *largest*

Library in this Nation, which might *not*, under that convenient word DIVERS, have been produced and have been attempted to have been read in Evidence upon the late Trials! (10-11).

Stanhope ridiculed the trial against Thomas Hardy, which had been opened with a nine-hour argument meant to demonstrate that Hardy's treason was "perfectly obvious". Stanhope warned that everything had to be undertaken to prevent an abolishment of the trial by jury.

In the appendix, Stanhope insisted that only published texts should be used against an accused person. Texts found in one's home should not be used in court because one could not rule out that these texts had not left the privacy of the home for the very reason that they had never been intended to reach the public.

Who knows, but that the printed Papers found in the House of *Thomas Hardy*, were part of some *cancelled* Edition? Of some Edition, *cancelled* for the very reason (perhaps) of its being *incorrect*? And surely, *that kind of Evidence* ought NOT to be *received*, upon a Trial, *to affect a Man's Life*... (15)[91]

91 Stanhope demands that only those texts should be read in court, which had been admitted. Otherwise none of the jurors might remember after nine days of trial which had been included in the chain of evidence.

8. "In an age so agitated by political convulsions as this," from: Anthony Pasquin [= John Williams], *Legislative Biography; or, an Attempt to Ascertain the Merits and Principles of the Most Admired Orators of the British Senate. Being Intended as a Companion to the Parliamentary Reports*. London: H.D. Symonds, 1795.

The author explained in the advertisment and the introductory remarks that he wants to inform his readers in a more objective manner than is usual (iv). John Williams had a reputation for publications of this nature. In 1793 he had published *The Life of the Late Earl of Barrymore. Including a history of the Wargrave theatricals, and original anecdotes of eminent persons* (London: H.D. Symonds). The *Legislative Biography* was followed by *Memoirs of the Royal Academicians, being an attempt to improve the national taste*, vol. 1 (London: H.D. Symonds, 1796), and *A Looking-Glass for the Royal Family: with Documents for British Ladies, and All Foreigners Residing in London. Being a Postscript to The New Brighton Guide. By John Williams, whose public Appellation is Anthony Pasquin* (London: H.D. Symonds, 1797).

Advertisment

In an age so agitated by political convulsions as this in which we exist, it may not be altogether unentertaining, or uninstructive, to aim at casting a new light upon those prominent characters, which are now considered, in a legislative sense, as actively employed in confounding or ascertaining the rights of human kind (iii).

In his article on "The Right Honourable William Pitt" (7-20), Williams also mentions the high treason trials of 1794 and the right of the opposition to call for reforms. Obviously, Williams was not as impartial as he claimed to be when he wrote of "the imputed fury of that studied ALARM" (13):

Under the influence of this pyebald privy council, he ventured to enforce a system of terror, which was rendered nugatory, if not ridiculous, by the beheft of a jury, who will be immortalized through the medium of virtue (13).

[...]

The nation is now arrived at that summit of woe, when the judgment is so stunned by the blows of calamity, and so confounded with apprehended evils, which the imagination first suggests to the understanding, and then embodies, for its own particular annoyance, that the faculties of thought have become partially suspended by terror; and all good men feel themselves *surprised* into a situation, which requires new habits of thinking, to justify new resolutions; yet, such is the danger by which we are environed, that while these resolutions are investigating and maturing, the Minister possesses so extraordinary a degree of power, as threatens the very existence of our most valued privileges! - THIS IS OUR STATE, and it belongs to the deliberate and virtuous part of the people, to compare the progress of Mr. PITT with the ends he has fulfilled; and, if, on due examination, it is proved, that from sinister and corrupt motives, he has raised up a tempest in the nation, to eclipse, or at least to dazzle the public vision so far, that no material and governing object shall have its own true and unequivocal appearance, I trust he will be devoted to that species of immolation, which should terminate a being unworthily employed (20).

The article on Pitt is followed by one on his main parliamentary opponent, "The Right Honourable Charles James Fox (21-37):

As it has been judicially declared that TRUTH IS A LIBEL, agreeably to the interpretation of the laws of this realm, I should deprecate the consequences of most honorably laboring to give perpetuity to Shame (23).

[...]

The abuses and mischievous tendencies of ORATORY are so numerous, that I have been led to regret, that our statesmen have a dominion so uncontrolled over the parts of speech; their pride seems involved in the furtherance of a verisimility, and not a fact, - they are eternally rotary, but never explicit; they argue more to bewilder than liberalize, and dedicate those powers to delusion, that were meant for truth! (30).

[...]

They pay more attention to the harmony of periods, than the spirit of the declaration, and seem to think that every sentiment, like every rascal, should be well received that is well drest! - Our professional talkers seem more sedulous to dazzle than to enlighten; and give that labour to captivate the passions, which should only be directed to the understanding (31-32).

[...]

As an orator he has always received more approbation than was due to his ability - though his *reasoning* is often very acute and convincing, he wants *perspicuity* in the arrangements of his matter: his zeal to confound his adversary hurries him into tautolagies [sic!] of expression, which would be certainly ruinous to his reputation, if his rapidity of delivery did not make every auditor an apologist for his weakness - his *assumption* of openness in opinion throws a faint charm around the fallibility of his judgement (35).

About Edward, Lord Thurlow (38-42), the Lord Chancellor at the time, Williams wrote the following:

In short, he is a living paradox of contrarieties, - classed by the discerning as a great man - without condescending to exercise many of those qualities which are generally reputed as good and amiable (42)

It was Thurlow, however, who refused to accept the charge of treason upon hearing of Sir John Scott's introductory speech: "Nine hours' address on a charge of High Treason! then there is no treason."[92] Following a literary portrait of Alexander Wedderburne, Lord Loughborough, born in Scotland in 1733 (43-48), Williams presents "Mr. Edmund Burke. The only true Portrait extant" (49-61).

He wandered through the mazes of the Machiavelian institutes, and gathered his earliest consolations from the tributary purse of Lord VERNEY! He occasionally amused himself with roasting the *King's turnspit*, and the defining the *sublime* and *beautiful*. In this singular work he had miraculously demonstrated that four things of soft are made of rough particles, and sweet things and smooth atoms (49).

About Burke's most famous book, *Reflections on the Revolution in France* (1790), Williams wrote:

---

[92] Mrs. Cecil Henrietta Boyle Thelwall, *The Life of John Thelwall. By His Widow*. In Two Volumes, vol. 1 (London: John Macrone, 1837), 240. The Earl of Derby is said to have quoted Lord Thurlow: "A Noble and Learned Lord [Thurlow] had said, that all the facts stated in the Report were highly seditious, but did not amount to Treason" (*Debates on the Report of the Committee of Secrecy*, 1794: 106).

When future generations shall read his pious lamentations at the sepulchre of Chivalry, and his deep groans for the extinction of savage habit, I hope they will not receive it as a primary feature of the age in which we breathe, and think all enamoured of absurdity (51).

[...]

What serious reply can be made to this polemic, furious, and unforgiving man, but coolly to inform him that we are not to estimate the merits of political principles, or to depreciate them, on account of any temporary effects which they may produce. In the awful rush of popular tumult and commotion, the indignant storm will often implicate in its baleful effects both the innocent and the guilty; as the lightning, while it blasts the poisonous plant, oft involves in similar ruin the beneficial oak. When the bosom of a nation heaves with convulsive throbs, it is vain to tell her, in the language of the poet, that 'Sunt certi denique fines/ Quos ultra citraque nequit consistere rectum (54).

Williams's conclusion is full of passion. He calls Burke's oratory "a disease in the commonwealth" (60).

The infirmities of a BURKE comprehend so much human degradation, that I cannot indite his weakness without a tear, - being what he is, I wish he had never been (58).

The Attorney General, Sir John Scott, later Lord Eldon (1751-1838), was the son of a Newcastle-on-Tyne coal factor. After he had been given a seat in Parliament, he became Solicitor-General, Attorney General, Lord Chief Justice and Chancellor (1807-1827). He delivered the opening speech for the prosecution at the Trial of Thomas Hardy in autumn 1794. Williams' portrait of Sir John Scott (62-64) is full of contempt:

During the prosecution of Mr. TOOKE, Mr. HARDY, and Mr.THELWALL, by the present government, for High Treason, it was the lot of this gentleman, in his capacity as Attorney General, to modify the evidence and illustrate the case: and it must be confessed by each party, that considering all the crooked and adverse circumstances of the solemn attempt, he conducted himself with as much liberality as he might be permitted to exercise, having the arduous toil to reconcile that to an agitated and inflamed world, which can never be reconciled to posterity. This struggle to connect delusion with ruin was a misappropriation of human intellect, for which he ought to receive a due reproof, but torment of the last poignancy must arise, whenever he reconsiders his labours on that melancholy occasion: - he argued in fetters, and was too obedient to his master. - I shall not say much of his coadjutor Sir John Mitford,[93] as the insignificance of his character precludes from animadversion. [...] It is but seldom that this gentleman delivers himself in the Senate, and then it appears in some degree compulsory: his speeches should be noted as the ramifications of a legal opinion, rather than the appropriate and bland declarations of a legislator, wishing to embrace in his position, all that was valuable to good men. - If he continues to speak upon a subject for three hours, his hearers can never forget that it is a mere Lawyer who is scudding like an eel, in every retrograde direction, through legislative mud, and is but seldom visible in the clear water of truth: the more such men are impassioned in their agency, the more they confound reflection, and give a strength to deception through the medium of art, which should have never been. The most acute speech I have heard him deliver, was his very sedulous endeavour to justify the suspension of the *Habeas Corpus Act*: and his reasoning upon that essential point was so thoroughly specious and imposing, that I shuddered for the existence of human liberty.

The late Trials (happily for the Liberties of this Country) have ended in the *honourable* acquittal of the Citizens accused: notwithstanding, the *complicated Difficulties* they had to contend with. Our view must, from henceforth, be directed to the FUTURE. And amongst the various Topicks, which I suggested for consideration, at the Celebration Meeting at the Crown and Anchor, or which are contained in this Appendix; there are *some* of *those Propositions* so peculiarly essential to the pure and impartial Administration of *Justice*, so obviously right, and so congenial to the mind and humane spirit of the best of our laws, that only *few* Men (one should hope) would be found so BLOOD-THIRSTY, as to give them opposition (63-64).

[93] Sir John Mitford (1748- 1830), first Baron Redesdale; prosecutor at many of the trials against reformers and Attorney-General after 1799.

9. "Imprisonment is attended, in many cases, with circumstances singularly distressing, and notoriously unjust," from: George Dyer, *A Dissertation of the Theory and Practice of Benevolence*. London: printed for Kearsley, 1795.

In his "Preface", George Dyer explains that this *Dissertation* is designed to be a sequel to his *Complaints of the Poor People of England* (1793). George Dyer[94] knew radicals such as Thelwall as well as Romantic poets such as Wordsworth and Coleridge. In his *Dissertation*, he explains and defends the benevolent thinking of the eighteenth century.

Part I.

Ch. i. Benevolence is independent in its Character

GOODNESS is defined by Johnson, to be, desirable qualities either moral or physical. In this Dissertation it stands for kindness, a gentle and humane propensity, that inclines to sympathy, and moves those who possess it to be interested in the happiness of others. A good man is the well-wisher, and, to the utmost of his power, the benefactor of his species: one, to whom the unfortunate may look with confidence, and call their friend. - To avoid, therefore, too frequent a use of the same word, goodness and benevolence will be made to express the same disposition.

Man is not only an imperfect being, morally considered, but frail, considered physically. The imbecility of his nature compels him to look beyond himself for protection; his social propensities require a junction of hearts in his gratifications and enjoyments. Hence connections are formed between man and man, and friendships cemented between persons of similar pursuits and inclinations.

Age is most pleased, when in sweet converse join'd
With hoary age, so youth delights in youth,
And female softness harmonizes best
With kindred tenderness, th' infirm, th' opprest

---

[94] There is a modern edition of *The Complaints of the Poor People of England* (Oxford: Woodstock Books, 1990) (= Revolution and Romanticism, 1789-1834). For George Dyer, see M. Ray Adams, "George Dyer and English Radicalism," in: *Studies in the Literary Backgrounds of English Radicalism with Special Reference to the French Revolution* (New York: Greenwood Press, 1968), 227-266; and "'Unremembered Kindness': George Dyer and the Poets," in: *The Politics of Nature* (2002), 19-42.

Bear to th' opprest, th' infirm, a sympathy of woe

Such a conjunction of minds and of interests may be considered as alliances, formes to resist a common enemy, and to obtain reciprocal attentions. [...] Benevolence, so far as human can operate, (and of divine I am not speaking) is the hope and guide of more enlightened periods. The theory of this amiable quality may, perhaps, lead to the practice.

Benevolence Is Independent in its character. - It being intended to consider this disposition as it resides in the human breast, it is unnecessary to observe, that the term independent cannot here be understood in the sense applied in the schools, as a necessary, self-existent, independent Being: nor can it express any superiority of mind, or separation of interest, authorizing a Being to say, I can stand alone - bound by no ties; exposed to no wants; affected by no calamities. The independence of a good man consists in a superiority to every influence, but of moral persuasion, and to every force, but of rational conviction. It proceeds from a sense of dignity, and personal rectitude: it is that decent pride, that characterizes generous minds; that high sense of honour, that will not suffer them to yield to profligacy, or to stoop to meanness: it is a kind of majesty, essential to virtue; or more properly speaking, it is the grace of ingenuousness, and of freedom of innocence.

This virtuous independence crowns the happiness of private life; and happy are the governments, that give it public security! In steady and pure governments this becomes a principal consideration of national regard. Their aim is to produce publick happiness, not to aggrandize or enrich individuals; to procure moral freedom through the medium of political justice. Offices are appropriated to talents; and, if virtues are not distinguished by honours, they are not, at least, exposed to penalties. The cultivator of the land enjoys the fruits without oppression; the legislator, and the magistrate are indemnified, if not rewarded. No one is tempted to exchange his principles for a livelihood; and each considers himself as an individual of a family, in which no one is a slave (3-6).

Ch. ii. Benevolence is free in its Design

Goodness retires from restraint [...] A proud man may be compelled to numerous acts of apparent humility: but a mere garb cannot conceal pride, which, like the charms of a prostitute, will always be obtruding on your notice (14).

Ch. iii. Benevolence is universal in its Influence

No system of theological opinions is, exclusively, essential to form the benevolent character. [...] The social affections are dictated by nature, and confirmed by habit; and dwell in the heart of that man, who is least corrupted by base passions, whatever his religion be.

The GOOD MAN from appearances of nature derives tender affections, generous principles, and human conduct. ... The good man thus acquires universal tenderness.

Art thou dejected? Is thy mind o'ercast?
Chain down some Passion; do some generous Good.
Teach Ignorance to see, or Grief to smile:
Correct thy Friend; befriend thy greatest Foe.
YOUNG'S NIGHT THOUGHTS, VIRTUE'S APOLOGY

The merciful man, says Solomon, is merciful to his beast; and the common saying, that a good man would not hurt a worm is full of significance: Go! said Uncle Toby, opening the window, and giving liberty to an imprisoned fly, the world is wide enough for thee and me.♣[95] - The old Pythagoreans, as well as many ancient and modern sects, believed in the transmigration of souls; that is, that the soul, being a distinct substance from matter, passed through different stages of existence, and, at death, migrated from one body to another. The system may be thought chimerical; but its tendency is benevolent. The reader will recollect some remarks on this subject in the SPECTATOR*. The Pythagoreans were peculiarly tender of the brute creation, and even abstained from animal food (19-20).

Ch. iv. Benevolence is persevering in its Labours

But the patriot and the philanthropist must be willing to be moral martyrs; must persevere amidst reproach, and be deaf to the voice of malevolence. [...] True benevolence is but justice exhibited in its most amiable form, and directing its energies to alleviate the distresses incident to hu-

---

♣ See Sterne's Tristram Shandy

95 "– Go, says he, lifting up the sash, and opening his hand as he spoke, to let it escape; – go, poor devil, get thee gone, why should I hurt thee? – This world surely is wide enough to hold both thee and me." Laurence Sterne, *The Life and Opinions of Tristram Shandy*, ed. Graham Petrie, intro. Christopher Ricks (Harmondsworth: Penguin, 1983), 131.

* No. 343

manity, and to remedy the evils forced on the world by a vicious state of society (23).

Part II.

Ch. i. Miscellaneous Cases: of uneducated youth; of poor and sick persons

[...]

Ch. ii. Poverty and Distresses of Men of Letters

However, to do the world justice, it should be acknowledged, that honest men are frequently led into mistakes: and, if a poor author is now and then starved to death, they, at least, should be acquitted of cruelty. When a writer has published a book, he is supposed to have procured a maintenance. Men suppose, that his profits keep pace with the reputation; and, who would suppose, that praise has been the only reward? (52)

[...]

There might be shew instances, in which a respectable list of subscribers, standing at the head of a publication, has been a most unfortunate circumstance for an author. Many readers have begun immediately to calculate pounds, shillings, and pence; and supposed, at random, that the author's pockets must be lined with bank notes. They are not aware, honest men, that the writer, during the long period of preparing his work, and of bringing it through the press, has not been living on the air: they forget, also, that printers and booksellers follow a profession as well as authors, and that they rarely work out of pure charity.

Will it be prudent in an author to throw himself among a host of criticks? An author runs no danger, but such as he ought to encounter, among real scholars, among criticks who possess the power of discrimination, and the principles of Justice. The real critick, if an honest man, will not wilfully mislead the publick taste: but he cannot be wantonly unjust (53).

[...]

But if a man of letters can obtain a patron, he may defy the critick -- True. But a patron is not always so easily found, as sought after: and it very often happens, that a writer obtains no patron, till he can either do tolerably well without one, or till disappointments and penury may have almost harrassed him out of the world. An able leader in the field of letters, may be flattered and over-powered with distinctions; while the pioneer of literature is frequently left to perish amidst the rubbish, which he was doomed to remove.

The notice of a great man, it is true, may prove beneficial: but such notice may eventually be the most unfortunate circumstance in a man's life. The GREAT are sometimes apt to make men of talents their tools, and to expect illiberal compliances, at which a delicate genius may recoil, or an upright conscience may revolt: a vague belief of the importance of such friendship, may lead to mistaken notions prejudicial to the author. And while the world may suppose the poor fellow has found a Mecænas, he may be fortunate to have escaped a Nero* (54-55).[96]

Dyer provided many more examples of impoverished ancient authors in his chapter "The Curiosities of Literature" (55-60).

To enlarge the above catalogue would be no difficult task: if any reader choose to pursue the enquiry, he will find abundant examples in Bayle's Dictionary, and in *de Infortunio Literatorum*. Enough has been noticed to justify the following conclusions: That genius, like beauty, my be ruinous to those who possess it; that literature, like virtue, must, sometimes, be its own reward; that poetry is allied to poverty, so as to justify the belief, that universal consent assigns poets to poverty; and that, after what has happened to Homer, Tasso, Milton, Spenser, and Butler, no poet has a right to complain of hard fortune ... (60-61).

[...]

Every one who thinks he can write, the publick are not bound to read, much less to support; but he who possesses the talents to instruct or amuse the publick, has the powers to procure a maintenance, by some course of industry. The man of fortune, who patronizes genius, is entitled

---

* Thomas Holcroft illustrated the circumstances alluded to in the above paragraph in the ADVENTURES OF HUGH TREVOR, a well-written novel: I refer to the conduct of the patriotic peer, and of the orthodox bishop. Vol. II.

[96] Originally published from 1794 to 1797; for a modern edition Thomas Holcroft, *The Adventures of Hugh Trevor*, 6 vols., ed. Seamus Deane (Oxford: Oxford University Press, 1973). See Joseph Rosenblum, *Thomas Holcroft: Literature and Politics in England in the Age of the French Revolution* (New York: Edwin Mellen Press 1995).

to esteem; but every man of fortune is not bound to be a patron, though every man of letters is bound to know how to live (62).

[...]

It is only within a year or two that a SOCIETY TO SUPPORT AUTHORS IN DISTRESS was constituted. The plan of this society is drawn up with much good sense, and, it is to be hoped, requires only to be more widely known, to be more generally encouraged (63).

Constitution of a Society to support Authors in Distress

Dyer complained that people in England might talk a lot about free press and literature, but nothing was done to improve authors' living conditions. While others were talking, impoverished authors died (63).

Dyer printed the entire constitution of this society to support Authors in Distress (63-66), which was founded by David Williams after he had been thrown into prison because of £40 worth of debts. The society helped authors organize themselves and support each other: "This institution confines itself entirely to the relief of authors" (66).

The utility of a society, that should unite in design the progress of elegant literature, with the means to assist distressed genius, has frequently struck my mind: and men of understandings more inventive than mine, and possessed of more influence and authority, might be able to realize a scheme, productive of permanent advantages in both those respects (67).

Dyer introduced the "Plan of a cheap Mathematical Society" and the constitution of such a mathematical society in Spitalfields as established in 1717 by Joseph Middleton (68-74). He warned that certain forms of institutionalisation had become something of an impediment to the circulation of knowledge in the past:

This fraternity, as before observed, is composed of persons in the middling classes of life; but from the inconsiderable expences attending their meetings, it is clear, that the lowest classes might form similar societies. The advantages would result from promoting reading societies through a country are too obvious to need pointing out. The monopoly of science is particularly injurious. It retards the progress of truth, the advancement of intellect; and encourages that insolence, not improperly called the aristocracy of literature, too common amongst academicks. The popular libraries, that abound in America, form the difference between the people of that country and of Great Britain. There is more polite literature in this country; but more general information in America (74-75).

[...]

Literary societies, consisting of persons of some degree of independence, and of sufficient talents and learning, answer the most valuable purposes. That of social intercourse in the highest degree agreeable and profitable. Societies of this kind might, indeed, pursue great designs: one object at least, they might without difficulty accomplish: they might amuse and instruct the publick. A body of learned men might easily effect what can rarely be obtained by individual exertion: and where there was sufficient stock of brilliant talents, abilities less splendid need not be disregarded. Works, stored with amusement, like certain well-known periodical publications; or tending to improve arts and sciences, to furnish important hints, and to exhibit useful discoveries, might proceed from such fraternities. But this Dissertation enters not into plans of such societies (75-76).

In this chapter, Dyer refers to the trials against Thomas Walker, Thomas Hardy, John Horne Tooke and John Thelwall (77-81).

Ch. iii. The Cases of Persons Lately indicted for Conspiracy, High Treason, and Sedition.

WE now proceed to consider the cases of

those, lately put on their Trials for Treason or Sedition; which, though the last in the order of this Dissertation, were the first in my mind.

In a legal and political point of view this subject has been treated of by various writers; and will, doubtless, undergo still further discussion. It occupies here a place of moral consideration: moral, not in regard to the justice or injustice of putting these men on their trials; nor to the principles or characters of the accusers; but in regard to the inconveniences and losses sustained by the defendants.

In the present view of the subject it is natural for the writer of these pages to feel not a little interested; approving, as he did, the object of their pursuit; for his opinion is, that their real object was the publick good: and they were evidently placed at the post of danger. They have, it is true, most justly escaped the punishment of traitors; but they have sustained considerable injury (76-77).

[...]

The first of those, lately tried for high Treason, at the Old Bailey, is THOMAS HARDY, Shoemaker, in Travistock Street. Concerning the crime imputed to this honest man, and the circumstances of his trial, I say nothing: and in a case, that involved so imminent peril, and was attended with such serious distress, as connects itself with the loss of a wife and child, there can be no calculation of damages, and no indemnification (77-78).

[...]

The English law professes a sacred regard to personal liberty of individuals: and with justice professes it: for the damage sustained by loss of time, and by length of imprisonment, is of the highest consideration, and may run out to a most ruinous extent. It may be questioned, indeed, whether our practices strictly accord with this profession; certain it is, that precedents do not harmonize with the fundamental maxims of law; with those principles, that are received as the basis of the English government, and to which our ancestors were accustomed to refer as the exemplars of Justice.* Imprisonment is attended, in many cases, with circumstances singularly distressing, and notoriously unjust.

This is particularly the case on a charge of high treason. The person may be innocent, but he is to be harassed with all the horrors of uncertainty, and the tediousness of delay. Embarrassments arise from considerations of time, and place, and from the nature of the fact. These circumstances may be rendered still more embarrassing from *closeness* of confinement, and the health of the prisoner. Such observations apply to the cases of all those, lately indicted for high treason; but more particularly to that of JOHN HORNE TOOKE, whose ill state of health, before, and during his confinement, rendered it probable, that he would not survive his imprisonment. To the serious expences, therefore, of attorneys, of counsel, and of witnesses, should be further added the damages consequent on a tedious

* See the Preface to the Mirror of Justice, and Ch. I.

imprisonment;* damages, which might have proved, and in some sort have proved, beyond calculation. But may the intelligent author of the DIVERSIONS OF PURLEY long live, to amuse and instruct mankind, by completing his most ingenious and learning undertaking.

And thanks to the fundamental MAXIMS of the English law, the courage and talents of an Erskine and a Gibbs, and the independence of an English jury! - Justice hath obtained a triumph. The worthy persons, indeed, knew themselves to be innocent; but where power intervenes, and power supported by corruption, even innocence is no pledge of security. It was not, therefore, without reason, that they at times expressed the most serious apprehensions of danger; and it may not be unamusing to some readers to be acquainted with the feelings of JOHN THELWALL, when in view of the impending storm.

The following composition is expressive of an innocent mind, and possesses poetical merit (78-80).

Dyer took this poem from John Thelwall's *Poems Written in Close Confinement*,[97] which had been published in the same year. He also further advertised Thelwall's book in footnotes.

On hearing, for certainty that we were to be tried for High Treason

SHORT is perhaps our date of life,
    But let us while we live be gay -
To those be thought and anxious care,
Who build upon the distant day.

Tho' in our cup tyrannic Power
    Would dash the bitter dregs of fear,
We'll gaily quaff the mantling draught,
    While patriot toasts the fancy cheer.

---

* Omnis pœna corporalis quamvis minima major est omni, pœna pecuniaria quamvis maxima, i.e. The smallest corporal punishment is greater than the largest fine.

97 John Thelwall's *Poems Written in Close Confinement in the Tower and Newgate, Under a Charge of High Treason* (London: J. Ridgway, 1795), 25-26. This poem was also published in Thelwall's autobiography, published by his widow, Mrs. Cecil Henrietta Boyle (1837: 195). For a recent edition, see *Poems Written in Close Confinement in the Tower and Newgate, Under a Charge of High Treason, ed. Jonathan Wordsworth* (1795; rpt. Oxford: Woodstock Books, 2000).

Sings not the seaman, tempest-tost,
When surges wash the rivven [sic] shroud -
Scorning the threat'ning voice of Fate,
That pipes in rocking winds aloud?

Yes; - he can take his cheerful glass,
And toast his mistress in the storm,
While duty and remember'd joys
By turns, his honest bosom warm.

And shall not we in storms of state,
At base Oppression's fury laugh,
And while the vital spirits flow,
To Freedom fill, and fearless quaff?

Short is perhaps our date of life,
But let us while we live be gay,
To those be thought and anxious care,
Who build upon a distant day.
Tower, Sept. 28, 1794 (80-81).

It appeared on Thelwall's trial, that he was a person of great integrity, maintaining himself, and others, who rested on him for support, by his personal industry. The means, therefore, during his confinement, were necessarily suspended; and his publick lectures, part of those means, have not as yet been resumed: These damages, therefore, are to be added to the expences of his trial; and is not entirely without design, that I have thrown the list of his publications in a note[98] (81-82).

In following paragraphs, George Dyer quotes from Thomas Holcroft's *Narrative of Facts* (82-83) and from Jeremiah Joyce's publications.

[98] Dyer mentions Thelwall's *The Peripatetic*, *Essay towards the Definition of Animal Vitality*, and his *Political Lectures*, which were published by Ridgway and Symonds. In his post scriptum, Dyer points out that Thelwall's Political Lectures had also been published in the meantime. All these texts are available in modern editions (see footnote 13).

J.A. BONNEY, STEWART KYD, JER. JOYCE, THO. HOLCROFT, J. RICHTER, AND J. BAXTER, though not brought to trial, have had separate counsel, and been involved in the unavoidable losses, which attended a long separation from business. There were also in the same indictment THOMAS WARDLE, MATTHEW MOOR, AND RICHARD HODGSON.

The expences of these three trials amount to between three and four thousand pounds. Yet each has been pronounced NOT GUILTY, and this verdict has been most cordially sanctioned by the publick voice.

JEREMIAH JOYCE has published a sermon, to which he has subjoined an Appendix, containing an account of his arrest, &c. In the last page of that appendix is the following passage (82-83).[99] Dyer quotes Jeremiah Joyce's *A sermon preached on Sunday, February the 23d, 1794* from the *Morning Chronicle* of 24 Nov. 1794.

In a footnote, Dyer mentions John Smith's address to allow readers to support his family. In his description of the "Cases of John Smith and others", Dyer emphasized the repercussions of imprisonment for the families of accused reformers.

There are still confined on a charge of high Treason, George Higgins, in Tothill-fields Bridewell, Paul Le Maitre, New Prison, Cold-Bath Fields; John Roussell, and John Smith, on the Felon's side, in Newgate.

The situation of the latter is peculiarly hard, and deserves particular notice. How long it may yet be, before Smith is brought to trial, cannot be ascertained. In the mean time, he has lost his employment of Clerk to Macklin's Picture Gallery, which brought him in sixty pounds a year; and this would not be restored to him on his enlargement. The profits arising from a small pamphlet shop are very inconsiderable: and he has a wife, four children, and an aged mother.[100]

Of Thomas Spence, Thomas Breillat, and William Winterbotham

There are several other cases, that deserve consideration: among others, that of THOMAS SPENCE, the publisher of PIG'S MEAT; and his requisition is so

---

[99] Dyer quotes this from the *Morning Chronicle* of Nov. 24, 1794. Jeremiah Joyce's sermon was also published separately in *A sermon preached on Sunday, February the 23d, 1794*.

[100] In a footnote Dyer mentions John Smith's address in order to make it possible top support his family.

modest, that it would be unpardonable to pass it unnoticed. In a short address to the publick, he expresses himself thus, "Fellow-citizens, I am again restored to my shop, after a tedious confinement of more than seven months, but change of circumstances readers my return productive of small joy. I beg leave, therefore, to observe to the friends of freedom and political truth, that by assisting in the sale of my book called the PIG'S MEAT,* they will essentially serve me (85-86).

Dyer mentioned not only the factual details of the cases of Thomas Breillat and William Winterbotham, including the charge brought against them and their sentence and punishment, but also the disastrous economic consequences of political prosecution: imprisonment and high penalties caused their bankruptcy. As in the case of the other reformers, Dyer published detailed information about the published works of the accused persons in order to help them to support themselves and their families in spite of the fact that they had to serve prison sentences (86-87).

Dyer also printed excerpts from a letter by James Ridgeway, H.D. Symonds and Daniel Holt, written to the authorities at Newgate prison in the second year of their imprisonment (3 Jan. 1795; 88-90).

Sir, Experiencing all the rigours of confinement, and daily feeling the severe and calamitous pressure of a long, distant, and ruinous separation from our business, our families, and our friends at large, without any prospect of speedy alleviation, we are, at length, reluctantly compelled to throw ourselves the humanity and benevolence of the Public, and to solicit from the generosity and justice of the British nation, that support which so long a suspension from our commercial concerns has rendered, in some measure, necessary (88).

The hardships the booksellers described in their letter destroyed their lives. Even without the fines, the imprisoned persons had to compensate for £3,200 of lost income per person. After two years in prison, they wrote a letter asking for "benevolent assistance" (88). Dyer wrote the following about the letter:

This letter was written previous to the meeting to celebrate the Trial by Jury, on the fourth of February, but it has never been circulated. For it

* This is a political work in two small volumes. Spence lives at No. 8, Little Turnstile, High Holborn.

being intimated to them, that a Subscription was to be opened for defraying the expences of the late Trials for High Treason, they indulged hopes, that their cases might pass under the consideration of those worthy and respectable persons, who will from the Committee. In expectation of that they keep back their letter (90-91).

Dyer included lesser-known political prisoners who were imprisoned in Newgate for sedition, such as Thomas Lloyd, an American citizen, the bookseller D.I. Eaton, and William Hodgson (not to be confused with Richard Hodgson, who was one of the accused in the treason trials of 1794). William Hodgson was …

... imprisoned under a sentence of two years confinement, a fine of two hundred pounds. He has two children. He is printing by subscription, in numbers, (price sixpence each) THE SYSTEM OF NATURE, translated from the French of M. Mirabeau: and, in the month of February, he intends publishing a work of his own, entitled, THE COMMON WEALTH of REASON. Hodgson is *now* on the state side (91).

In his next chapter, Dyer talked about the "Cases of Joseph Gerrald, William Hudson, William Lloyd, and others" (92). Joseph Gerrald, a deputy from the LCS,

... has been in different prisons near a twelve-month He is, at present, in close confinement in the New Compter, opposite Newgate. He is the author of a pamphlet, that affords proof of very superior talents, entitled, *A Convention the only means of saving the Nation from ruin*, printed by D.I. EATON. He is uncertain yet, as to his future destiny; but whatever it may be, Gerrald behaves himself as one that is invulnerable. He closes his well-written DEFENCE in the following spirited manner: "Impressed wit the justice of these sentiments, dungeons, fetters, exile, carry no terror to me; for I say with the immortal Sydney, that though I have a particular love to my country, of which, I hope, that I have given some testimony; though I think that being exiled from it is a great evil, from which I would redeem myself with the loss of a great deal of my blood, yet, when that country of mine, which used to be esteemed a paradise, is now like to be made a stage of injury; the liberty which we hoped to establish oppressed; the best of our nation made a prey to the worst; the parliament, court, and army corrupted; the people enslaved; all things vendible, and no man safe, but by such evil and infamous means as flattery and bribery; what joy can I have in my own country in this condition?" (92-93).

Dyer mentioned the cases of C. Sinclair, John Franklow (tailor and ladies habit maker), and John Hiller (bookseller). "Ridgway's situation, indeed, is singularly hard, and merits a distinct consideration" (96). Dyer pointed out that none of the imprisoned persons had deserved such a ruinous treatment.

There are numerous other cases of the kind indifferent parts of the country, which ought to be specified, and laid before the publick. I have not been able to collect them, but, I doubt not, that others will pursue the enquiry (97).

[...]

To speak once for all on this subject: - Publick utility is the basis of moral obligation and of political truth: and a consciousness of having discharged the duties of social life is the reward of publick virtue. He, whose only object is praise, never merited it; and he, who under a mask of patriotism, merely pursues his own interest, is a mean and a wicked man. "Act well on your part, there all the honour lies." - POPE. But where men unite, on legal and constitutional ground, in the case of liberty, they pledge themselves to encounter common hazards. To such persons *suum cuique*; is applicable in a participation of difficulties, as of duties; of degradations, as of distinctions; of losses, as of profits; of sympathies, as of enjoyments. Each man, indeed, possesses a right to select his friend: no one is obliged to approve the conduct of a bad man: nor can individuals, though of the most enlarged humanity, remove the inconveniences, or satisfy the wants of every sufferer. At the same time, a just man will not shrink from his duty: he will guard against harbouring illiberal suspicions, or forming unreasonable prejudices; he will not impute to persons imaginary crimes, nor listen to false and injurious representations: he will do justice to acknowledged virtues, and make allowances for human frailties. In short, one who is just cannot be malevolent: nor will he regulate his conduct by such principles, as would leave any worthy man to be the abandoned scape goat of a party; doomed to bear away either the virtues or the crimes of others, and to perish in the wilderness.

On dismissing this chapter, it may be necessary to guard against any mistaken conceptions. The author is aware that he has thrust himself into a province, where he must expect to have his sensibilities put to the trial. He says, thrust himself into it; because, he has undertaken an office to which he finds himself unequal. And must he obtrude on the reader's notice the grounds of his conduct?

Must he acknowledge, that he was acquainted in a greater or less degree with most of the above persons? That many of their cases he knew to be distressing? That he possessed a disposition to befriend them, but was destitute of the power? That he also possessed little influence with others? And that by repeated applications to a few friends on former occasions, even that influence was diminished? Fully convinced, then, that there are some cases, and that these are such, which need only to be known, to be attended to, and that hints thrown out at random by insufficient observers, are sometimes seriously taken up by powerful advocates, he has taken the present measure.

And here the exertions of the author must, he fears, slacken: he can go little further. Henceforth his own affairs must obtain his attentions: his favourite pursuits, which have been long suspended *must* be resumed: and care must be taken, that in attempting to be generous, he lose not the means to be just. It is with pleasure, he has been given to understand, that a plan is now forming among some respectable persons, to bring before the publick several of the above cases; and it is to be hoped, the plan will comprehend every case of real distress throughout the country, connected with pretended treasons and sedition. But feeble subscriptions will produce little benefit to the numerous sufferers, and reflect little honour on the publick. What has been said concerning the places of confinement, the abodes, or the publications of the above persons, were meant as hints to benevolent readers (98-101).

Chapter iv: Conclusion

THE reader further is requested, before he forms a judgement concerning the present publication, to consider its precise character, and its avowed object. The former part of it only is Dissertation; the latter is a Narrative of Facts: the former delineates the principles of Benevolence; the latter presents objects for its exercise. The detail is, sometimes, given in the exact words of respective Reports, - not with a view to save labour, but to preserve accuracy. For it is easy to see, that less patience was necessary to take a general view of those matters, than to acquire accurate information, and to reduce it to order.

With respect to the THEORY of Benevolence, few men, it is apprehended, of much reflection, will materially differ; though persons of very serious minds, and of the most benevolent intentions, may differ widely about the PRACTICE. To ascertain a truth is one thing; to apply it quite another (101-102).

[...]

Some persons, I know, object to whole system of publick charities: and they are not likely here to find an antagonist. It has been admitted, that if justice formed the basis of society, charity, in the common acceptation of the word, might slacken her exertions: her schools, her workhouses, her hospitals, and her infirmaries might, perhaps, be converted into workshops, warehouses, or granaries: human wants and miseries would be diminished: and man in his most distressed and feeble moments would receive in the sphere of private life all those succours and supports, which he is now taught to expect from the publick charities. It has even been asserted, that these institutions far from being blessings to a community, are rather its bane: and that the man who contributes largely to their support, would be more usefully and more benevolently employed, in relieving the distresses of individuals (103-105).

[...]

Hence the necessity of keeping open all the avenues to knowledge, and of allowing the freest scope of human investigation: and where knowledge precedes improvement, and peaceable measures follow steady principles, society ameliorates as it alters: men become as willing to correct their mistakes as to discover them, and advance in benevolence, as they advance in wisdom. But certainly Administration may exceed the limits of Justice.

In conclusion too, it should be observed, that Censure and Punishment also may exceed their just limits. - In the cases of the persons lately indicted for a conspiracy, treason or sedition, it should be recollected, that many of them have been pronounced NOT GUILTY by a JURY of their COUNTRY. Justice, therefore, requires that they at least should receive no pecuniary injury. In this pamphlet, indeed, those convicted of sedition, whether justly or unjustly, are coupled with such as have been pronounced innocent of higher crimes. - They are here, it is true, stated merely as cases of distress, without any reasonings; and the reader must make what use of them he thinks proper. He must, however, be reminded, that the bill of rights has declared, that excessive fines ought not to be imposed, nor cruel and unjust punishments inflicted: that the reasonableness of fines too ought not to be imposed, nor cruel and unjust punishments inflicted: that the reasonableness of fines too ought to be regulated by the determination of MAGNA CHARTA, one clause of which is, that no freemen shall be amerced for a small crime, but according to the measure of his crime, and that the amercement *should be in mercy*; and that this amercement should be according to the *particular* circumstances of the *offence* and the *offender*. In the present instance the persons are utterly incapable of paying their fines; and if they are not assisted, they and their families must be in danger of perishing (105-106).

10."I shall not be satisfied with general declarations of their love to the constitution," from: *Two Letters: The First Containing Some Remarks on the Meeting Held 5th November, 1809, to celebrate the Acquittal of Messrs. Hardy, J.H. Tooke, Thelwall, and others, in November 1794: with an Abstract of the Facts Proved on Those Trials, and also of the Confession of James Watt, Executed at Edinburgh for High Treason in October 1794. The Second containing A Short Comparative Sketch of Our Practical Constitution in Ancient Times and The Present; with some Observations on certain Assertions made by the Modern Reformers.* By A Freeholder of Cornwall. London: J. Hatchard, 1810.

Both these letters were written in response to a meeting of reformers held on the occasion of the anniversary of the acquittal of 1794. In his first letter (1-27), the anonymous author, who calls himself a freeholder of Cornwall, informed his readers about the old reform movement from a loyalist perspective: "I shall confine myself to their public character, as disclosed by their public conduct" (3). Like many earlier meetings of the London Corresponding Society, this meeting also took place in the "Crown and Anchor" tavern. On 5 November 1809, some 200 persons gathered in order to celebrate with Thomas Hardy and Jeremiah Joyce.

The author asks whether the two reform societies, the London Corresponding Society and the Constitutional Society had not tried to abolish the monarchy.[101] Univer-

[101] The Society of the Friends of the People was founded by radical Whigs in April 1792. Fox did not join, but many of his supporters did, such as members of Parliament Grey, Francis, Sheridan, Lambton, Whitbread and Erskine. The Friends of the People were more aristocratic and moderate than the working class London Corresponding Society. After the treason trials of 1794, the

sal suffrage and annual parliaments could be interpreted in this way (13). This understanding of reform had never been rejected by the reform societies. Mr. Frost and Joel Barlow had been sent to Paris as British representatives to the National Convention (13). The author quotes a paper of the Constitutional Society, whose authors believed that there might be an English National Convention soon: "This is tolerably explicit," writes the author, pointing out that, in the same year the French National Convention was established, the King was arrested and executed (14). People such as Thomas Paine and Joel Barlow had not only served as envoys of the reform societies, but were also widely read in France (14). From all of this, the author drew the following conclusion:

Summary of the Facts proved

I think it may be fairly admitted, there being no proof to the contrary, that the views of the Constitutional and London Corresponding Societies were, in their beginnings, turned only to a reform of parliament by the mode of "universal suffrage and annual parliaments." However extravagant, or even wicked (if we contemplate its almost inevitable consequences), such a project may be, I should conceive, that, by the law of England, there is nothing criminal in taking the usual and ordinary steps for its accomplishment.

But it will be seen how long these societies continued to have this object alone in view, and also whether the methods which they adopted were legal and constitutional, and consistent with the safety, or even with the existence, of any constitution in any country.

I shall observe, that these societies (of one of which Mr. Hardy was a member, and the secretary of the other) at a very early period contrived to maintain a correspondence with similar societies in Great Britain and in France. This act alone, if there were no guilt in the actual letters, is not criminal; but the practice is too much in unison with that of Jacobins of Paris, and the Affiliated Societies of France, not to afford matter and ground for the most jealous suspicion. Such, indeed, was the fact, as it

---

Friends of the People disappeared again. Holcroft referred to the London Corresponding Society and the Constitutional Society, which was founded by Tooke and his associates in 1771. Tooke reactivated the Society for Constitutional Information (SCI) in 1791 and helped to found the London Corresponding Society (LCS). The LCS was founded at the Bell Tavern, Exeter Street, Strand, on 25 January 1792. Thomas Hardy was its treasurer and secretary. "The Society was a poor man's club and its penny a week subscription was modelled on the journeymen's clubs of the time", as Cobban 1960: 119, explains.

appears, that, in very early days, a society in London, called "The Friends of the People," of which many of the most distinguished characters of opposition were members, did venture, in a letter addressed to Mr. Hardy, to find some fault with their proceedings; after which I do not find further traces of their correspondence.

But two very striking and remarkable facts, which throw considerable light on the views of the Society, occurred nearly about the same period, 1792, 1793.

In the correspondence that took place with a society at "Stockport", the Chairman of this Society (Mr. Frost) expresses his doubts whether the grievances he complains of can be redressed "*whilst the House of Lords retains its present authority in the Legislature*," and "*whether liberty of conscience can ever be obtained whilst the Bishops maintain their seal*." On this the society at Stockport request an explicit opinion.

A society at Norwich ask the Societies, through Mr. Hardy, in express terms, whether their language about Reform is only ostensible, *or "whether it is not their private design to rip up monarchy by the roots, and place democracy in its stead?"*

I think nothing can be more clear, than that if the views of these Societies had been fairly directed *to reform only*, their disavowal of such designs should have been prompt and explicit: no such disavowal appears in their answers, which are worded with the most studied ambiguity and caution. They talk of their hatred to *despotism* and *aristocracy*, the meaning of which terms is pretty well understood; and they then announce their intention of sending a deputation to the National Convention of France; and they invite the Stockport society to unite with them, adding, *"That they shall not enter into the probable effects of such a measure - effects which your Society will not fail to discover"* (11-13).

[...]

I am fully sensible that I could furnish you, from the Trial of Mr. Hardy, with many more facts, which clearly explain and prove that the views of these societies extended far beyond *any mode of Parliamentary Reform*. I shall not detail to you the patriotic songs that were given, all of which inculcate popular revolution, and soften of disguise its attendant horrors (15).

One paper, presented as a playbill, is too remarkable to be passed over. It is entitled, "*The Guillotine; or, George's Head in a Basket.*" It states: "In the course of the evening, will be exhibited *Tight-rope Dancing from the Lamp-post, by Messrs. Canterbury, York, Durham, &c.* The whole to conclude with *a grand Decapitation of Placemen, Pensioners, &c.*"[102]

Now I will not say, that this is a direct exhortation to a deluded and irritated mob, to murder the King, the King's servants, and the Bishops; but I will say, it was an atrocious attempt to lessen the horror which the minds of genuine Englishmen, of all classes, feel on the contemplation of assassination and regicide. It is impossible not to connect these sentiments, so artfully promulgated and impressed on the minds of the unwary, with the repeated attacks made, in those days, on the person of our gracious Sovereign.

I here close my account of the facts that develop the probable views of these societies (15-16).

One of the texts distributed by the opposition was entitled "The guillotine; or, George's Head in a Basket". What annoyed the Freeholder of Cornwall most was the fact that the members of the London Corresponding Society and the Constitutional Society regarded themselves as the legitimate representatives of the people, and therefore believed that they had the right to call an English National Convention (15).

The author claimed that Hardy was in contact with Watt and Downie before the Edinburgh Trials (21). The meeting at Chalk Farm, on 14 April 1794, was particularly "violent" (22). He quoted Justice Eyre, who had called the resolutions of this meeting a call for an uprise. The author regarded the resolutions of the reform societies as extremely dangerous. He quoted from one of the resolutions which promises:

... that the social contract would be actually dissolved, and that they should be driven to an immediate appeal to that incontrovertible maxim of eternal justice, That the safety of the people was the supreme, and, in cases of necessity, the only law.

---

[102] See also David Bindman, *The Shadow of the Guillotine: Britain and the French Revolution* (London: British Museum Publications, 1989).

But these societies did not confine themselves to resolutions; they provided pikes from Sheffield; they purchased muskets in London; they formed armed associations at Lambeth and in London, for disciplining and training the different members of the societies, and for the express purpose of supporting the Convention by force; -- an offence which is most distinctly declared to be treason by Mr. Justice Eyre.

But, from Mr. Hardy's acquittal, we are to conclude that the jury decided that this proof (though the facts are undeniable) did not *personally* attach on *him* (22).

The author maintained that the reformers had not only passed dangerous resolutions, but had also purchased weapons:

... they provided pikes from Sheffield; they purchased muskets in London; they formed armed associations at Lambeth and in London, [...] But from Mr. Hardy's acquittal, we are to conclude that the jury decided that this proof (though the facts are undeniable) did not personally attach on him (23).

The author asked his readers not to trust the radicals. He believed that the meeting in 1809 still had traitorous intentions:

One method by which they will attempt to evade the accusation does occur to me. They will tell us, that the only object of the meeting was to celebrate the honesty of the jury that acquitted Mr. Hardy (24).

The Farmer did not understand why the jurors, who acquitted the accused reformers in 1794, were praised more than any other jury in the 16 years following the treason trials.

But if they wish to give a fair colour to their assertion, let them again meet at the Crown and Anchor, and let their club-room, for once, resound with a language never yet held within its walls.

I shall not be satisfied with general declarations of their love to the constitution, nor with their drinking the king's health with the acclamations of three times three. No; this will not do. Let them distinctly set forth and specify the overt acts proved on the trial of Mr. Hardy, and let them, in strong, clear, unequivocal resolutions, declare their abhorrence of such proceedings, as tending to subvert the constitution of the country, and place in its room an ungovernable and tyrannical representative government, which, after involving all classes, rich and poor, in one common scene of desolation and calamity, would itself become the prey of the first military adventurer who had address and courage enough to attack it!

A FREEHOLDER OF CORNWALL
March, 1810.

VIII. Radicals and Reformers

The Treason Trials are embedded in a larger political context that was defined by the repercussions of the American Revolution and the traditions of the old reform movement, the agenda of which had been voiced for the first time in the 1770s by people such as John Wilkes. The radicals' understanding of the War for Independence and the resulting experiment in government was rooted "in a complex network of social attitudes, spiritual values, intellectual principles, and ideological requirements" typical of the middle ranks of society (Bonwick 1977: 3). Most of the radicals were concerned with parliamentary reform, and many of them were particularly interested in ending discriminatory legislation directed against them as religious dissenters. Bonwick suggests the term "ideology" to describe "their corpus of ethical values, political principles, and empirical programs" (4).

The impact of the French Revolution and the centenary of the so-called "Glorious Revolution" also contributed to the political agenda of the 1790s, which was dominated by the campaign for democratisation, on the one hand, and the fear of Revolution in Great Britain on the other hand.

Michael Scrivener emphasized that the "LCS advocated and practised a participatory democracy that had its finest moments in the late 1795 demonstrations against the Gagging Acts: tens of thousands of artisans, laborers and middling-class shopkeepers, professionals and tradesmen, nonviolently protested and discussed the proposed legislation."[103] Scrivener points out that it is not sufficient to regard the so-called Jacobins as dissatisfied dissenters and as radical reformers who wanted to change the parliamentary system: "'Jacobin' also signifies participatory democracy, an expanding public sphere, activism, internationalism, and a rationalistic rigor" (*ibid.*).

Therefore, among the most original contributions to this public sphere are the countless songs, published on single sheets and in pamphlets, which constituted an attempt to gain the attention of readers with original images and satirical exaggerations. Some of the most notorious authors and publishers, such as Richard Lee, were as prolific as they were short-lived. Others, like Isaac Eaton, fought a more than yearlong struggle for freedom of the press.

---

[103] Michael Henry Scrivener, *Seditious Allegories: John Thelwall and Jacobin Writing* (University Park: Pennsylvania State University Press, 2001), 42.

Radical authors did not just try to oppose the cultural hegemony protected by the loyalist Tories (and to a lesser degree by the Whigs), but also tried to establish a counter-culture that they hoped would help to change people's minds and democratise the political and legal systems. The following two sections on the political culture of the 1790s complement the more specific selection of contributions from the legal culture of the Treason Trials in the preceding chapters. They illustrate the opposing literary reactions to the specific political positions. These texts are intended to achieve a certain effect in contested public spheres in which political opponents claim the same narrative and metaphorical resources.

1. "But Reason and Philosophy,/ Began to plant Democracy," from: *The Tree of Liberty, A New Song. Respectfully Addressed to the Swinish Multitude, by their Fellow Citizen, William England.* London, [1794?]

There are several songs of this title, which differ slightly, bearing witness to the success of this sort of publication. Barrell points out that Richard Lee, who lived at his mother's shop in St Ann's Court, Dean Street, Soho, probably set up as a bookseller and traded under the sign of 'The Tree of Liberty' by February 1795 (2000: 611). Only one month later, Lee had to move the Tree of Liberty to a new shop at 47 Haymarket. Barrell believes that this was due to an attack on the St Ann's Court shop by Church and King rioters (*ibid.*).

FRIENDS of LIBERTY a while attend,
To these remarks that here are penn'd;
A most tremend'ous story:
Some short time since, each bold Briton
Boasted of freedom, such as none
In Spain, or France, or any one,
In Italy, or Germany,
'Till the contest with America[104],
Curtail'd proud Albion's glory.

The spirit of brave America,
First stood forth for liberty;
Tho' then 'twas but in theory.
But the despot Louis did incline,
And Spain and Holland did combine;

[104] The author refers to the Declaration of Independence (1776) and the ensuing War for Independence (1776-1783).

Not knowing of the grand design,
To plant the Tree of Liberty,
By ambition prompted on were they,
To crop great George's glory.

Those worthies never dreamt this plan,
Was to establish Rights of Man,
And doom each tyrant's downfall.
Brave Washington the MAN WAS HE,
Who nourish'd up fait Freedom's Tree,
Which brought forth fruit abundantly:
A noble treat, delicious, sweet,
And PAINE declar'd it was complete,
So wish'd it universal.

The slaves of despots view'd this Tree,
And hop'd such fruit at home to see,
When they returned tither.
Some seeds procur'd during their stay,
They brought across th' Atlantic sea;
But their soil and them did not agree,
To cultivate so speedily,
For Priest-craft and Aristocracy
Were so combin'd together.

But Reason and Philosophy,
Began to plant Democracy,
And root out all the evil:
Of superstitious Priest-craft vile,
And Bigotry, Belzebub's child;
Which had the land so long defil'd,
By it's Infamy and Sophistry,
First introduc'd by Popery,
Which sprung up from the Devil.

Democracy so deep it struck,
That the old System quickly shook,
And totter'd all together.
Blind Superstition tumbled down,

And Louis[105] cry'd my Crown! my Crown!
The summon'd all the despots down;
Who did resolve that he should flee,
And they'd establish Monarchy.
More safe and sound than ever.

This speedy flight of Lewis prov'd
His people by him were not belov'd,
And that he was unfaithful.
Yet Louis did his vows renew,
That he'd be loyal, just, and true,
Tho' sole Monarchy was all his view,
For nothing less for him would do;
And it justly prov'd his overthrow,
And made him mount the Scaffold.[106]

This news when Numps[107] our King had got,
He goggl'd, grinn'd, and cry'd What, what!

---

[105] Louis XVI, King of France, had been imprisoned in August 1792. In January 1793 he was condemned and executed. One month later, France declared war on England and Holland. In *Rights of Man*, for which he was prosecuted in December 1792, Paine made a distinction between the King and the system he served: "It was not against Louis the XVIth, but against the despotic principles of the government, that the nation revolted. These principles had not their origin in him, but in the original establishment, many centuries back" (1998: 97).

[106] For Barrell, the unique significance of Louis' execution for British politics is the starting point for his study on *Imagining the King's Death*: "It is high treason in British law to imagine the king's death. But after the execution of Louis XVI in 1793, everyone in Britain must have found themselves imagining that the same fate might befall George III" (Barrell 2000: n.p.). See also John Barrell's earlier research, "Sad Stories: Louis XVI, George III, and the Language of Sentiment," in: *Refiguring Revolutions: Aesthetics and Politics from the English Revolution to the Romantic Revolution*, ed. Kevin Sharpe and Steven N. Zwicker (Berkeley and Los Angeles: University of California Press, 1998), 75-98.

[107] According to Barrell (2000: 215), "Gosling saw a mock playbill exhibited in Edwards's shop, which Edwards said Baxter had given him, and which advertised the 'new and entertaining Farce' Of 'LA GUILLOTINE; or, GEORGE'S HEAD IN THE BASKET', to be played, in one version of the bill, on 30 January, the anniversary of Charles I's execution, in another on All Fool's Day 1794. The central character, 'Numpy the Third', would be played by 'Mr. Gwelp' himself '(Being the last time of his appearing in that character'). The climax of the piece would be an exhibition of 'Tight Rope Dancing, from the Lamp Post' by the bishops; the singing Of 'BOB SHAVE GREAT GEORGE OUR-'; and, finally, 'A GRAND DECAPITATION', apparently presided over by Fox, Sheridan, Grey, and Erskine." For the text, which was also quoted in the *Trial of Thomas Hardy*, 1794 (*State Trials*, XXIV, pp. 681-3), see Cobban 1960: 285-6.

What! have they slain my brother?
Is this the fruit of Freedom's Tree,
That grew in England antiently?
Which was so cut and hewn away,
Down to the root it to destroy?
But, perhaps, the same may me annoy; --
Oh! how PAINE makes me shudder.

Go, go, go search if you can find,
Any of the Stump remain behind,
That's likely to recover.
In PAINE they sought, in PAINE they found
Some shoots were springing up around
And rooting in the solid ground,
Which hastily they cut down,
And sent far off across the sea*,[108]
In hopes thereby to smother.

But other roots so deep had struck
And grafted in the solid rock
Of Justice, Truth, and Reason;
That all the arts that could be found,
By Mitre's, Maces, and the Crown,
To root them up and pull them down,
Or blast them by Corruption,
Liberty so firmly held her ground,
And e'en def'y High Treason.

The tyrants continu'd to combine,
Our Rights and Reason to purloin,
And threaten all their thunder.
But they may labour with all their might,
And vent at Reason all their spite,
The grumbling swine will still unite,

---

* In allusion to those Patriotic Worthies, MARGAROT, MUIR, SKIRVING, PALMER, GERALD, &c. now suffering Exile in the Cause of PARLIAMENTARY REFORM.

[108] This is a reference to the 1793 Edinburgh Trials in which Joseph Gerrald, Thomas Muir, Thomas Palmer and Maurice Margarot were tried for sedition and sentenced to transportation to Botany Bay. Gerrald (or Gerald) died at the age of 33, not long after his arrival in Australia.

And with grunting sound,
Their proud feelings wound,
And Liberty proclaim around,
To their dismay and wonder.

2. "Hang them, and bang them, and hang them up all!" from: *Brother Burke to Brother Wyndham, A New Song, for the New Year*. London, [1794?][109]

This anonymous song presents an imagined conversation between the two main opponents of the radical movement, Edmund Burke and William Wyndham (1759-1834), who conspire against the radicals and seem to agree in killing them all. Made Baron Grenville in 1790, Wyndham became leader of the House of Lords. He was Home Secretary from 1789 to 1791, and Pitt's Secretary of State for Foreign Affairs from 1791 to 1801. His greatest achievement was the abolition of the British overseas slave trade. Grenville introduced the *Habeas Corpus* Suspension Act in 1794 and both, Burke and Wyndham, played a major role in constructing the case against Thomas Hardy and others in 1794.[110] Unconstitutional in the means suggested, but recognizable as a satirical hyperbole in the context of the Edinburgh and London Trials, this song must be from the pen of a radical author who wants to denounce the government and reduce the trials to their alleged purpose of executing the major figures of the radical movement.

---

[109] There are no details available on the date of publication. *The Eighteenth-Century Short Title Catalogue* suggests the year 1794; Barrell believes that it might have been published one year later, in 1795 (2000: 18).

[110] For more on the character differences between Burke, Wyndham, Dundas and Pitt in the perception of reformers such as Thelwall and Holcroft, see Barrell (2000: 18).

AIR. -- LORD CHESTERFIELD'S, O BROTHER SANDY, &c.

I.
O brother Wyndham! what must we do,
  Hang them, and bang them, and hang them up all!
To smash and to smother that Jacobin crew?
  Hang them, and bang them, and hang them up all.

To arms, to arms, REEVES' boys[111] to arms,
  Our true TORY cause for courage doth call:
In country and city, against the banditti;
  Hang them, and bang them, and hang them up all.

II.
They're a numerous host, and a desperate band,
  Hang them, and bang them, and hang them up all;
Who propagate *Heresy* over the land;
  Hang them, and bang them, and hang them up all.
To arms, to arms, &c.

III.
They say they are *Whigs*, but they're no such thing,
  Hang them, and bang them, and hang them up all;
They care not a fig for the CHURCH, or the KING:
  Hang them, and bang them, and hang them up all.
To arms, to arms, &c.

IV.
They say they are *Christians*, but that's a mere trope,
  Hang them, and bang them, and hang them up all!
They laugh at the *Prelates*, they laugh at he POPE![112]
  Hang them, and bang them, and hang them up all.

---

[111] John Reeves (1752?-1829), King's printer, lawyer, legal writer, and founder and organizer of the Association for Preserving Liberty and Property Against Republicans and Levellers in 1792, was himself prosecuted in 1796 for his absolutist ideas on the English Government. For one of Reeves' resolutions, which was agreed upon in a meeting of the Association, see Cobban 1960: 276-277. In a speech which Thelwall delivered in the Beaufort Buildings and which was published in *The Tribune* (No. xxviii, 123), he called Reeves "the grand arch inquisitor!" (Claeys 1995: 234).

[112] This malicious statement denounces the Tories as Roman Catholics.

To arms, to arms, &c.

V.
A plant they have lately imported by sea,
Hang them, and bang them, and hang them up all:
They call it, what impudence! LIBERTY'S TREE!
Hang them, and bang them, and hang them up all.
To arms, to arms, &c.

VI.
'Tis a plant of a dangerous, damnable breed:
Hang them, and bang them, and hang them up all!
Reformation its *root* -- *Revolutions* its *seed*!
Hang them, and bang them, and hang them up all.
To arms, to arms, &c.

VII.
They pretend it was *once*, an endemial shrub:
Hang them, and bang them, and hang them up all!
But this is no more than the *tale of a tub*:
Hang them, and bang them, and hang them up all.
To arms, to arms, &c.

VIII.
It may grow on the *Seine*, it may grow on the *Po*:
Hang them, and bang them, and hang them up all!
But we trust we shall ne'er on the *Thames* see it grow:
Hang them, and bang them, and hang them up all.
To arms, to arms, &c.

IX.
What thanks, my dear Wyndham, what praises are due,
Hang them, and bang them, and hang them up all!
To Grenville and Portland, to Pitt and to You?
Hang them, and bang them, and hang them up all.
To arms, to arms, &c.

X.
But let not, ah! let not your efforts decrease;
      Hang them, and bang them, and hang them up all!
I tremble to think of a Regicide Peace!
      Hang them, and bang them, and hang them up all.
To arms, to arms, &c.

XI.
But what joyful tidings this moment I hear:
      Hang them, and bang them, and hang them up all!
Lord MUM is come back, with a flea in his ear:
      Hang them, and bang them, and hang them up all.
To arms, to arms, &c.

XII.
I foresee his return will raise clamour and noise;
      Hang them, and bang them, and hang them up all!
But stop up your ears, and regard not the voice!
      Hang them, and bang them, and hang them up all,
To arms, to arms, &c.

XIII.
'Tis only the barking of Jacobin dogs!
      Hang them, and bang them, and hang them up all;
'Tis only the grunting of Jacobin hogs!
      Hang them, and bang them, and hang them up all.
To arms, to arms, &c.

XIV.
Should Sinclairs,[113] or Joneses,[114] or Thelwalls, or Tookes,

---

[113] Charles Sinclair was accused of sedition in Edinburgh. His trial had begun in February 1794 and was abandoned after a month. This "led him to be suspected of having become a Government informant", but he might have been saved by the influence of his family, as he was the nephew of Sir James Sinclair (Barrell 2000: 149).

[114] John Gale Jones was a missionary delegate from the London Corresponding Society and was sent to rural reform societies to explain to them how to evade and not challenge the Two Bills of 1795. He was accompanied by Binns. Both were arrested and imprisoned in Birmingham. Jones was convicted of sedition, although never sentenced. The cost of defending them contributed to the downfall of the London Corresponding Society. John Gale Jones supported the use of violence, if necessary, to achieve reforms (see Barrell 2000: 217 and Goodwin 1979: 398-402).

Hang them, and bang them, and hang them up all!
Assemble their auditors -- shoot them like rooks!
Hang them, and bang them, and hang them up all.
To arms, to arms, &c.

XV.
The strings of our statutes more rigidly draw:
Hang them, and bang them, and hang them up all!
And make a Procrustian bed -- of the law:
Hang them, and bang them, and hang them up all.
To arms, to arms, &c.

XVI.
Steal in a new Bill, 'ere the end of Recess,
Hang them, and bang them, and hang them up all!
And the relics of Liberty tear from the press:
Hang them, and bang them, and hang them up all.
To arms, to arms, &c.

XVII.
Then, let some Inquisitor watch that --- no elf:
Hang them, and bang them, and hang them up all!
Write politic pamphlets --- save Reeves and MYSELF!
Hang them, and bang them, and hang them up all.
To arms, to arms, &c.

3. "The Law is the only expression of the public will," from: *The Rights of Men and Citizens [and other songs and prayer]*. London: printed for Citizen Lee, [ca. 1794?].

This pamphlet was printed on both sides of a single sheet. The text on "rights" and "duties" is presented in two parallel columns; the prayer is printed below "Rights and Duties", on the front side. "Citizen" Lee summarized the essential ideological assumptions of the radical movement; thus, popularising the political theories of Tom Paine and others. The emphasis on a civil religion suggests that the author may have read Paine's *Age of Reason*, published in 1794.[115] In France, the Rousseauist de-Christianising campaign, which had tried to replace Christianity with a civil religion, came to an end in 1794.

---

[115] See Wilson Carey McWilliams, "Civil Religion in the Age of Reason: Thomas Paine on Liberalism, Redemption, and Revolution," in: *Social Research* 54,3 (1987), 447-490.

The Rights of Men and Citizens.

ALL Men have equal Rights.
These unalienable Rights are Liberty, Security, Property, and Resistance of Oppression.

Liberty is the Right of saying, writing, and doing whatever we please, without injuring our Neighbour, the State, or ourselves.

Security is the Right of being protected by the public force against evil doers.

Property consists in every one doing what he pleases with his own, excepting those who are under age, or deprived of their reason.

Resistance to Oppression is the Right of taking up arms against open violence, and illegal or tyrannical compulsion.

The Nation is the only sovereign; all power is delegated by her, and ought to be employed for her service.
Every one entrusted with the public power, is answerable to the Nation; but must only be tried by the tribunal established for that purpose by the Nation.

The Nation only, of her Representatives, freely elected, can pass laws, or impose taxes.

The Law is the only expression of the public will, and the supreme rule for all the particular powers. No one can either elect of be elected, judge or be judged, no one ought to obey or disobey, but in virtue of the Law.

Without these RIGHTS the PEOPLE are SLAVES.

The Duties of Men and Citizens

ALL Men are bound by reciprocal Duties.

These inviolable Duties are Subordination, Benevolence, Justice, and Obedience to the Laws.

Subordination is the respect and tractable disposition due from children to their parents, from scholars to their masters, and from inferiors to their superiors in office.

Benevolence consists in the regard, the care and assistance which we owe to each other in all the troublesome situations of life. Justice requires us to keep our promises, to respect property, to be grateful for favours received, and ready to do favours when needful.

Obedience to the Laws comprehends the observance of Regulations, fidelity to the Magistrates, and the union of the Citizens to suppress tumults.

Insurrections are never allowable, but in cases of the utmost extremity, and after legal remonstrances.

Every disturber of the public tranquillity deserves not only to be seized and punished, but also to be executed by the public.

The Nation only, or her Representatives, freely elected, can interfere with the established order, and the government.

The Law, passed by the Legislative Body, the Representatives of the People, is a kind of *civil religion*, which ought to unite all hearts and all arms; the very name of the Law ought to act, instead of muskets and bayonets.

Without these DUTIES the PEOPLE are SAVAGES.

THE PRAYER of a TRUE CITIZEN.

SOVEREIGN of Nature! Thou Supreme Legislator, who maintainest the world in such wonderful order, who governest it by immutable laws, without which this vast machine would fall in pieces, all the elements be out of order and confounded, and the most dreadful disorder succeed to that harmony which commands our admiration! Teach us to respect thy laws, which alone can bind and keep in order the various parts of the body politic: Teach us to respect the Magistrates who superintend the execution of

the laws: Enable us to love our country, which, by the wisdom of her laws, restores to man his native dignity, and procures to him all the happiness which he can enjoy in this life: Enable us to love that pure and holy religion, of which thou art the Author; which will direct all our actions to thee, as to their only end; which will lead us, by every thought, word, and deed, to promote the advantage and good order of the society, as being continually in thy sight!
(From the Catechism of the French Constitution)

Printed for CITIZEN LEE, at the British Tree of Liberty, Haymarket.

The Tree of Liberty

Tune - *Mulberry Tree*

I.
The great Reformation approaching we hail,
'Gainst Statesmen and Priests, Truth and Reason prevail,
Triumphant the Planters of LIBERTY see
Preparing the Soil of the Globe for the Tree.

CHORUS.
All shall yield to FREEDOM's fair Tree,
Bend to thee
Blest Liberty!
Heroes are they now planting thee,
And all their great Names immortal shall be.

II.
Away with the Splendour and Pomp of a Court,
Our Toil shall no longer the Baubles support,
No longer the Slaves of a Statesman and King,
Inspir'd by the Muses of Freedom we Sing.
All shall yield, &c.

III.
Ye Trees of Corruption in Courts that abound,
The Fruits ye produce are a Curse to the Ground;
In the Soil where ye flourish no others can grow
But now see the Axe at your Root aim the Blow.

All shall yield, &c.

IV.
May Heav'n guard the PEOPLE of Britain and France,
And crush all their Foes where'er they advance,
An end to the Councils of Traitors combin'd
The downfall of Tyrants and Peace to Mankind.
All shall yield, &c.

V.
How great in the Ages to come, and how dear
Your Names and your Conquests great Heroes appear,
With Rapture they'll read, and your Actions review,
While under the Shade of the Tree rais'd by you
All shall yield to FREEDOM's fair Tree,
      Bend to thee
            Blest Liberty,
Heroes are they now planting thee,
And all their great Names immortal shall be.

The SWINISH MULTITUDE's
Address to Mr. BURKE[116]

Tune - Derry Down

I.
Apostate! give over your Eloquence, pray!
No more on the subject of Monarchy say,
Exalted in Office, and fed by the Swine, -
If we should desert you, you'll catch a Decline,
      Tumble down! down! down! come ye down!

[116] This poem was written and published by Thomas Spence in 1792 under the title "Burke's Address to the 'Swinish Multitude'" [Satirical verses by Thomas Spence] and "The Swinish Multitude's Reply to Burke's Address" (London, [November 1792?]). Lee's version omits the first part of the publication, "Burke's Address to the 'Swinish Multitude'" and does not include all the stanzas of the second part of the original.

II.
But we cannot well brook to be called *the Swine*,
Let Man have his Rights, and *the Epithet's thine*;
Apostate thou art, -- and allur'd by the Hire,
Return'd like the *Sow* that was wash'd -- *to the Mire*.
Tumble down! &c.

This stanza is from Spence's 1792 version of this poem:

Our thanks we return -- You may think it a joke,
For the blessed enquiry your writings provoke;
We thank you for thwarting your own base design,
The Bacon and Pork are restor'd to the Swine.
Tumble down! &c.

III.
No longer like Asses we tamely submit,
And tremble like Fiends at the Mouth of a *Pit*:
You are but our Servants, our delegate *Powers*,
If we speak but the Word, you must fade and like Flowers
Tumble down! &c.

IV.
Too long, it is true, we resembled the Swine,
And stood in the Market all passive as Kine,
But no longer the grunting of Swine shall ye hear,
The Voice of the LION now pierces your Ear.
Tumble down! &c.

Apostate! Beware, and with Caution advance,
The Ground you are treading, is fertile as France;
If you once overheat and inflame the *Old Bull*,
He'll toss the rich Dogs from their soft *Packs of Wool*.
Tumble down! &c.

VI.
No longer, *Oppressor*, insult the Opprest,
Our Grievances *may*, and they *shall* be redrest;
In the Fable your Picture - behold in that Glass --
"The LION was rous'd by the Heel of an Ass!"

The following (perhaps more learned) stanza is from the 1792 version of Spence's original poem; it cannot be found in Lee's more popularised version.

No longer, thou Sophist, attempt to deceive,
To plunder, and blind us, and laugh in your sleeve;
Apostate, thy payment, for pimping -- depends
On those you're insulting -- and with them it ends.
Tumble down! &c.

VII.
The Faults of the People you freely make known,
While a Mantle of Charity covers the Throne;
But in France 'tis a Doctrine the People know well,
That Kings are as apt as the Mob to rebel --
and come down! &c.

VIII.
Proclamations we dread not, - but rather desire,
They say to the Sleepers - "Arise and enquire!"
For the Good of the Nation no more do we seek,
Than a *new Proclamation* at least once a week.
Tumble down! &c.

IX.
The Pow'r of Enquiry no Despot can bind,
For Millions already have Freedom of Mind
Let *Reason* be heard, and let Reason go round,
And soon on the Globe, not a Tyrant be found.
Tumble down! down! down! Tumbled down!

Sold by R. Lee, at the TREE of LIBERTY, No. 2, St. Ann's Court, Dean-street, Soho.

4. "Thus shall thou speak unto the children of Albo," from: *The Book of Bobs. Being a Serious Caution to the Pensioned Tribe of Albo.* London: Printed for R. Bedford, and Sold by all the Patriotic Booksellers [1795?].

The eight-page pamphlet is written in the fashion of a prophet's warning to the government to save peace and order by carrying out reforms. In the *Book of Bobs* the king's death is imagined, fulfilling God's retribution for oppression and persecution. It describes, as Barrell points out, "persecution, from the beginnings of organized popular radicalism until late 1795, in the mixed form of a chronicle of a past and a prophecy of a future time" (2000: 543). One of King George's punishments will be a return of his madness; and he will eventually be punished with a rod that will transform into a poisonous serpent. The poem directly attributes to the treason trials of 1794 a special status in the English history of the 1790s. In his concluding line, the author warns the ruling class, "the pensioned tribe", to "redress the grievances of the starving Swine, least the multitude devour them like hogs-wash" (1795: 8).[117]

Chap I

1 Know ye not that I heard a voice in the night-time speak unto me, saying thus shall thou speak unto the children of Albo, and say unto them.

2 The rulers of the Earth, and the King thereof oppress thee, and ye are become Slaves, unto men, and ye have worshiped them as gods and idols, which are no more then ye yourselves.

3 And it shall come to pass in the days of Avaricious King of Albo that the children of Albo shall assemble and meet together in great and mighty bodies in various parts of the Kingdom.

---

[117] The allusion to Burke's "swinish multitude" was a popular motive in polemical writings of the radical movement. Burke coined the expression for the French revolutionaries in Reflections on the Revolution in France: "... learning will be cast into the mire and trodden down under the hoofs of a swinish multitude" (Burke 1981: 130). For the most popular radical replies to Burke, see Spence 1792 and Parkinson 1793. See Scrivener (2001: 110): "Spence parodies Burke's swinish trope and its attendant class attitudes, while focusing principally on issues of taxation in such a way as to raise the question: whose society is this? to whom does Britain belong? Spence's Burke dismisses the democratic reformers as presumptuous overreachers [...]. The contradiction Spence exploits is that the disenfranchised pay most of the taxes, which are then in turn used as welfare for the rich."

4 And they shall send the wise men from the East and from the West, from the North and from the South.

5 And they shall say unto the rulers of the land, and the King thereof, and unto him that is over the tribute.

6 Thus hath the Children of Albo commanded us to speak unto you saying.

7 Ye have erred and strayed from their ways and led them away like lost swine, and taken the rooting, which they have rooted from their nose, for thy own stye.

8 Ye have followed too much the vices, and desires of your own hearts, ye have offended against their lawful ways.

9 Ye have left undone those things, which ye ought to have done, and done those things, which ye ought not to have done, and there is no *truth* in you.

10 They ask for peace and ye gave them war, ye have sent their brethren to battle, and they have been slain with very great slaughter.

11 And those whom thou hast not sent to battle have thou oppressed with very great taxes, and ye have divided the taxes amongst yourselves, and to whom it pleaseth thee.

12 Thou hath lived in pomp, and in pride, and in luxury, and hath been wanton, and the lord our God hath not chastised you.

13 But the time draweth nigh unto hand, that ye shall repent of the evil which ye hath done, but he people will not hearken unto your voice.

14 They said unto you make our yoke a little lighter, that we may get bread for ourselves, for our wives, and for our children; but ye would not hearken unto their voice.

15 But instead thereof, ye chastised them with whips and with scorpions, and gave their bread unto strangers, which fighteth for your lust, the gold and the silver, also, hath thou taken from thy people, and given unto foreign PRINCES, as it pleaseth thee,

16 And the children of Albo, said unto thee REFORM, and ye hallowed out TREASON, TREASON!

17 And these men whom the children chose to say unto you REFORM, cast ye into dungeons, and sought to take away their lives, that ye might pursue on in your wickedness, but the lord their God saw that they had done no evil, and so he delivered them from out of your hand, and from your wrath.

18 But because thou hath done this and was not ashamed, will the lord God cause the people whom thou hath opprest, to forsake thy laws, and resist from thy power for thou hath dealt wickedly with men.

19 And it shall come to pass in that day, that an evil spirit shall come upon thee, and thou shall be much troubled, because of the evil, which thou hath done.

20 And thou shall send for the player upon harps, the organs, the symbols, and flutes, to play unto thee to make thee merry, yet thou shall be sad, neither shall the evil spirit depart from thee.

21 The *Wallisite* and the *Docterites*, and all the *Parisites* shall attend thee, and thee shall know what aileth thee, yet they shall not comfort thee, because of the evil which thou hast done unto this people.

22 And when the *wise* men have done speaking that which the children of ALBO have commanded, them, and thou answer them roughly, and will not yet hearken unto their voice, nor make their yoke lighter, but addeth thereto and oppress them more and more, and continue to rule them with a rod of iron, then shall the *wise* men return and say unto the people, all that which thou hath said unto them.

23 Then shall the people say one to another what portion have we in an-over, or in the elector thereof, or in *William the Bastardite*, then every man will haste to the King's palace, and return not until he spake unto them, and if he answers them yet roughly, then will they bring down the kings house and the walls thereof, even unto the ground, and make the king to flee from their presence lest they smite him.

24 Then shall he haste to the house of God, which is called *Sanctus Paulus* unto this day, and he shall pray unto the lord, and the lord will not hear him because he has done evil in the sight of God.

25 And so it shall be that while the king prayeth unto the lord, that the people shall pursue after him and shall mock him, and the king shall be afraid.

26 And the graven image which standeth on the front towards the west of the church, shall be thrown down, and broken into many pieces, and cast unto the king, and the people will curse him even to his face.

27 And he shall haste to his chariot to flee unto *Anover*[118], but shall not escape because of the multitude of people.

28 And they shall cast the pieces of the graven image, unto the chariot and break it so that he shall not ride therein.

29 Then shall he go unto Dear-side! and there shall he behold a man standing in the midst thereof with a rod in his right hand whose name is SATAN sir-named LUCIFER, and he shall haste to him and say, unto him save me Oh! thou true prophet.

30 Then shall the prophet liftup the rod that is in his right hand to smite the people therewith, and so it shall be that while the prophet lifteth up his hand to smite the people,

31 The rod which he holdeth in his right hand shall become a serpent, and shall *spit in* the KING's face, so that it *sting* him, and he dieth therewith.

The Author being an enemy to riots, and tumults, strenuously advise the pensioned tribe to redress the grievances of the starving Swine, least the multitude devour them like hogs-wash.

Finis

---

[118] i.e. Hanover

5. "We live in times when any sentiments in favor of Liberty are dangerous to their author," from: James Sansom, *Oppression; or, the Abuse of Power, with the Recovery and Establishment of Freedom in America and France. A Poem. Interspersed with Occasional Strictures on many of the most Celebrated Characters of the Present Age. Addressed to the Reforming Societies in Great Britain*. London: Printed and sold by J. Davenport, 1795.

James Sansom, the liveryman of London, hopes that the achievements of the French Revolution – freedom and sovereignty for the people – may find their way to Great Britain. In the preface to his five-part poem, he addresses the "Reforming Societies":

To all Reforming Societies in Great Britain

"We live in times when any sentiments in favor of Liberty are dangerous to their author; when the contemptible ignorance and tameness of individuals gives every encouragement to the rapid advances of tyranny, and when every delusion is practiced to stimulate the base passions of fear and interest, to a blind subserviency to the ruinous conduct of Oppression's Prime Minister.

It is to your efforts the world look for a renovation of Rights, long lost, much talked about, little understood or felt; and of which only so much of the shadow remains, as to enable to produce a sort of stage-effect in our senates, for the amusement of the public. When we see Ministers and Opposition wrangling in public, and drinking in private; when the most cruel, wanton, or ruinous measures pass unnoticed, or in concert, we must lament the deplorable farce, and despise the actors.

From the amazing accessions daily to the number and respectability of your societies, the most lively hopes arise - TRUTH is mighty! and must prevail, when the corrupting durst of Ministers is forgotten!

I remain, Gentlemen,
With the most ardent Wishes for a speedy,
radical and effectual REFORM,

And with every Sentiment of Respect,

Hounslow,

October 19, 1795 THE AUTHOR

(iii-iv)

Oppression

Part One

Rise, rise, my Muse, with kindling fire,
And Freedom's sacred love inspire!
No vulgar strain demands the strings,
No mean attempt to flatter Kings;
Oppression rouses all my patriot mind,
And Liberty the cause of all mankind!

And rise with sacred veh'mence strong,
With energy unknown to song;
With HAMPDEN's zeal[119] and MILTON's rage,
Expose to scorn a despot age;
Of pow'r explore the strange, the guilty dream,
And rise to verse, exalted as my theme.

Tho' hard the task in humble verse,
The crimes of tyrants to rehearse;
Nor stars of Heaven in number more,
Nor sands upon great NEPTUNE's shore,
Tho' num'rous courtly dangers round me croud,
Like threat'ning seas tumultuous roaring loud.

Tho' Freedom's friends have all to fear,
From proud Oppression's mad career:

---

[119] John Hampden (c. 1595-1643), an important opponent of Charles I, was regarded as a hero by the radical movement. He was often named together with Sidney and Russell; e.g., in Baxter's History of England (1796: xi) and in Thelwall's *Poems Written in Close* (1795: 12 and 20). The Hampden Clubs were founded between 1812 and 1817 (Bonwick 1977: 63-64, Goodwin 1979: 494, and Gerald Newman, *The Rise of English Nationalism. A Cultural History. 1740-1830* (rev. ed. New York: St. Martin's Press, 1997), 229.

If dungeon's threat, or ling'ring pains,
Malicious exile, death, or chains --
Yet will I advocate fair Freedom's cause,
Unaw'd by tyrants, or their junto laws.

Say, Muse, whence came the horrid birth,
How came Oppression upon earth?
To plague mankind in evil hour,
Oppression came from lust of pow'r --
That fatal fountain-head of mortal strife,
Which stains, with endless ills, this troubl'd life.

This lust is not confin'd to time,
It reigns in ev'ry heart and clime;
It enters nearly with our breath,
And scarcely leaves the hour of death;
A fever of the soul, perhaps design'd
To punish, or instruct, our guilty kind.

Unbounded ever in its rage,
Uncheck'd in youth, untam'd by age;
Like PHILLIP's son, insatiate still,
Altho' the world it holds at will:
Create some place or pension ev'ry hour --
Will it in GRENVILLE[120] sate the lust of pow'r?

This pow'r, with strength of virtue join'd,
Dispenses blessings to mankind;
Joy springs, still new, a thousand ways,
And Nature smiles beneath its rays:
When pow'r and goodness reign around the land,
With rapture nations own th' Almighty hand!

But when it reigns without control,
When passions base enslave the soul;
It sweeps, like whirlwinds, all away,

---

[120] For William Wyndham Grenville, Lord Grenville (1759-1834), son of prime minister George Grenville, see my introduction to "Hang them, and bang them, and hang them up all!" (Ch. VIII, text 2, 194)

And teems with varied crimes each day;
Wide and more wide the swelling tempests spread,
And guilt and slaughter heap the plains with dead.

And Heav'n sometimes, in happy hour,
Exalted virtue binds with pow'r!
HENRY of France, Rome's ANTONINE,
Seem offspring of the hand divine;
And add, O Muse, great ALFRED's honest name,
With WASHINGTON - to virtue and to fame!

Sansom regrets that there are only a few exemplary kings in British history like Alfred the Great: "Alfred, a bright example made/ was lov'd, was honor'd, and obey'd":

"Nor less in arts or arms we find,
Great WASHINGTON amongst mankind!
To honest fame his mind aspires,
An ALFRED's soul his bosom fires;
Peace, Heav'ns best gift, is still his god-like plan;
And ev'ry act proclaims him -- friend of man!

Sansom refers to Poland's fight for freedom and warns that any form of oppression may provoke an uprising of the people:

O pow'rs unjust may you yet find,
The rising vengeance of mankind!
Heav'n ever just, and angry Fate,
Will crown deeds with endless hate;
The baleful cup you sent to injur'd men,
With tenfold poison shall return again.

End of the first part.

To entrust one person with all the power, can never have been God's will. God knows that no human being is perfect and without faults. Therefore, the monarchy is justified for irrational and wrong reasons. Sansom asks his muse why kings become murderers and destroyers of freedom.

Part Second

The crown is now a mystic sound,
To spread a juntos arts around;
Borne by its sacred riddling force,
Secure the courtier runs his course;
Swears, lies, corrupts, and taxes ev'ry hour,
The Lord of all things by this magic pow'r.

And despots long, by wanton sway,
Have lesser despots made each day;
Thus proud Nobility began
To domineer o'er prostrate man:
And right hereditary was design'd,
Hereditary mischief to mankind.

The American Revolution had brought new hope "from pole to pole" to many people who were discouraged by omnipresent corruption. However, the British destroyed this hope with "infant hands":

'Twas on America's fam'd shore,
To which all Nature's mercies pour,
On an auspicious glorious morn
Was Herculian Freedom born:
And sporting as he lay in childish bands,
The British serpents crush'd with infant hands.

In contrast to such a corrupt government, Sansom conceived of a freer political order, achieved by young people who feel the patriotic zeal for change.

There social order first began,
And man was reverenc'd as man,
All were obedient, all were free,
And God's own law -- equality --
Dispenc'd its blessings with a lib'ral hand,
And banish'd vile Oppression from the land.

The state was form'd on Heav'n's own plan,
On this sole rule - THE GOOD OF MAN;
The laws were lenient, few, and wise,
Made to protect -- not tyrannize:

Mild pow'r, with justice join'd, was ever found,
And universal joy diffus'd around.

No proud distinctions scornful mien;
No modest merit starving seen;
No juntos tempt with plunder'd bags,
Nor sinking toil o'ertax'd in rags;
No royal pow'r usurp'd the mercies giv'n,
But all - enjoy'd the equal gifts of Heav'n!

'Tis here, and here alone we find,
True wisdom governing mankind;
Where delegated pow'r is just,
In all things to th' important trust:
A state fast-rising to immortal fame,
More glorious than the Greek or Roman name!

No partial laws -- invade the fields --
But toil receives what nature yields:
No strength o'er weakness can prevail,
For all are equal in the scale;
And pow'r -- created by the public mind,
Flows back in plenteous mercies to mankind!

O may this country ever know,
Those blessings which from Freedom flow!
And may Heav'n smile on all that pour
To this fam'd renovated shore;
What thousands hourly fly by pow'r opprest --
To heal their sorrows in a mother's breast.

Such - are the grand effects, and joy,
Diffused by the Heav'nly boy;
Oppression shrunk from Freedom's sight,
To hide its shame and guilt in flight:
And to long darkness may the fiend be hurl'd,
And endless Freedom bless the western world!

Thus lust of powers mad career,
Was timely check'd - and taught to

Its snakes still twisting with design - fear;
The glorious birth to undermine;
Still platting, venom fraught, fresh toils succeed,
More victims to prerogatise must bleed.

In the third part, the poet's "humble muse" praises Washington (17), Paine (18) and the Polish freedom fighter Kosciuszko (19). The muse speaks of "Europe's despots" and reminds her reader that some sold their subjects to America as mercenaries: "They sell their subjects' blood for gold".

Part Third

PAINE, thou firm friend of Liberty,
This verse, the Muse, inscribes to thee;
Thy daring soul and upright mind,
The plaudits claim of all mankind:
Thy mighty genius was inspired by fate,
T' unfold the treasons of the despot state!

Hail Freedom's champion! -- thy great name,
With WASHINGTON shall rise to fame;
Tho' Kings and Ministers engage,
In plots against thy matchless page;
Thy truth -- resistless -- yet shall pour its ray,
While all BURKE's splendid nonsense melts away!

In the stanzas following, Sansom explores the causes of the French Revolution and the reactions to it. All continental powers ought to have bowed down to French freedom (19-22). Then in part four of his poem, Sansom focuses on the war between England and revolutionary France:

Part Fourth

Degraded Britons -- lost to shame --
No longer boast your former fame!
Must Britons aid a tyrant cause,
And basely fight 'gainst Nature's laws?
Must Britons -- for each noble purpose born,
Be Europe's dupes, the ridicule, and scorn?

Shall a vile junto's ill-got pow'r,

Team with Oppression ev'ry hour?
Have they for plunder or for pride,
All laws of earth and Heav'n defi'd?
O gen'rous Britons: - vindicate your fame,
And to the junto leave th'eternal shame!

The members of such a regime betray their country and their friends for greed of power. Mankind will condemn their crimes:

Let Jesuit PITT, the nation's curse,
With madness drain his country's purse;
With sullen pride, and ranc'rous hate,
His own opinions reprobate:
His country sacrifice -- himself to save --
A nation's tyrant -- and a junto's slave.

While P--TT, for ignoble ends,
Of feelings talk'd -- and left his friends,
And ruthless BURKE, with vulgar rage,
Disgrac'd his genius, fame and age:
But infamy yet higher play'd its part,
When venown'd-malice flow'd from W--MS heart.

Let meanness stain the first in sway,
Let endless av'rice rage each day;
While each in pow'r invention racks,
To form each hour some fruitful tax;
Falsehood and cruelty disgrace the law,
And to corruption's vortex all things draw.

Sansom believed that Great Britain should stop waging a senseless war against France (27).

Part Fifth

O MERCY! -- may thy gentle pow'r,
Its sacred influence shed each hour;
Offspring of Heav'n, descend and rest,
Supreme within each mortal breast!
May thy bright element illume each soul,
And love of GOD and man pervade the whole.

While Freedom rises ev'ry day,
May Mercy guide its rising sway;
With honest Pow'r go hand in hand,
And rise sublime in ev'ry land;
Make wars, remote or near, for ever cease,
And just reform begin -- and end in peace.

The author hoped that the message of freedom might reach the British coasts. He accuses the government of William Pitt of despotism (29-30), and he calls for the people to claim their sovereignty (30-31):

This then is clear -- all government,
Shou'd flow from national consent;
This is the source of lawful pow'r,
A right ne'er lost a single hour;
The people must create, support, protect,
And with full sov'reign power its vice correct!

All power -- however it may shoot,
Which springs not from this sacred root;
Is pow'r that tramples on mankind,
And may usurp, but cannot bind:
Most European pow'r is fraud -- or might --
Rais'd on the ruins of the people's right!

But Liberty is now defin'd,
And beams extensive on mankind;
Court craft is melting fast away,
Before the ever-friendly ray;
Heaven o'er th' Atlantic rais'd the grand design,
And France with rapture own'd the work divine!

In vain the tyrants of the age,
Conspire against the honest rage,
The clouds are passing swift away,
And all shall hail the coming day!
The world shall see the golden age again,
And tyrants be exalted into men!

From small beginnings mountains rise,
Swell o'er the base, and prop the skies;
Young liberty from year to year,
Shall fill fast-expanding sphere;
And rising still, some distant time may find,
His giant-arms embrace all human kind.

Then shall the simple negro find,
His equal rank among mankind;
Th' accursed Christian's whip no more,
Shall lash him from his native shore;
But rise to know his God, and milder fate,
And boast the honors of the sable state.

Accurs'd Oppression, how each hour,
Growns with examples of thy pow'r,
And Av'rice, joining hand in hand,
For sudden vengeance marks that land:
Where WILBERFORCE[121] and mercy plead in vain,
And sordid senates lengthen slav'ry's chain.

O France, to thee the Muse shall raise,
With trembling notes her utmost praise!
With honest zeal the wreath is sent,
The faint expression of intent;
O rais'd by Heav'n, fair Freedoms dearest friend,
From thee, Oppression, and its vices end.

The golden clouds shall cease to move,
The stars no longer shine above;
The planets from their orbs shall fly,
And anarchy -- unsphere the sky --
The sun's bright animating soul shall fail,
Ere tyrants can against thy cause prevail!

---

[121] William Wilberforce (1759-1833) was a friend of Pitt and was strongly anti-Jacobin in his views. He converted to religion in 1784 and founded a society for the suppression of vice three years later. As a parliamentary leader, he led the struggle for the abolition of the slave trade. In 1794-5 he called for peace with France. Hannah More, through her friendship with the abolitionist philanthropist Wilberforce, was inspired to publish her cheap repository tracts, admonishing society to improve its moral standards and to reject the French Revolution.

Secure thy Liberty shall stand;
Beyond the pow'r of mortal hand;
Thy slav'ry shall no more return,
But Freedom's fire for ever burn;
One clear, one constant, still encreasing flame,
With blessings ever new and endless fame.

Time shall record thy deathless praise,
And nation's grateful altars raise;
Old age shall fire at thy great name,
And infants lisp thy wond'rous fame:
From France new joys with years successive roll,
And Freedom clasp mankind from pole to pole.

While Nature pours the rapid Rhine,
Or Belgic plains with Freedom shine,
While the long Pyrenean's rise,
And frozen Alps invade the skies:
Shall the great globe thy fame and glory know,
While rivers wind their course, or oceans flow.

O Muse -- restrain thy feeble wing,
Nor dare attempt this praise to sing;
Not VIRGIL's, nor great HOMER's lyre,
Nor sweeter SHAKESPEARE cou'd inspire.
This theme sublime -- their force conjoin'd were vain,
No mortal strength can reach the lofty strain!

THE END

6. Thomas Spence, *The End of Oppression; or, a Quartern Loaf for Two-pence; being a Dialogue between an Old Mechanic and a Young one. Concerning the Establishment of the Rights of Man*. London: printed for the Author, and Sold by T. Spence, [1795].

Thomas Spence (1750-1814)[122] was a bookseller who devoted his life to the propagation of land reform and phonetic spelling. He was the founder of the Society of Spencean Philanthropists. On the first page of *The End of Oppression*, Spence advertised another book: *Pigs' Meat: The Honey of Politics, Is now finished in Seventy-two Penny Numbers, making Three Volumes*; Price half-bound 7s. 6d – "This is the only Book that in a direct Manner teaches the real, honest, and pure RIGHTS of MAN: and that shews an easy and practicable Way to enjoy them." The effort to translate complex political messages into an entertaining conversation between a young worker and an experienced, old man is reminiscent of Hannah More's cheap repository tracts – extraordinarily successful loyalist propaganda literature of the mid-nineties.

Thomas Spence was committed to an agrarian reform in England which would achieve the *Establishment of the Rights of Man* (Spence 1795) for the rural population. In this context, the old mechanic explains to the young man how the "Usurpation" of the rights of the people might be brought to an end. In a similar way, Thelwall criticised the aristocracy for usurping more and more land through land enclosures: "Law and liberty are alternately in their mouths; but their liberty is the unrestrained license of monopolizing oppression, and their law the arbitrary exercise of their own discretion for their usurpations".[123] Both Thelwall and Spence wrote of restoring the distribution of property that had been existed before the usurpation of the land by the aristocracy.

The End of Oppression.
Young Man. I hear there is another RIGHTS of MAN by Spence, that goes farther than Paine's.
Old Man. Yet it goes no farther than it ought.

---

[122] For his famous trial, see *The Restorer of Society to its Natural State, in the Important Trial of Thomas Spence, on May 27th* (London, 1801); for background on Spence, see O. Rudkin, *Thomas Spence and His Connections* (London: Allen and Unwin, 1927).

[123] John Thelwall, *Sober Reflections on the Seditious and Inflammatory Letter of the Right Hon. Edmund Burke to a Noble Lord. Addressed to the Serious Consideration of His Fellow Citizens* (London: Symonds, 1796); quoted from Thelwall 1995: 329-388; here 342.

Y.M. I understand it suffers no private Property in Land, but gives it all to the Parishes.
O.M. In so doing it does right; the earth was not made for Individuals.
Y.M. But people of all conditions have been so accustomed to think that the completion of all earthly felicity consisted in the possession of Landed Property, that it is not likely they will generally be brought to give up the darling hopes of one time or other possessing a snug Estate.
Y.M. It is true, if there were no injustice attending the state of a Landlord, it is the most desirable and enviable state in the world, even infinitely more so than that of a King, or any State Placemen or Pensioner whatsoever.
O.M. It is indeed. Every body knows that well. For the landlord is entirely supreme, independent, and arbitrary in his own Domains, hence the title Lord, and nothing binds him but his own Leases, which he for his own interest grants. He is in danger of losing, his revenues, for he pays himself in a most haughty and lordly manner, without process, and without hardly condescending to ask. And when his rents are brought to him on the very hour they are due, his Dignity will not permit him to be thankful.
O.M. Why, I find you are left half a Spensonian:[124] You understand something of the nature of the enemy; and I dare say we shall not differ much in opinion.
Y.M. I have heard, read, and seen enough of their oppressions to make me wish them an end, if possible.
O.M. Whether it be possible we shall see by and by. But for reasons before mentioned, unless it be necessary that there should be in a State Freemen and Slaves, Lordly Men and Mean Men, Landlords cannot be suffered.
Y.M. But most people believe it would be unjust to deprive Landed Men of their Property, as many of them have purchased their Estates.
O.M. Landed Property always was acquired, either by conquest or encroachment on the common Property of Mankind. And as those public Robbers have never shewn any degree of conscience or moderation in their Usurpations, it cannot be expected that the multitudes thus disinherited and enslaved for ages, should in the Day of reclamation, through an effeminate and foolish tenderness, neglect the precious

[124] A government report of 1801 describes Spence and his followers as "treasonous levellers, encouraging food riots and welcoming foreign invasion" (Scrivener 2001: 141). Spensonianism was regarded to be a dangerous marriage of secular and religious dissidence, being equally dangerous to the established authorities. Scrivener (2001) dedicates an entire excursus to the radical underground of Spence (and Wedderburn).

an effeminate and foolish tenderness, neglect the precious opportunity of recovering at once the whole of their Rights.
Y.M. But I am speaking of the seeming hardship of depriving modern Purchasers of their Property.
O.M. Those modern Purchasers are not ignorant of the manner in which Landed Property was originally obtained, neither are they sorry for it, not for any other imposition by which they can get Revenue. And every one knows that buying stolen Goods is as bad as stealing.
Y.M. You are intirely right, The conduct of our rich Men is not such as to create much respect for their Property. The whole of their study is to create Monopolies and to raise Rents and Revenues; and like the Grave, their endless cry is, Give! Give!
O.M. And what was originally obtained by the Sword, they determine to detain by the Sword. Are not they and their Minions now in Arms under the Name Yeomanry? And what means the inveterate War commenced by the Aristocracy against France? They know that Mankind once enlightened will not brook their lordliness, nor be content with Rights by piece-meal; therefore they exert every nerve to prevent light from spreading, and the union of the People.
Y.M. Indeed there cannot be anything said for them. They exhibit to us too plainly all the properties and practices of Robbers. Plunder, spoil and contributions they will at all events have though their ill-gotten Lands should swim with blood, full declaring themselves the worthy Heirs and Successors the ancient nimrods from whom they hold.
O.M. Then let all Men say Spence has done right in rooting up such a combination of Spoilers, and setting the world free from the all exactions, in posts, and abuses, at once and for ever.
Y.M. The reason is evident: They have no chance of being Kings, but many of them are already, and the rest foolishly and wickedly hope to be sometime or other Landlords, lesser or greater.
Y.M. But do you think Mankind will ever enjoy tolerable degree of Liberty and Felicity by having Reform in Parliament, if landlords were still suffered to remain.
O.M. You should first ask if the Landed Interest will let you have a Reform, which they will take care to prevent. For a Convention of Parliament of the People would be at eternal War with the Aristocracy. But granting they should so far gorge their interest, they would soon recollect their mistake and set about their true interest again, which is to counteract every species of public good. And full well are they qualified with every requisite for the diabolical Work. The perpetual influx of wealth by

their Rents without toil of study, leaves them at full Liberty and Leisure to plot against the interest of the working part of the Community and turn their Labours to their own advantage.
Y.M. Yes, it is natural to expect that whether in the legislature or out of it, their whole study will be, under every kind of Government, to encrease the prices of what their Estates produce, that their rents may rise. What shall we then account such a body of people, whose interests are only their own, and so opposite to all others, but a public Enemy, a Banditti that must always be watched and sometimes resisted.
O.M. There you are wrong with your watching and resisting. Who is to watch and resist? Must not all the rest of the world do something for their Bread? And are they not disarmed by the Game Laws, and by Monopolies, State Tricks, Rents and taxes reduced to continual Drudgery and Starvation? How many Days do you think such a brood of Beggars could maintain themselves in a state of Insurrection against Oppressors? They must away to their work again. The cries of their famished Families break up their Campaigns before they are well begun, and they must return again to the yoke, like other starved animals, for mere subsistence.
Y.M. O hopeless state of Mankind!
O.M. No, it is not yet hopeless, though the enemy, like a numerous Army, be garrisoned and quartered every where among us, and have all the strong Holds, all the Arms, and every advantage that triumphant and cruel Invaders could wish for, yet will a true and universal knowledge of Spence's plain and simple System overturn them, and sweep all their Greatness and Lordliness away in one Day, and leave the world in perpetual and perfect Peace.
Y.M. Some seem to apprehend the mismanagement of the Parish Revenues, and so discourage People from thinking of it.
O.M. That is the natural work of the Enemy, and must be expected. But it does not become Democracy to doubt concerning it. For if Man cannot manage the Revenues and affairs of a Parish, what must they do with a State? It is almost as absurd to answer such quibbles as to make them. How strange that Men will turn the world upside down to get the management of a Nation, and yet pretend to despair concerning a Parish!!! It is too bad. The villainy is too barefaced. I am weary with combating the vile sophistry of Scoundrels that are Oppressors, and Scoundrels that would be Oppressors. But in Spence's Pig's Meat, you will find the parish System represented in a variety of ways, evidencing to every Reader, the easy and practicable transition from this scene of Oppression and Woe, to perfect Freedom and Felicity.

Y.M. Now suppose a whole nation, (no matter which) were fully convinced of the excellence of this System, and universally wishing its establishment, I should be glad to know the most easy method of doing so and wish least bloodshed.
O.M. I a Country so prepared, let us suppose a few Thousands of hearty determined Fellows well armed and appointed with Officers, and having a Committee of honest, firm, and intelligent Men to direct their Actions to the Proper Object. If this Committee published a Manifesto or Proclamation, directing the People in every Parish to take, on receipt thereof, immediate possession of the whole Landed Property within their district, appointing a Committee to take charge of the same, in the name and for the use of the Inhabitants; and that every Landholder should immediately, on pain of Confiscation and Imprisonment, deliver to the said parochial Committee, all Writings and Documents relating to their Estates, that they might immediately be burnt; and that they should likewise disgorge at the same time into the Hands of the said Committee, the last payments received from their tenants, in order to create a parochial Fund for immediate use, without calling upon the exhausted People. If this Proclamation was generally attended to, the business was settled at once; but if the Aristocracy arose to contend the matter, let the people be firm and desperate, destroying them Root and Branch, and strenghthening their hands by the rich Confiscations. Thus the war would be carried on at the expence of the wealthy enemy, and the Soldiers, of Liberty beside the hope of sharing in the future felicity of the country, being well paid, would be steady and bold. And wherever the lands were taken possession of by the People, which by all means should be as early accomplished as possible, the grand resource of the Aristocracy, the Rents, would be cut off, which would soon reduce them to Reason, and they would become as harmless as other men.

FINIS

IX. Loyalists and Reactionaries

It was conservatism, not Jacobinism that won the battle for the popular mind in the early 1790s. In the short term, the reaction provoked by Paine [...] proved stronger than the radicalism he excited. Compelled to answer the democratic Jacobin challenge, opponents of reform developed an intellectual and moral defence of the existing order.

This is how John Belchem summarized the outcome of the struggles of the 1790s in his study on *Industrialization and the Working Class*. On the one hand, this assessment has become common opinion and can hardly be denied. On the other hand, the radical movement of the 1790s not only created a continuity between the old movement of the 1770s and the new reform movement, which came into being after the Napoleonic wars, but also taught its supporters to create and organize public spheres which democratised the values and attitudes of a developing civil society. People gradually developed social activities that allowed for intervention and participation in the decision making of established institutions. Even though "the plebeian radicals were unable to counter the loyalist propaganda victory"[125] and had to withdraw from the political scene, they continued their activities as poets (Thelwall), dramatists (Holcroft), authors of popularised textbooks on chemistry and physics (Joyce), and etymologists (Horne Tooke).

The publication campaign of the radical movement, in which participation in all fields of learning and knowledge was suggested and offered to a critical public sphere, found a committed answer from those who had the established and powerful institutions of the state on their side and, therefore, were less dependent on the word. Hannah More's cheap repository tracts are the most ready example that the loyalists reacted to the success stories of the radical press. The unprecedented sales of Paine's *The Rights of Man* (I, 1791; II, 1792) – "approaching or exceeding a million by the start of the new century – illustrated that the literary market for democratic literature was far greater than anyone at the time had imagined was possible" (Scrivener 2001: 7).

[125] John Belchem, *Industrialization and the Working Class: The English Experience, 1750-1900* (Portland, OR: Areopagitica Press, 1990), 68.

Because of these impressive sales, loyalist literature was neglected for a long time. However, since Butler's *Romantics, Rebels and Reactionaries* (1982),[126] the number of research studies accounting for all political attitudes and no longer neglecting loyalist literature and propaganda has steadily grown. In a recent research survey, Matthew Grenby suggested dividing "Jacobin from anti-Jacobin novels, and because of their much greater numbers, group[ing] the conservative fictions according to their primary literary-political tactic".[127] However, such a distinction simplifies the situation, Grenby warns, because "the novels of the 1790s were not as politically polarised as has generally been thought" (46). Grenby points out "that a noticeable tension at times arises from the intersection of an author's desire to be radical and the social or commercial necessity of ideological orthodoxy" (46). Consequently, he regards "the idea of a binary Opposition of conservative and radical texts" as highly problematic (46).

The following texts, which were written by conservative authors, illustrate that these pamphleteers and writers were well aware of the fact that they were reacting to the literary public of the radical movement. In contrast to novels and poems, however, these propagandistic texts offered a clearer political message and were less open to interpretation –an indication that the concept of literature had become more and more exclusive.

---

[126] Butler, *Romantics, Rebels and Reactionaries* (New York and Oxford: Oxford University Press, 1982).

[127] Matthew O. Grenby, "Politicised Fiction in Britain 1790-1810: An Annotated Checklist," in: *The European Messenger* 9,2 (2000), 47-53; here 46. For further secondary literature, see Grenby's bibliography in which is listed among the publications from the 1990s: Chris Jones, *Radical Sensibility: Literature and Ideas in the 1790s* (London: Routledge, 1993); Gary Kelly, *Women, Writing and Revolution 1790-1827* (Oxford: Clarendon Press, 1993); and Eleanor Ty, *Unsex'd Revolutionaries: Five Women Novelists of the 1790s* (Toronto: University of Toronto Press, 1993).

1. "So well balanced is our Constitution," from: *Opinions Delivered at a Numerous and Respectable Meeting in the Country, Lately Held for the Purpose of Signing a Declaration for the Support of Government in the Present Lamentable Crisis*. London: R. Edwards, 1793.

This anonymous pamphletist warned of the "universal equalization" of the French Revolution, which was responsible for unspeakable atrocities in the days of its terror. He believed that the radical press had tried to deceive the British public about the true nature the Revolution:

Clubs are formed in London, and in many parts of the kingdom, where the deluded people are taught to reverence sedition, and embrace rebellion, under the *mask* of liberty and happiness. The members of a club in a northern county are all sworn: they receive regular pay, and are ready to follow those who may call them forth to any desperate enterprise. Incredible pains have been taken throughout Great Britain and Ireland to stir up discontent and commotions - it has been attempted to plant the Tree of Liberty at Dundee in Scotland by a mob of six hundred persons. Every wall in London has been covered with inflammatory and seditious writings - the fidelity of the soldiers has been attempted in more places than one: but they shewed themselves by no means behind *any* description of Englishmen in love to their Constitution: they immediately *seized* on the offenders, and delivered them up to justice.

At the head of a long list of seditious writings stands that most infamous of all productions, *Paine's Rights of Man*. In *my* opinion no title to a book ever so completely belied its contents; for if it be the right of man to substitute confusion in the place of order, and to destroy all the bonds of law, humanity, and religion, (without which no civil society can exist) - if it be right of man to level all property, to divide all substance from one end of the world to the other, and to give to each man an equal share, by which the dissolute spend thirst would be placed on an equality with the industrious œconomist - if it be the true right of man to decree, that when I have improved my farm, or got a little money by any Divide with me your profit, because by *nature* we ought to be *all equal* - if *such*, I say, are the rights of man, we have lived indeed to *little* purpose to be so completely *ignorant* of them, and all the happiness we have enjoyed under our excellent Constitution is discovered to be an empty dream, or, at best, a pleasing delusion (2-4).

The author quoted from a speech delivered by John Frost on a meeting of the Society for Constitutional Information (SCI). He believed that all the resolutions and reports on the revolution in France were lies and treason (14ff.). The author suggested comparing English happiness with French misery (19f.).

The number of persons murdered in France within these four years, is, by fair computation, full 50,000. But the history of the events that happened at Paris on the 10th of August, and 2nd and 3rd of September last, is *written* in blood. Human nature on the 10th of August, seems wholly to have lost those feelings that are hardly ever extinguished under the impulse of the most violent passions. The hearts of the slain were torn from the bodies, and the women, *dead to every sense of shame*, committed such *cruelties* on the dying men, as it would be equally disgusting for me to repeat, as it would be shocking for you to hear.

The 2nd and 3rd September surpassed, however, the horrid transactions of the 10th of August. It was reserved for those days to prove, that cool intention and premeditated proscription were more sanguinary in their nature than sudden fury and ungoverned passion. On those two days the channels of Paris absolutely flowed with human blood, and the streets were strewed with the dead bodies of those wretched victims, whose imaginary crimes served as a pretence to the real ones of their enemies, and whose accuser, judge, and executioner, was often one and same person. In some places the mockery of a trial rendered the approach of death more terrible; on the table before those men called judges, tobacco and wine held the place of the laws and statute books; and how hard must it have been for the purest innocence to command sufficient presence of mind to defend itself, where the sword of the executioner was (during the trial) raised over its head, waiting to strike down its victim (16-18).

[...]
Let us now turn our eyes from these scenes of blood, and compare our happy situation with the misery of France. So well balanced is our Constitution, consisting of King, Lords, and Commons; so just and equal are our laws, so protected and secure do all ranks of people live under them, let their religious tenets and principles by what they may, so long as they conduct themselves as good and peaceable subjects; that no one who feels for his freedom, or enjoys his property, can for a moment think of exchanging these certain advantages for the destructive plans of those levellers whose wish it is to lower all men to their own level, but will by no means descend themselves to an inferior station, though in general

men of desperate and broken fortunes; and while they are telling us what we are to gain by their plan, it would be wise in us to consider what we should lose by it (19-20).

2. "Tis time the World should grow more sage," from: Sir John Ramsea, *The Head and Limbs. A Fable.* London: Harrison, 1794.

Sir John Ramsea admonished his reader to learn from history. He used the traditional metaphor of the body politic[128] to explain the consequences of revolutionary politics. He denied having taken the idea for his fable from Æsop, since his interpretation is "favourable to a rational or limited MONARCHY", which is represented by the head. The author leaves the public to judge his fable.

What Sir Ramsea did not mention is the fact that the metaphor of the "body politic" was still quite popular in late eighteenth century among political authors. John Thelwall, for instance, regarded himself as a "political physician", administering to the body's diseases. In contrast to Sir Ramsea, "Thelwall is somewhat anxious about the authoritarian implications of the metaphor of the political physician."[129] The body metaphor was widely used in legal texts: "The destruction of the physical body of the condemned transformed the individual into a restorative example capable of re-establishing the health of the social body."[130] In the second half of the century, however, reformers tried to ground punishment in interest (McGowen 1987: 674). Legal authors such as William Eden, for example, believed that "soci-

---

[128] See, e.g., the sociologist Donald MacRae, "The Body and Social Metaphor," in: *The Body as a Medium of Expression*, ed. J. Benthall and T. Polhemus (London: Penguin, 1975), 59-73, who considers the body as one of the richest sources of metaphor that we have.

[129] Michael Henry Scrivener, "John Thelwall and the Press," in: *Romanticism, Radicalism, and the Press*, ed. Stephen C. Behrendt (Detroit: Wayne State University Press, 1997), 120-136; here 123. The body metaphor could also be found behind the charge for high treason, as Barrell explains: "... this extension of the statute by construction would be deplored [...] as part of a long and deliberate policy on the part of the executive to represent Opposition to the Government for the time being as Opposition to the king, and so to represent as high treason actions that could be represented as such only figuratively or analogically, only by confusing the king's actual body with his political body, his head with his hat [...] They were, in short, 'imaginary treasons'" (2000: 40).

[130] See Randall McGowen, "The Body and Punishment in Eighteenth-Century England," *Journal of Modern History* 59 (1987), 651-679; here 665. McGowan studied mid-eighteenth-century texts such as Joshua Fitzsimmonds's *Free and Candid Disquisitions on the Nature and Execution of the Laws of England* (London, 1751).

ety did not seem like a body composed of organs", but rather emerged from a more perfect union between the individual and society.

Warn'd by the Wise, of ev'ry Age,
'Tis time the World should grow more sage;
And not, to make each Lesson vain,
Act it's old Follies o'er again.

EACH downy pinion'd CHILD OF SONG,
When first he tries his tuneful tongue;
The source of evil, or of good,
As yet but little understood;
With zeal, that's felt, would fain impart,
The dictates of his infant heart:
Then let a BARD, whose frequent strains
Have fill'd the groves, have chear'd the plains,
Matur'd on firmer wing to rise,
Tell what EXPERIENCE bids him prize.

ADVERTISMENT

It will be quite natural for the Reader to suppose, not only that the Author of the HEAD and LIMBS has adopted the familiar metre of LA FONTAINE, which is in some measure true; but that Æsop's *Belly and Members* furnished the idea of the Fable itself. This, however, is not the fact. It arose from an accidental and sudden reflection, that the HEAD was, by *Nature*, calculated to *govern* the Body; and an instantaneous transition in the mind of the Author, favourable to a rational or limited MONARCHY. To a Man who feels himself a native of the *freest* and *least imperfect* state on earth; and who wishes to see a just value set on that Constitution which was formed by the wisdom, and has been transmitted to us by the valour, of our Ancestors, the smallest suggestion of this kind was sufficient.

The Fable of the HEAD and LIMBS was accordingly produced; with what success, the Public are to determine.

The Head and Limbs. A Fable.

In days of *ignorance* -- that is, of *yore* --

For now we're all PHILOSOPHERS, and *wise*;
Such days, Heav'n bless us! can return no more --
There chanc'd strange, graceless, gumblings to arise,
Among the *lower orders* of the plan,
On which our *once thought* MAKER first form'd *Man*.

It seems, the *Being* -- no more call'd CREATOR --
For in our schools of grand, *omniscient* REASON,
Such language, we're aware, would be high-treason:
In short, that great FIRST CAUSE,
Sage moderns, with applause,
Have *christen'd* MISTRESS NATURE ---

Had, as these grumblers judg'd, been full of *whims*,
Acting much like a silly noddy;
To frame so many *joints, members* -- nay, *Limbs* --
In one fair, *large*, compacted BODY;
Then, spoiling all, from where the *Shoulders* spread,
Erect, and *crown*, as SOVEREIGN of the *whole*,
That *small*, that useless *gewgaw*, call'd a HEAD,
And make *them* SUBJECTS of it's *weak* controul.

For many years they did the *burden* bear,
Faring as well as any of their neighbours;
But, *lately*, grown more *knowing* than they *were*,
They *found* the HEAD was nourish'd by *their* labours;
And when they once had made this *grand discovery*,
Their peace of mind was lost, past all recovery.

'Tis hard to say, *where* treason first began,
While some accuse the LIMBS, and some the *Heart*;
But swift as lightning the contagion ran,
And with it's venom poison'd *ev'ry part*.
-- would they be *Slaves* to such a stupid *thing*?
No, curse their vitals, if they *kept* a KING!

The *where*, we cannot tell -- but yet, the *why*,
Perhaps we may -- at least, the Muse shall try.

I've heard, when LUXURY has made *too fat*

Certain most thankless creatures;
Favour'd with *human* features,
And even, now and then,
Deservedly call'd MEN,
The brutes know scarcely *what they would be at*;
And are, like *drunkards*, fullest of pretences
To *wond'rous* wisdom, when they've *lost* their senses.

Then, if this mad intoxication
Seizes a whole *corrupted* nation,
Swift sinks its boasted grandeur to decay,
And all it's pomp and pride are swept away!

In such a fit, the LIMBS, so mighty *wise*,
Forming a *Grand*, a NATIONAL CONVENTION,
Resolv'd to vote against the Head's *supplies*,
And thus to *merit* HONOURABLE MENTION.

Quite at a stand
Was either *Hand*,
Each gout-swoln *Toe*
Refus'd to go,
And neither *Leg*
Would move a peg,
To furnish new supplies for ROYAL JAWS:
Tho' not a single grinder HE could stir,
Knew ev'ry growling, discontented *cur*,
That did not help to stuff their own vile maws.

The *Tongue* of Eloquence to speak essay'd;
To drown his voice, the senseless mob huzza'd.
That fawning *Courtier* they had heard too much,
The devil a morsel more should he e'er touch!
They knew him well - the *Tongue*, a specious elf,
Whate'er he *said*, spoke only for *himself*!

The *Eyes*, the *Ears*, the *Nose*, advanc'd their claim;
They, too, were *Courtiers*, and their fate the same.

In short, the *Crowd*,

With clamours loud,
Pronounc'd them PLACEMEN, full of mere pretences;
To own their smallest *use*,
Was a most vile abuse:
For soon the *world* should see,
To be *compleatly* FREE --
Tho' they might stare -- they must *discard* their SENSES!

Besides, were *such* things wanted,
It is by REASON granted,
Maternal NATURE, kind alike to *all*,
Made *equal*, at their birth,
In *wisdom* and in *worth*,
Each creature that inhabits earth's vast ball;
Then how should saucy *Tongue*, *Eyes*, *Ears*, or *Nose*,
Smell, hear, or see, or speak,
Judg'd idly by the *weak*,
Better than *Hands*, and *Arms*, and *Legs*, and *Toes*?
It could be no such thing:
Each was *himself* a KING!
And soon presuming *Nose*, *Eyes*, *Ears*, and *Tongue*,
Who thought them *weak*, should find that they were *strong*.

And now, as usual, when the *base* Inferiors
Possess the *means* to harass their Superiors,
Eager they strive their guilty *pow'r* to shew,
By meanly striking the most *barb'rous* blow:

For foes to REASONS's mild and gentle *sway*,
Loud tho' the *Ideots* bawl,
That they are *Freemen* all,
With *slavish* zeal wild ANARCHY *obey*.

Like BEDLAMITES,[131] when *Pride* has fir'd their brains;
Who, with a *Sceptre* straw,
Fiercely *direct* the law,
Themselves, poor *Slaves*! in *chains*.

---

[131] See footnote 48.

Thus MADNESS *rules*
The brutal fools;
And on it leads
To deadly deeds:
For with destructive Pride elate,
The savage monsters rush on fate!

With shouts of joy,
The maniacks cry -
Tho' all our strength in war we spend,
Tho' ev'ry drop of blood we shed,
And tho' *success* in DEATH must *end*,
Yet will we be -- *without* a HEAD.

Off, in an instant, at th' accurs'd command,
The MONARCH fell, beneath th' *unnatural* HAND;
But with him fell the *Hand* that gave the blow,
And ev'ry *rebel* LIMB was quickly laid as low.

There stretch'd, a *dread* EXAMPLE to the World!
Laid the huge Mass, in loathsome ruin hurl'd;
Till Birds obscene, Reptiles, and Beasts of prey,
Who with delight
Beheld the sight,
Rejoicing bore the horrid *Spoil* away!

The End

3. "To defend poor Old England -- Huzza! boys, huzza!" ***King, Liberty, Laws. (Tune, -- "Hearts of Oak.").*** **London [1794?].**

This loyalist song promised explanations in a time of uncertainties. The author believed in a conspiracy common of his period: he believed that the French enemies had control over the British radical movement, which tried everything possible to deceive compatriots in order to deliver them to the Revolution. The author used the usual national stereotypes, praising the British wealth in contrast to France.

This text exemplifies the paranoid style the conservatives had developed, "a totalising discourse of self-aggrandizement and persecution," which would last well into the period of Shelley and Byron[132] and which served to propagate a society that would support Britain's imperial project.

Ye true-hearted Britons, so brave and so free,
Come lend your Attention, and listen to me;
I'll shew you most clearly the Plots, that are laid
Each Comfort to steal, ev'ry Blessing invade:
But to join in the Cause
Of King, Liberty, Laws,
We always are ready,
And steady, boys, steady,
To defend poor Old England -- Huzza! boys, huzza!

II.
The French most perfidious have ever been known;
Old England they hate, and would fain pull her down;
Our Glory they envy; our Happiness too;
And would change our old Gold for Tinsel so new:
But we'll shew, in the Cause
Of King, Liberty, Laws,
We always are ready,
And steady, boys, steady,
To defend poor Old England -- Huzza! boys, huzza!

III.
Afraid lest the Lion of England should wake,
They try to filch that, which by Force they can't take:
They pay wicked men to seduce us with lies,
And to rob us securely, throw Dust in our eyes:
But they'll find in the Cause
Of King, Liberty, Laws,
We always are ready,
And steady, boys, steady,
To defend poor England -- Huzza! boys, huzza!

---

[132] See for instance Carla J. Mulford, "Joel Barlow, Edmund Burke, and Fears of Masonic Conspiracy in 1792," in: *Secret Texts: The Literature of Secret Societies*, ed. by Marie Mulvey Roberts and Lennon Hugh Ormsby (New York: AMS, 1995), 169-187.

IV.
No Religion nor Laws the vile Jacobins own,
Their God they deny, and their King they dethrone;
To gain their own ends, the poor people they cheat,
Then leave them to starve, scarce a morsel to eat:
Then let us in the Cause
Of King, Liberty, and Laws,
Be ever more ready,
And steady, boys, steady,
To defend poor Old England -- Huzza! boys, huzza!

V.
Their Trade is all gone, there is None now to buy;
The Rich being banish'd, the Poor left to die;
No Corn in their markets, no Coin in their states,
No Ships in their ports, nor no Faith in their gates:
But they'll find in the Cause
Of King, Liberty, Laws,
We always are ready,
And steady, boys, steady,
To defend poor Old England -- Huzza! boys, huzza!

VI.
But look, Oh, hold Britons! around you, and see,
The contrast how great -- *We are happy and free*!
Here Peace spreads her Olive, and Plenty her Store;
And Justice alike guards the rich and the Poor;
Then shew in the Cause
Of King, Liberty, Laws,
We always are ready,
And steady, boys, steady,
To defend poor Old England -- Huzza! boys, huzza!

VII.
Our Commerce is great, Manufact'rers well paid;
The World is our Mart, so extensive our Trade;
All, all have employment, the idle alone
Have cause of complaint, but the fault is their own:
Then firm in the Cause
Of King, Liberties, Laws,

We always are ready,
And steady, boys, steady,
To defend poor Old England -- Huzza! boys, huzza!

VIII.
Our Nobles for Liberty freely will bleed,
Since they planted her first in the fam'd Runnymede;
Most sacred our Gentry her Boughs will sustain,
From the blows of vile France, or their engine *Tom Paine*:
Then firm in the Cause
Of King, Liberties, Laws,
We always are ready,
And steady, boys, steady,
To defend poor Old England -- Huzza! boys, huzza!

IX.
Our Soldiers are loyal, brave, honest, and true;
And our Sailors unmatch'd, if you search the World thro';
The Poor, when industrious, have plenty and ease;
And Charity shelters old age and disease:
Then firm in the Cause
Of King, Liberty, Laws,
We always are ready,
And steady, boys, steady,
To defend poor Old England -- Huzza! boys, huzza!

X.
Great GEORGE is our Father, Protector, and Friend,
And firmly our Rights and his own will defend;
Then uniting our Hearts and our Voices, we'll sing,
And pray for long Life and long Reign to our King:
And staunch in the Cause
Of King, Liberties, Laws,
Be ever more ready,
And steady, boys, steady,
To defend poor Old England -- Huzza! boys, huzza!

4. "A race of Democrats [...] Atheists, Assassins, Traitors, Regicides," from: Dickinson, Charles. *The Travels of Cyllenius. A poem. In Sixty-six cantos.* London: Printed for the Author, 1796.

Charles Dickinson (fl. 1780-1796), a name that appears to be the pseudonym of an anonymous author, published this work in 66 cantos; cantos 1-4 are continuously paginated; cantos 4-66 are each separately paginated; the register is continuous throughout. Each canto was possibly published separately in 1795, as the *Short Title Catalogue* suggests, and later published together in this 1796 edition.

The conservative author warned of "the little embryos of politic woes" which might turn into serious problems faster than expected. Similar to the speaker of the preceding song, the author believed that the situation in England was more dangerous than acknowledged. The "race of democrats" – i.e., the reformers – want to import the French Revolution to Britain.

Dickinson compares "the last good man" in Pitt's cabinet[133] with Milton's "dreadless Angel", the loyal Abdiel, who fought on God's side in the battle with Satan and his apostates (*Paradise Lost*, Book VI, ll. 1-28) and was regarded as the epitome of a loyal patriot in eighteenth-century literature. The opposed pair of Satan and Abdiel presents a character loyal to conservative moral issues in contrast to radical traitors: "So spake the Seraph Abdiel faithful found,/ Among the faithless, faithful only hee;/ Among innumerable false, unmov'd,/ Unshak'n, unseduc'd, unterrifi'd/ His Loyaltie he kept, his Love, his Zeale".[134]

The Fortieth Canto:

He spoke; whilst from the mingled crowds around
The smothered groans of discontent resound
And deep despondence sat on every brow,

[133] See the pamphlet "Speedily will be published", Price 3l. 6s. in Boards, *The Travels of Cyllenius. A poem. In Sixty-six cantos* - a satire in the form of an advertisement and list of contents [4 pp; 1796], sometimes cotributed to John Horne Tooke, in which the 40th canto is summarized in the words: "A Guide to the Cabinet, containing the leading features of Mr. Pitt's Administration. "I do see the bottom Justice Shallow." Dickinson's *Cyllenius* could be found in John Horne Tooke's library. See *A Catalogue of the valuable Library, late the property of John Horne Tooke, Esq. ... which will be sold by auction ... May 26, 1813, etc.* London, 1813, no. 173.

[134] *Paradise Lost*, Book V, ll. 896-900; *The Oxford Authors: John Milton*, ed. by Stephen Orgel and Jonathan Goldberg (Oxford and New York: Oxford University Press, 1991), 468-9.

To hear their patriot friend such thoughts avow
As must the credit of their sect impair,
Which still they watch with ever anxious care;
Still view their country's good with looks askance
Or solely for their private ends advance;
To these their thoughts, to these their lives devote,
And tease and fret and foam and rail and vote.
Their last good man like Abdiel withdrew
Amid the taunts of the rebellious crew.
New themes at length 'midst high debates arose
And the warm conflict still more warmly glows.
Here crowds at once with mingled accents rise,
"To order" there, some thundering voice replies;
Here their weak sides contending foes descry,
There winged with wit their tingling arrows fly;
Here of the bankrupt state the wrongs deplore,
There high jest augments the general roar;
Here eager to explain the veteran stands,
There the raw youth his sluggard frame expands,
Or sounds with insolence and wine replete
O'er the rough floor the signal of retreat;
Here the vexed Patriot finds his wishes crost,
There blushing merit in a trope is lost.
Some o'er the crowd their threatening aspects rear,
And bold defiance strikes the wondering ear;
Some to politic measures gently dose,
Lulled by the general cadence to repose,
Or sacred by dreams prophetic of their fall
With raven croakings fill the echoing hall.
The ministerial phalanx some arraign
And loudly of encreasing debts complain,
Whilst with mistaken zeal the Patriot rails
And feeds the sickle crowd with idle tales,
Mine be the task those measures to defend
That solely to the public welfare tend.
What though corruption reign with boundless sway,
And public delegates their trust betray?
Though laws be dwindled from their ancient form
And countless myriads clamorous for reform?
Though prostitution openly carest

And the great mass of subjects sore opprest,
Though all be granted, still new forms arise,
With tenfold lustre charm our wondering eyes;
Commerce and opulence at once increase
And glorious wars ensure perpetual peace.
Nor even corruption should we rashly blame
That still of government promotes the aim,
Since among those who feel its magic force
And draw from Ministers each proud resource,
Who by no sense of honor are restrained,
Our ends at least are in a trice obtained;
Since the vast opulence from whence it flows
From ministerial wisdom first arose;
Which surely may employ the means it gave,
To spur the restive and reward the brave.
Whilst over earth and main our banners fly
And ample revenues each want supply,
Reforms must be most studiously supprest:
If commerce prospers who can be distrest?
Which through all ranks the means of life expands
And crowns the festive board with lavish hands.
The Minister should be the Monarch's friend.
A chain 'twixt Prince and People to extend
And firmly rivet is the Statesman's boast:
Break but a single link and all is lost:
Long may this golden chain our wishes bind;
In one harmonious league forever joined.
Whoe'er the state of nations would define
Must to their revenues his thoughts confine,
Since these alone have sovereign power to bless,
The true criterions of happiness;
And clearly prove that industry must thrive
From whence our grand resources we derive.
I too by wild reforms have been beguiled,
In years a man, in wisdom but a child.
But since by sage experience better taught
Have learnt to reprobate the audacious thought;
Since this profound arcanum stands confest,
Must needs avow we are supremely blest.
Not that on earth an object can be found

For which my character I would compound,
Nor can the bribes of power or vain applause
Induce me to desert the better cause;
But what contributes to the public weal
Have ever thought my duty to reveal;
And through all ranks and ages would extend
Those truths that to our future welfare tend.
[...]
But grant they have incurred a people's curse,
A race of Democrats are surely worse;
Atheists, Assassins, Traitors, Regicides,
Whose every act, all right, all sense derides.
Shall we on terms with such banditti live,
Or even the pledges of their faith receive?
Shall we thus stoop from our meridian fame,
And taint the glory of the British name?
No, rather let the flames of war increase,
Let us shut up each avenue to peace;
Though from the labouring poor each dolt we strain,
Though not the least resource untaxed remain,
Though the last column of the state should fall,
And general bankruptcy involve us all;
Till at our feet these murderous ruffians bend,
And solely on our clemency depend.
Though views like these inferior minds bemoan,
Though some beneath the weight of taxes grown,
Yet will the grand majority approve,
And still more firm beneath their pressure move.
But whilst one spark of genuine worth remains,
Or great atchievements fire the Briton's veins,
The pride of conquest, Victory's spreading plume,
The laureate honours that around us bloom,
Must such vile trash in our esteem outweigh
And all we lose a hundred-sold repay.
Still on politic themes the vulgar dwell,
And woes that never yet have dawned foretell;
Even ministerial schemes attempt to scan,
But he who fathoms must be more than man.
Even as the general features of the world,
That some have vainly thought at random hurled,

In beauteous order to the elect appear,
So these promiscuous scenes of hope and fear
That form of Ministers the varied scheme,
Which unconnected in their parts may seem,
Contemplated with confidential eyes,
Clear as the day's first dawn through Chaos rise,
And every presage of approaching fate
Still adds new vigour to the exhausted state.
But when by the licentious crowd pourtrayed [sic!],
In folly's garb even Premiers are arrayed,
Caught in their own invented snares they stand,
Sunk the high crest, and dropt the magic wand:
Their dreams of greatness in a trice decay,
And all their air-built castles melt away.
End of the fourtieth CANTO.

The Fifty-Sixth Canto:

In Canto 56, Dickinson describes a petrified and despotic state in which the smallest reforms bring down the whole government. However, Dickinson does not refer to England, but to France.

Let states where arbitrary power prevails
Be influenced by such preposterous tales.
Where will is law and all remonstrance vain:
Where ignorance and tame submission reign;
That are by frowning Despots overawed;
Founded in violence, upheld by fraud;
Hang o'er their base like some dismantled wall,
If even a stone were moved the whole must fall;
From radical defect have never swerved
In hopeless uniformity preserved.
Well might this abject state our thoughts restrain;
Where all is wrong 'tis treason to complain.
Changes howe'er expedient must annoy,
Since to reform the state were to destroy.
Those that with genuine Liberty are blest
When most secure are not in perfect rest.
That were the presage of approaching ill;
They thrive when moved, degenerate when still.

Like the pure wave in circling eddies tost
Where each putrescent particle is lost;
But by the breeze no longer winnowed o'er
With baneful dews infects the neighbouring shore.
The germs of virtue quicken in each heart
And through all ranks a generous warmth impart.
That active spirit which pervades the whole
Is of politic liberty the soul.

The author recommends the improvement of the economic situation of a country rather than the reform of social rights:

Of industry and commerce is the source
And of all laws should regulate the course.
The mind to new atchievements still incites
And swells the narrow bound of social rights.
Resents what with our interest disagrees
And of the state corrects the high decrees.
Have we forgot that memorable hour
When freedom bursting from despotic power
First raised her standard on the British coast?
The noblest seat our history can boast!
The state then prospered too, and all seemed well,
When headlong from his throne the Sovereign fell.
No factious chiefs laid waste our peaceful plains
Nor of our government assumed the reins,
Nor did a ruthless mob the land o'erawe
Or drown the voice of justice and of law.
No vile usurpers o'er our heads were placed.
No massacres the splendid scene disgraced.
Calm and serene amidst a host of foes
With one accord an injured people rose;
In every act a temperate zeal displayed.
Repair the breach that bigot rage had made;
Their trampled laws and liberties restore;
And shine more great and glorious than before.

End of the Fifty-Sixth CANTO

The Fifty-Seventh Canto

Nor was a state of freedom ever found
In which this golden chain we might not trace,
That holds the future bound in strict embrace.
[...]
Not wait until those mischiefs be displayed
That may our own peculiar rights invade;
But rouze at once and loyally expose
The little embryos of politic woes;
Impress the treacherous slave with awful fear
Who dares to sport with all that is most dear;
Watch every storm that o'er our heads may lower
And mould events while yet within our power.
The Patriot embraces every part
And has of all alike the good at heart.
Distinguishes the truth from vain surmise
And learns from past disasters to be wise.
Surveys the future with prophetic eye
And in suspicion finds reality.
These are the maxims of politic truth,
Which can preserve the state in plight and youth;
To which all freemen should direct their aim.
The probable and real are the same.

The Fifty-Eigth Canto

Nor can a single reason e'er be found,
If we perceive that all is calm around
Nor of rebellion fear the gathering storm,
Why any moderate system of reform
That may the outworks of the state repair
And cleanse the obnoxious weeds that harbour there,
Should not with generous ardour be received,
And to the utmost of our power atchieved.
Or why the few who have such schemes proposed
Should still to public odium be exposed;
Still eyed with looks askance and visage four;
Save the enormous thirst of wealth and power,
The abject meanness of that servile crew,

Who for some paltry end, some selfish view
Are pleased to see our jealousies increase
And sap the very base of public peace,
To see corruption mine her treacherous way,
(The happy prelude of despotic sway!)
Nor care though ruin should o'erwhelm us all
So to their share some splendid fragment fall.
So the wild schemes succeed to which they trust
Would see our laws and charters laid in dust.
Who like the vermin that infest our plains
Find in our loss the source of all their gains.
[...]
The general object of the wisest laws
That ever have been framed in freedom's cause,
The insidious arts of traitors may illude,
When through a series of years pursued.
Till nations, lost to every sense of shame,
Virtue and liberty at once disclaim.
Renounce themselves the honours of their race,
And become parties to their own disgrace.
Till all the ends of despot power are gained
And all the forms of freedom still retained.
If nought but laws our liberties ensure
Are we admidst corruption then secure?
But I would ask these advocates for power
If from the accession to the present hour
Essential changes have not of occurred?
And if it may not fairly be inferred
But for the vigilance we have displayed,
The noble stand that patriot zeal has made,
(Which neither frowns could awe nor smiles seduce)
Against the shameless champions of abuse
Our rights had dwindled to a mimic show?

The Sixty-Sixth Canto

Of sublunary blessings most esteem
Yet Traitors all who would retrieve them deem.
Still to support their government pretend
Though nought but forms are left them to defend.

What might the spirit of the laws restore
As earthquakes, plagues, or hurricanes deplore.
Find amidst those who burn with patriot zeal
The sworn Assassins of the public weal.
Still despotic sway all order found
And liberty with anarchy confound;
Still place the sole criterion of sense
Upon the honied lip of eloquence.
[...]
And that politic frenzy erst concealed
To many a patriot breast has now revealed.
[...]
The very mention of reform abhor,
And scatter o'er the earth the flames of war.
Prophets of ill, insidious Traitors call
Whose timely aid would intercept their fall;
And treat with more contempt the great design
Than Teucer's[135] Sons their Prophetss [sic!] divine.
The Patriot far more distracted deem
That those that he from ruin would redeem:
His body still to dungeons have consigned
And to the flames the efforts of his mind.
At length a Bard, the meanest of the throng,
Strove as he past the vale of life along
(Discouraged by the ill success of prose)
In rustic rhymes the secret to disclose.
Britannia listened to his artless lays
And blest the Harbinger of better days!

FINIS

[135] Teucer was the first King of Troy. Teucer's sons are the Trojans who would not listen to Cassandra's prediction. Cassandra, the daughter of Hecuba and King Priam (the rulers of Troy during the Trojan War), foresaw the fall of Troy according to Homer's Iliad. See also Shakespeare's description of Cassandra as a prophetess in Troilus and Cressida.

Bibliography[136]

Barrell 2000: Barrell, John. *Imagining the King's Death: Figurative Treason, Fantasies of Regicide, 1793 - 1796* (Oxford: Oxford University Press, 2000).

Bonwick 1977: Bonwick, Colin. *English Radicals and the American Revolution* (Chapel Hill, NC: University of North Carolina Press, 1977).

Burke 1981: Edmund Burke, *Reflections on the Revolution in France*, in: *The Writings and Speeches of Edmund Burke*, ed. by Paul Langford, L. G. Mitchell, William B. Todd, vol. 8 (London: Clarendon Press, 1981).

Cobban 1960: *The Debate on the French Revolution, 1789 - 1800*, ed. by Alfred Cobban (London: A. & C. Black, 1960).

Godwin 1968: *Uncollected Writings*, ed. Jack W. Marken and Burton R. Pollin (Gainesville: Scholar's Fascimiles, 1968).

Godwin 1993: *Political and Philosphical Writings of William Godwin: Political Writings II*, ed. Mark Philp and Austin Gee (London: William Pickering, 1993).

Goodwin 1979: Goodwin, Albert. *The Friends of Liberty: The English Democratic Movement in the Age of the French Revolution* (London: Alan Hutchinson, 1979).

Hostettler 1996: Hostettler, John. *Thomas Erskine and Trial by Jury* (Chichester: Barry Rose Law Publishers, 1996).

Scrivener 2001: Scrivener, Michael Henry. *Seditious Allegories: John Thelwall and Jacobin Writing* (University Park: Pennsylvania State University Press, 2001).

Thelwall 1995: *The Politics of English Jacobinism. Writings of John Thelwall*, ed. by Gregory Claeys (University Park: Pennsylvania State University Press, 1995).

Thelwall 2000: Thelwall, John. *Poems Written in Close Confinement in the Tower and Newgate, under a Charge of High Treason 1795*, ed. by Jonathan Wordsworth (Oxford: Woodstock Books, 2000).

[136] Only books which appear more than twice and in different parts of the book are included.

BRITANNIA
Texts in English:
Literature, Culture, History from early modern times to the present

Edited by Jürgen Klein, Ernst Moritz Arndt Universität Greifswald

Vol. 1 Ewald Mengel (ed.): The Railway Through Dickens's World. Texts From Household Words and All The Year Round (With Illustrations). 1989.

Vol. 2 Peter Wagner (ed.): Erotica and the Enlightenment. 1991.

Vol. 3 Elizabeth Schlömer, Alex Atkins: The Patriot Game. A Play. 1990.

Vol. 4 H. George Hahn (ed.): The Country Myth: Motifs in the British Novel from Defoe to Smollett. 1991.

Vol. 5 James Fanning: Literaturwissenschaftliches Wörterbuch. Deutsch-Englisch. Englisch-Deutsch. 1993.

Vol. 6 Horst Höhne: Life and Literature. Eine Auswahl von Texten zur englischen und amerikanischen Literatur 1959-1996. 1996.

Vol. 7 Jürgen Klein (Hrsg.): T. S. Eliot, poeta doctus, Tradition und die Konstitution der klassischen Moderne. Mit einem Beitrag von Wolfgang Iser. 2003.

Vol. 8 Tatjana Schäfer: The Early Seventeenth-Century Epigram in England, Germany, and Spain. A Comparative Study. 2003.

Vol. 9 Stefani Brusberg-Kiermeier / Jörg Helbig (eds.): Sh@kespeare in the Media. From the Globe Theatre to the World Wide Web. 2004.

Vol. 10 Christoph Houswitschka (ed.): Freedom – Treason – Revolution. Uncollected Sources of the Political and Legal Culture of the London Treason Trials (1794). 2004.

Vol. 11 Of Remembraunce the Keye: Medieval Literatur and its Impact through the Ages. Festschrift for Karl Heinz Göller on the Occasion of his 80th Birthday. Edited by Uwe Böker. In collaboration with Dieter A. Berger and Noel Harold Kaylor, Jr. 2004.

www.peterlang.de

FSC
www.fsc.org
MIX
Papier | Fördert gute Waldnutzung
FSC® C083411

Kolibri 360 GmbH
Ferdinand-Jühlke-Straße 7
99095 Erfurt, Deutschland
produktsicherheit@kolibri360.de

Druck:
CPI Druckdienstleistungen GmbH
im Auftrag der
Kolibri 360 GmbH
Ferdinand-Jühlke-Str. 7
99095 Erfurt